Joyful Learning in Kindergarten

Joyful Learning in Kindergarten

REVISED EDITION

Bobbi Fisher

Heinemann
Portsmouth, NH

Heinemann
A division of Reed Elsevier Inc.
361 Hanover Street
Portsmouth, NH 03801-3912

Offices and agents throughout the world

The authors and publisher thank those who generously gave permission to reprint borrowed material.

The Natural Learning Model (page 21) is adapted from the model adapted by Intercultural Training and Resource Center, Roslindale, Massachusetts.

Chapters 3 and 14 appeared in different form in the journal *Teaching* K-8 (August/September 1989; November/December 1989).

The book in the cover photo is *I'm the King of the Mountain* by Joy Cowley (Katonah, NY: Richard C. Owen).

Library of Congress Cataloging-in-Publication Data
Fisher, Bobbi.
   Joyful learning in kindergarten / Bobbi Fisher.—Rev. ed.
      p.   cm.
   Rev. ed. of: Joyful learning. c1991.
   Includes bibliographical references (p.   ) and index.
   ISBN 0-325-00038-7 (alk. paper)
   1. Kindergarten—Curricula.   2. Language experience approach in
education.   3. Reading (Preschool)—Language experience approach.
4. Language arts (Preschool)   I. Fisher, Bobbi.   Joyful learning.
II. Title.
LB1180.F57   1998
372.62—dc21   97-50311
                                                                          CIP

Editor: Scott Mahler
Production: Melissa L. Inglis
Cover design: Jenny Jensen Greenleaf
Manufacturing: Louise Richardson

Illustrations in Chapter 17, Chapter 18, and Appendix D:
Emily Fisher Medvic

Printed in the United States of America on acid-free paper
03 04 05   EB   9 10 11

To Mary Kurth,

my friend and teaching assistant

Contents

Foreword by Don Holdaway

Traditional wisdom accepts that one of the hard facts of life is that school learning is inescapably dull, pointless, and painful, even sometimes for our brightest, and therefore fails to read the very visible failure of many children as forms of inefficiency or injustice that might sensibly be avoided. Obsessed with measurement that scorns the obvious and the real, it has no way to measure the *invisible* waste and inefficiency represented by mindlessness whenever it occurs, and *especially* in our brightest. It mandates more of the same pain as the inevitable cost of excellence.

Committed teachers around the world are currently developing a new, and at last more sane, set of wisdoms that entail a radically different perspective on human development, learning, and expectation. Such a perspective sees the learner as operating in a social environment that should reflect the purposeful accomplishments and joyful satisfactions of real thought and action, and make it possible for every child to share in the consummations of developing human skill from the earliest stages. The requirement of all effective human learning is that it makes sense: that it is complete or whole within the experience of the learner at the time of learning; that it is perceived by the learner as issuing from personal control or *ownership*, and that it certifies acceptance or *membership* in the community of learners. Traditionally, those ends were regarded as permissible by-products of an education for the few who excel—but for daily classroom learning? For all children? For *kindergarten*? They must be joking! Teachers like Bobbi Fisher accept the challenge of such principles with joyful seriousness, and display with great precision how it may be done.

In historical and cultural terms, the nature of the shift is unprecedented for teaching, for curriculum, and for the whole educational enterprise. Naturally, everyone is a little confused when change is far-reaching and unprecedented, and we are very much in need of sensible and confirming models that transcend the merely trendy. This book has those qualities to a marked degree. It represents a significant contribution, at the level of early schooling, towards the expression of deep modern sensitivities about education in the practical form of efficient and concrete ideas for the classroom.

In the last ten years or more, these new developments towards efficient, holistic, and process-oriented education have centered around language learning. This is the most distinctive of human tasks and, in terms of indicated reform, it has been the most urgent. The growing body of insights has fallen quite appropriately under the banner of "whole language," although the implications are much wider than language alone—especially as they impinge upon the social context of learning, personal relationships within the classroom, and the irreducibly self-regulated nature of complex human learning.

Properly understood, whole language accommodates the genuine richness and diversity that have always been the hallmark of great teaching—it promotes imagination, initiative, inventiveness, commitment, and professional skill above any concerns for a "right" way of doing things. This is as it should be, for the vision of great teachers always transcends any particular philosophy or narrow set of formulas. *Joyful Learning* embodies such a vision within a responsible context of theory and research. It is both a model of sensible and creative teaching in the new paradigm and an enticement to creativity and autonomy on the part of teachers.

Over the last ten years I have moved regularly among classroom settings in Australia, New Zealand, Canada, and America, often as a visitor to classrooms where "interesting things are happening." Increasingly, I have been struck by the astonishing diversity of teaching strategies in classrooms identified as whole language environments. At the same time, there has almost always been an identifiable coherence of practice around central ideas—a new and vigorous pedagogy. Considering the restrictions placed on innovative teachers in very similar ways the world over, one can only marvel at this determination by grassroots teachers in their thousands to reshape schooling in powerful ways to meet the needs of modern society. Both the coherence and the diversity are deeply gratifying.

Purely superficial changes at the level of teaching methodology alone, however, miss the point of what it is all about, and it is difficult in the extreme to avoid the inevitable band-wagon effects of a popular trend. This is a challenge to the teacher who wishes to retain authenticity as a top priority, and to the writer who wishes to capture the incredible complexity of whole language insights. The satisfying thing is that so many teachers have understood the "movement" in deeply authentic ways displayed in a great diversity of innovative practice shaped by coherent structures of principle. Both as teacher and as writer, Bobbi Fisher represents this remarkable generative approach to the modern classroom.

Diversity of practice, rather than an externally imposed rigidity, is exactly what is to be expected from the paradigm: firstly, as a result of confident self-regulation on the part of teachers; and secondly, as a result of the freedom to meet special individual and cultural needs displayed by children—a genuine responsiveness to the real diversity of children's development under varying conditions. The unique capabilities and talents of teachers have an opportunity to flower within whole language classrooms because they not only feel free to make their own instructional decisions in moment-by-moment engagement, but also possess in their own awareness the understandings necessary to make those decisions. Furthermore, they perceive their students as something more than the dehumanized "subject" of behaviorist theory. Children are their *real clients*, before administrators, the public, or even parents, and they feel empowered to respond to the unique developmental personhood displayed by their children in the course of longitudinal observation and evaluation.

Not surprisingly, then, healthy whole language classrooms cannot be described by any stereotype of methodology—they are remarkably creative and varied environments coordinated by overriding insights about learning and development. Nor are the limited technologies of instruction, variously promulgated as solutions during the decades of "methodology," entirely wasted. Rather, older methodologies are being reformed and enlightened by thoughtful teachers to serve more purposeful, holistic answers to children's varied developmental needs.

However, this diversity cannot be characterized as chaotic or lacking in soundness of form or intellectual rigor. Whenever I enter a whole language classroom, regardless of what part of the world it is in, I become aware of a solid basis of consensus, a distinctive difference of tone and relationship that informs the environment. This display of coherence in practice is also predictable as an outcome of whole language strategies when they are deeply understood and authentically applied. Mindlessness, boredom, incomprehension, and despair are disappearing from classrooms where the new paradigm reigns. Cooperative strategies begin to replace competitive structures in the social dynamics of the classroom, in such a way that *all* children can be seen to profit from the positive expectations placed on them. Real engagement, responsibility, and personal commitment on the part of children characterize both their styles of working and the quality of their products. If the politically in-word must be used, this is the true excellence we have been waiting for.

It is an exciting challenge to participate in these great changes, and Bobbi Fisher presents the invitation with justified assurance and a pragmatic flair.

1991

Acknowledgments

Since I wrote the first edition to *Joyful Learning*, I have continued to keep up with the people mentioned in the first acknowledgment, and have been blessed with new friends who have supported me on my teaching and learning journey.

Dawn Boyer, Carolyn Coman, Pat Cordeiro, and Mary Glover have stretched my thinking and encouraged me in my work. I thank them for their support and friendship.

I also want to thank the many dedicated teachers across the country who have shared their classroom practices and ideas with me.

The staff at Heinemann has continued to be extremely supportive. Lois Bridges, Melissa Inglis, Scott Mahler, and Susie Stroud have helped me as editors and friends.

I continue to receive suggestions, laughter, and love from my husband, Jim, my son, Tim and his wife Carin, my daughter Emily, who drew the illustrations for new material in this book, and her husband Stephen.

1998

To paraphrase Robert Fulghum, "All I really needed to know about kindergarten I learned from my students." Therefore, it seems fitting that I start my acknowledgments by honoring all of the kindergartners who have been in my classes. They have been my most important teachers and will continue to be so. Along with the children, I need to acknowledge their parents, who throughout the years have appreciated and valued their children's literacy development. They were always willing to come in and help in the classroom, thus joining their families with the school community.

My colleagues at Haynes School are part of this community. I know I couldn't find a staff more committed to each other both personally and professionally, and I thank them for their support and friendship. I would also like to thank my principal, Chet Delani, who in creating a school community of learners enabled me to create a community of learners in my classroom, and who has encouraged my professional growth.

During the past year, members of the Whole Language Teachers Association steering committee cheered me on to get up early and write in the morning before school, and many of them contributed ideas and suggestions for the text. Jackie Finn answered many of my questions. Don Holdaway acted as mentor and friend throughout and graciously wrote the foreword for this book.

I am grateful to Harold Raynolds, Massachusetts Commissioner of Education, and to my Lucretia Crocker fellows who, during the 1988–1989 fellowship year when we shared our various classroom programs with teachers all across Massachusetts, encouraged me to start the draft for this book. I also want to thank the many classroom teachers who, after attending my workshops that year, urged me to "put your workshops into a book."

I would especially like to thank Sally Wilson for reading the entire manuscript and devoting many Sunday mornings to phone conversations between Colorado and Massachusetts to share her ideas and suggestions.

When I first talked with Philippa Stratton, editor-in-chief at Heinemann, about writing a book for kindergarten teachers, she saw the need for such a book, and has supported me throughout the process. Cheryl Kimball, the production editor, was always available for discussion and advice, and has been a pleasure to work with. Heinemann sales and marketing directors Bob Thomas and Tom Seavey were both enthusiastic and helpful, and Wes Hays, the Heinemann representative in the Boston area, provided continual encouragement.

And finally, the biggest THANK YOU goes to my family: to my children, Tim and Emily, who may forever picture their mother sitting in front of a computer; and to my husband Jim, who read and reread the manuscript and provided enthusiastic support for this book throughout the whole process.

1991

Introduction
to the Second Edition

Why a second edition? When *Joyful Learning* was first published in 1991, many teachers were just becoming aware of the theory and practice of whole language. Since that time, many have told me that my book has helped them understand and apply the conditions of natural learning in creating caring classroom environments that support all their students as lifelong learners. Additionally, many of these teachers have shared with me the new routines, activities, and strategies they have developed for their classrooms.

Because I felt these teachers' ideas deserved to be shared with all kindergarten teachers, and because I, too, had made some further adaptations and developed new procedures since writing *Joyful Learning*, I decided to update the book with this new material.

In this second edition, the original sixteen chapters remain unchanged. I believe that their message and content are still appropriate and timely. To these I have added three new chapters, plus a second epilogue, appendices of teachers' ideas, and a comprehensive index. I have also updated the original bibliographies.

Chapter 17 discusses classroom organization and schedules. First, I revisit I CARES (the management system outlined in Chapter 7), answer some of the questions that teachers have asked, and describe some of the practical innovations they have developed for their classrooms. Next, I share some ways that teachers can effectively organize an extended or full-day kindergarten.

Chapter 18 focuses on language arts. It extends the possibilities for the shared reading described in Chapters 5 and 6, and for reading and writing during choice time, outlined in Chapters 8, 9, and 14.

Chapter 19 discusses generative curriculum and provides a framework for planning and organizing different curriculum structures. It also expands upon the concepts of the dramatic play environments described in Chapter 12.

In an added appendix entitled "Learning from Each Other," I have shared ideas given to me by kindergarten teachers from all over the country. These ideas reflect the teachers' enthusiasm and imagination in figuring out new and better ways to do their jobs to keep learning joyful in their classrooms.

Introduction
to the First Edition

As I look back on my twenty years of teaching, I realize that I was a whole language teacher much of the time. My kindergarten classroom always had sand and water tables, big blocks, unit blocks, puppet theaters, a dramatic play area, math manipulatives, easels, an art table, a workbench, a table where children could draw, and books. I read to the children and we sang songs together. They were busy and happy, and I knew they were learning.

But, what's different now? First, my classroom looks about the same as before, except for one very noticeable difference *there is an abundance of print around the room*. Second, the children are involved in many of the same activities as in previous years, except for one major difference: *they are involved in planning and managing their learning*. No longer do they spend time doing worksheets; instead they are engaged in authentic literacy demonstrations and involved in their own reading and writing process. Finally, I am either facilitating group time or working with individuals or small groups of children as I've always done, except for one important difference: I *trust the children as the authorities of their own learning*.

What initiated the changes in my approach to how children learn? In the fall of 1984 I watched Don Holdaway demonstrate shared reading with a group of children at the Lesley College Kindergarten Conference, and I was fascinated by the joyful way he engaged them in literacy. Curious to find out more, I took a course on evaluating and assessing emergent and initial readers with Don Holdaway and Mary Snow at Lesley College the following spring. I was hooked. I have read Don's book *Foundations of Literacy* several times and return to it regularly for understanding and clarification during the course of the year. His natural learning classroom model is the basis for the structure of my kindergarten class day and my guide for interacting with the children.

The works of Holdaway and others have provided me with the theoretical base to clarify my beliefs about how children learn and to help define my role as a teacher. Like many teachers throughout North America, I am continually "kid watching," sharing ideas with colleagues and visiting their classrooms, attending and presenting at workshops and conferences, and reading professionally. My kindergarten program has developed and evolved, reflecting theory and practice learned from these various sources, and the process continues daily.

I view my role as planner, observer, and teacher so that my beliefs about how children learn are realized in my classroom. I plan so children develop as authorities of their own learning. I organize the physical environment and daily routine in my classroom to encourage participation in a variety of experiences that are interesting, meaningful, and developmentally appropriate. I plan opportunities that offer rich literacy, math, social studies, and science experiences, and that facilitate the children's social, emotional, and physical growth.

I observe the children in a variety of situations throughout the day. This "kid watching" enables me to assess their intellectual, social, and emotional development, and to teach when my observations indicate that I should step in and support the child who I observe is ready to learn something new. Vygotsky calls this "the zone of proximal development" and refers to this zone as "the distance between the [child's] actual development as determined by independent problem solving and the level of potential development as determined through problem solving with more capable peers" (1986).

At workshops I give, kindergarten teachers often ask me if there is a whole language book for them, a practical guide to classroom practice that links practice and theory. Most of the content of my workshops is just that—I explain what goes on in my classroom throughout the day, and why I do what I do.

This book is essentially an extension and elaboration of these workshops. I hope that my ideas can act as a catalyst for classroom practice for all early childhood teachers, whether they work in rural, suburban, or inner-city schools, whether they teach multicultural, bilingual, economically advantaged, or disadvantaged populations. The book is intended as a guide or springboard for teachers as they develop programs that match their own teaching style and school culture to the needs of their student and parent population, and that satisfy the curriculum goals of their school systems.

1

My Beliefs about How Young Children Learn

As a whole language teacher I have developed certain beliefs about how children learn, which guide my responses to individual children and group situations, and which are the foundation for my classroom curriculum and daily schedule. These beliefs are based on whole language theory and personal experience and can be summarized as follows:

- Children learn naturally.
- Children know a lot about literacy before kindergarten.
- All children can learn.
- Children learn best when learning is kept whole, meaningful, interesting, and functional.
- Children learn best when they make their own choices.
- Children learn best as a community of learners in a non-competitive environment.
- Children learn best by talking and doing in a social context.

Children Learn Naturally

Our daughter, Emily, was an early reader. We really didn't know why, although we knew that reading to her, especially her favorite stories over and over again, and giving her a "quiet hour" every day (when she read to her stuffed animals) were important. What I discovered as I began learning about whole language was that Emily had learned to read, as well as talk and play, in the natural learning environment in our home.

Whole language learning theory and practice are modeled after natural developmental learning, specifically the acquisition of oral language. Cambourne (1989) examined the conditions under which young children learn to talk and which enable some children to learn

Figure 1-1 Holdaway: Natural Learning Model

to read before formal school instruction, and he understood the implications for literacy learning in the classroom. In my classroom, whenever possible, I duplicate these conditions for natural learning. I *immerse* the room in print, *demonstrate* reading and writing that *engages* the children in literacy activities. I have a high *expectation* that the children will take the *responsibility* to become readers and writers. I value their *approximations*, giving them opportunities to *use* and practice language and to share and *perform* what they can do.

Holdaway explored the implications for language teaching through examining the "homely models" of spoken language acquisition, emergent literacy, and developmental learning (1988). He has applied these conditions, which take place in the social context of the home and involves interaction with family members and friends, to literacy development in the school setting. This natural-learning classroom model, which includes *Demonstration, Participation, Role-playing* or *Practice,* and *Performance* (Holdaway 1986), provides the framework for what happens in my classroom (Figure 1–1).

Children know how to learn because it is the nature of the brain to make sense (Smith 1986). They learn from the people they admire in their lives. Parents, siblings, relatives, and care givers talk to them and engage them in meaningful and authentic conversations and activities. Holdaway (1986, p. 58) refers to these people as "significant others," " 'bonded' adults," and "superior skill users." Cambourne (1988, p. 32) calls them "user experts," and Smith (1988, p. 2) refers to them as "experienced members of the club."

As Emily's parents we were the bonded adults in her life. At school the teacher becomes the bonded adult in the child's life. Therefore, as I establish the natural learning conditions in my classroom, my first goal is to develop trust or bonding between the children and me. I believe that when they trust me, they will learn from me in the environment I create.

Candace is sitting in the rocking chair with about seven Sunshine Books on her lap. As she finishes one, she puts it on the floor and takes another. I am helping Justin hang the chart with the words to the chant "I woke up in the morning" so he can read it, but I am also "kid watching" (Goodman 1985) I'm watching Candace out of the corner of my eye. I notice that she is pointing to the words in *Faces*, and then I remember that that was the same book she chose as her expert book last week. However, I'm not surprised when she opens *The Birthday Party* and makes up her own story as she looks at the pictures. Justin volunteers to read me the chant, and Candace stops to look up and listen. Then she reaches for *Faces* again and asks if I would like to hear it. Of course I would

Meanwhile, Justin is happily hanging up another chart, by himself this time. As I leave the reading area to hear about a battleship that Chris and Mariah have made with the unit blocks, I jot down what I had just noticed about Candace and Justin. In about three minutes I have observed what kinds of reading materials these two children enjoy and how they handle the materials and I have heard them read. I'll keep watching.

This scene is similar to many scenes that go on in homes where young children are involved with literacy events, and my role is similar to the role of many parents who support their children's endeavors. Candace has chosen a relaxing place to read. I don't interrupt her, but when she invites me to hear her read, I accept with pleasure. Justin is as interested in learning to hang charts as in learning to read them. Both children show they trust me, and I show that I trust them.

Children Know a Lot about Literacy Before Kindergarten

Jackie is a reader. "There's McDonalds," she shouts as her father pulls into the parking lot.

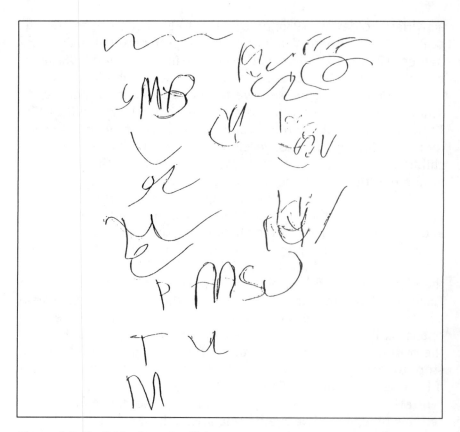

Figure 1-2 Scribble shopping list

Mandy is also a reader. She is reading one of her favorites, *Wilfred Gordon McDonald Partridge*, by Mem Fox. She holds the book with ease on her lap and tells the story in her own way, including much of the language of the text that she has memorized from hearing it many times. She looks at the pictures and sometimes at me as she reads. Her story is fluent and her voice expressive.

Sam is another reader. He has also chosen a favorite book, *Hairy Bear*, with a simple, familiar text. He reads slowly, word by word, and his voice often lacks expression. He is focusing on the words in the text.

Allie is a reader, too. She is reading *Spot's First Walk*, by Eric Hill, a book she has not heard before. Her reading is supported by the meaning of the story, the flow of the language, the pictures, and what she knows about phonics.

Jerry is a writer. He tells me about the picture he has drawn about his visit to the playground.

Taisha is a writer. She has just written a grocery list (Figure 1–2) in the housekeeping area. The paper has several lines of scribble-like writing.

Figure 1-3 Writing sample: "A boy is coming out of his home."

Joey is a writer, too. He has drawn a picture of his house and written mostly random letters from his name all over the page. He has labeled the house "H." He reads me his story.

Stefanie is a writer. She has written a story about a boy coming outside after the rain (Figure 1–3). Her accompanying picture has detail and action, and her story describes past, present and future events. She uses many conventions of writing. For example, she leaves spaces between words, spells some words conventionally, applies temporary (invented) spelling in others, uses vowels in every word, and starts two of the three sentences with uppercase letters.

In this book the definition of children's reading and writing encompasses a wide variety of reading and writing behaviors demonstrated by children. For example, reading might be reading environmental print (such as McDonalds, exit, favorite cereal names on boxes), role-playing and telling a story, pointing carefully to the print, or beginning to read independently. Writing might be a drawing, scribbling, writing random letters, or inventing spelling. When we refer to writing in my classroom, the children and I know that we mean picture drawing and symbols in writing. Ruth Hubbard, in *Authors of Pictures, Draughtsmen of Words* (1989), encourages us to examine the relationship between growth in children's pictures and in their writing.

Children arrive in kindergarten knowing a lot about reading and writing (Durkin 1966; Clay 1972; Holdaway 1979; Bissex 1980; Yetta Goodman 1984, 1986; Harste, Woodward, and Burke 1985; Doake 1985; and Wells 1986). Teale and Sulzby (1986) have adopted the term "emergent literacy" to describe this literacy development in young children, specifically before the ages of five or six when they begin to read and write in conventional forms. By "literacy" they mean reading and writing and the relationship between the two. They use "emergent" to suggest that development is taking place, that there is something new emerging in the child that had not "been there before" (p. xx). They sum up what has been learned about emergent literacy in the past two decades with the following conclusions:

1. Literacy development begins long before children start formal instruction.
2. *Literacy* development is the appropriate way to describe what was called *reading* readiness: the child develops as a *writer/reader*.
3. Literacy develops in real-life settings for real-life activities in order to "get things done."
4. Children are doing critical cognitive work in literacy development during the years from birth to six.
5. Children learn written language through active engagement with their world.
6. Although children's learning about literacy can be described in terms of generalized stages, children can pass through these stages in a variety of ways and at different ages (xviii).

All Children Can Learn

It is Valentine's Day and the children are distributing valentines to their friends in the mailboxes we made from grocery cartons. When they need help they ask Dicky, because he can read the names of all the children in the class. Dicky can also point word for word when he reads In a Dark Dark Wood, a story very familiar to him. He can draw a picture with detail and tell an elaborate story about it. When he hears a *b* sound in a word, he says *b* and then writes it down. Even though he can only give the names of seven letters, Dicky knows a lot about reading. No question, he knows how to learn and he knows that he can learn (Smith 1988).

One of my primary goals is for the children in my class to know that I believe they can learn. I want them to have the same high

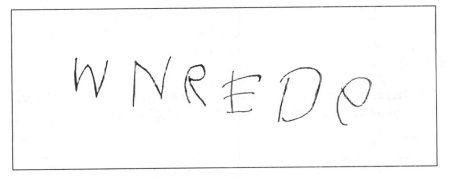

Figure 1-4 Writing sample: "We need red paint."

expectation for their own learning as I have for them. I want them to trust themselves as learners just as I do. I want all of them, just like Dicky, to join the literacy club (Smith 1988).

Therefore, I treat them all as readers, writers, and mathematicians, regardless of where they are developmentally. For example, when I introduce a new big book I invite everyone to read along with me. If a child informs me that we are out of red paint, I suggest that he or she write me a note reminding me to get some (Figure 1–4). If we need pencils, I ask someone to count them to see if we have enough for everyone. The assumption underlying my actions and attitudes is that everyone can read, write, and do math for a variety of meaningful and functional purposes.

I also believe that children learn in their own unique way, and I plan opportunities for them to develop and follow their own style. For example, during shared reading I demonstrate a variety of reading strategies used by successful readers. If the children are trying to figure out a word in a text, we might look at the pictures, reread the sentence, read ahead, look at the beginning letter, skip the word, or spell the word to help us discover what it is. During choice time the children choose the book they want to read, their own topic and genre for writing, and the kind of blocks with which to build.

I am continually evaluating my curriculum, methods, and attitude, and making adjustments to fit the needs, interests, and styles of the children. When children are struggling to learn, I look closely at what they can do, as opposed to what they can't do.

David avoided drawing whenever possible, and when he did give it a try, his pictures were like those of a three-year-old. However, I noticed that he seemed confident painting at the easel, and his paintings were similar to those of his classmates. I decided to help David build upon what he could do well by encouraging him to write about his paintings. His confidence grew, and eventually his success as a painter showed up in his drawings.

Children Learn Best When Learning is Kept Whole, Meaningful, Interesting, and Functional

"I'm going to make some money for our bank," claimed Ryan as he took some green paper to the art table. "Lincoln is on a five-dollar bill. I'll make that."

I gave the group that gathered a one, five, and ten dollar bill as models, and they were on their way, talking about the different bills and explaining what they knew about money and banks. Soon the money was in use at the environmental play area, which the children had made into a supermarket and bank. The next day I read a book about the United States Mint to the class.

Learning was whole, meaningful, interesting, and functional to the children in this activity (K. Goodman 1986) It was initiated by Ryan, who had previously shown an interest in money in his drawings, and expanded upon by several of his classmates, who had built the supermarket and bank and who saw a need for money in their play. I capitalized on this interest by supplying the real money and by reading a book on the subject. This was an example of what Holdaway calls a "generative" or "developmental curriculum" (personal conversation, 1989).

When materials, activities, and discussions develop from the interests of the children, curriculum remains

- whole, not broken into bits and pieces;
- meaningful, not irrelevant;
- functional, not artificial and contrived; and
- engaging, not boring.

During shared reading we read complete books and stories, always focusing on meaning, but as the need or interest arises, we discuss parts of the text within the whole. For example, one day while reading Mrs. Wishy-washy, probably for the twentieth time, we started to discuss the author's use of "screamed" when Mrs. Wishy-washy wanted to wash the animals. On the chalkboard I wrote, " 'In the tub you go,' she screamed," and the children brainstormed words that would sound right and make sense in place of "screamed." The children were engaged and learning writing skills in a meaningful context, as I modeled writing while listing their suggestions.

Children Learn Best When They Make Their Own Choices

"I'm going to the library."
"Sally and I are going to draw a picture together."
"I'm going to start with snack."
"We want to play under the loft."

As the children leave the group area to begin the hour-long choice time, they tell me their starting plan. Opportunities for choosing and planning continue throughout the day. I'm continually watching the choices they make and asking:

"What is your choice?"
"What is your plan?"
"Do you want to stay with that choice or make another choice?"
"Why did you choose to put red in your sky?"
"Why do you read *Counting Sheep* every day?"
"Tell me about your picture."

I want children to know that they are the primary directors of their own learning, to gain confidence that they can make appropriate choices, and to take responsibility for their choices.

There are teacher choices and student choices in my kindergarten. Teacher choices are managerial, such as the physical arrangement of the classroom, materials, supplies, and books; the daily routine; and the overall curriculum. Within these managerial parameters, the children make choices about their learning, such as what and how they want to read, write, create, and play.

For example, I have decided that the children should read every day—a managerial choice. I plan time for reading and supply reading materials—books, magazines, newspapers—from many genres of fiction and nonfiction. Within this framework, the children choose what and where they will read, whether they will read alone or with a friend, and when they will read (Figure 1–5). While reading, they are making moment by moment decisions, usually not consciously about their reading. They are predicting, sampling, approximating self-correcting, and confirming that the text makes sense to them so *they* can feel success as readers.

Why is it so important for children to make these choices? I believe that when encouraged to choose activities that are whole, meaningful, and functional to their lives, children naturally engage in activities that meet their intellectual, social, emotional, and physical needs. As Holdaway (1979) states, "There is no better system to control the complexities and intricacies of each person's learning than that person's own system operating with genuine motivation

Figure 1-5 Choice reading

and self-determination within reach of humane and informed help"
(p. 170).

Children Learn Best as a Community of Learners in a Noncompetitive Environment

When I interviewed the children in my class about reading at the end
of the year, each child said that everyone in the class could read and
that they knew this because they saw their classmates reading a lot
(Fisher 1990). I believe that optimal learning occurs for all children
in an atmosphere free of competition. The teacher is the catalyst in
creating this atmosphere by demonstrating through daily interactions that everyone can learn, that confidence in one's self as a
learner is the most important ingredient in learning, that we all can
learn from each other, and that children learn best in a social context.

I work with the children to create a community of learners in
which we care about each other, and learn from and with each other.
This sense of community develops during community circle time,
when we share what is happening in our everyday lives. It also occurs
during shared reading time, when through group singing and reading the children are free to regulate their own learning through

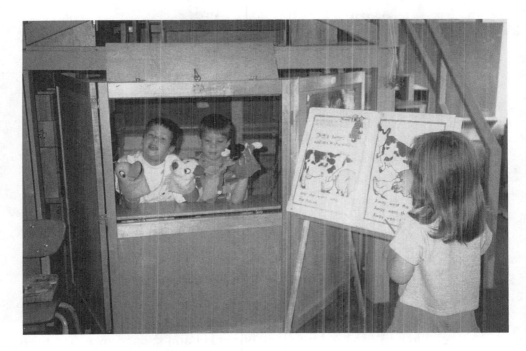

Figure 1-6 Children learning together—puppet show

sampling, approximating, self-correcting and confirming in the safety of the group. This noncompetitive atmosphere creates the trust necessary for the children to learn as they collaborate and cooperate with each other during independent choice time (Figure 1–6).

What are some of the specific ways that we develop a noncompetitive atmosphere? As we sing, read, and talk about texts as a group during shared reading, the children are not singled out because they are accurate, have the 'right' answer, or express a particularly creative idea. Although I play a dominant role as the demonstrator during this time, each child's response and participation is unique to his or her interests and developmental needs. Often when I ask a question, each child responds individually. Some of the techniques I use are to ask the children to think their answer, to whisper it, or discuss it with the person sitting next to them. This takes the emphasis away from the extrinsic motivation of being right in front of the group and teacher and shifts it to the intrinsic motivation of being engaged in meaningful and interesting ideas and activities.

When I ask individuals to respond to a question in front of the group, I usually ask for volunteers. I want the children to take the responsibility for choosing when to participate, and I don't want them to feel they have failed because they don't have a response or "correct" answer. I have found they are more willing to be risk takers as learners when they have control over their participation. The following questions allow for this control and elicit a variety of responses.

- What do you notice?
- What do you know about _____ ?
- How do you know?

These open-ended questions focus on what the children know and are interested in, and enable us to share what we know as a community of learners, with everyone having something equally important to contribute. Sometimes we discuss what the child has noticed, and sometimes I just acknowledge the responses. Regardless, I accept each reply without putting a value judgment on it. For example, I nod my head or say, "Yes," or "Uh, huh." Comments such as "Wow," "What a great idea," or "Aren't you smart" encourage children to compete for the right answer and my approval, and take away from self-evaluation and self-monitoring.

This noncompetitive environment during shared reading continues during choice time, when the children practice their own reading, writing, and math. I notice children talking about their writing (or drawings), asking each other how to write and spell words, reading to each other, and working collaboratively on pictures, block building, etc. They're engaged in the task, not in trying to please the teacher or be "better" than a peer.

Children Learn Best by Talking and Doing in a Social Context

In my classroom children are allowed and encouraged to talk about what they are doing, as they read books and as they write, as they are actively involved with math, science, and art materials, and as they play in the dramatic play area. The following are examples of learning occurring through social interaction in my classroom:

- David and Sara went to the library together
- Stefanie and Ian took turns reading *I Am Freedom's Child*
- Julie gave Andrea change at the grocery store in our dramatic play environment
- Mary and Dicky helped Clare figure out how she could divide her snack in thirds to share with them

- Three children built a tower of Unifix Cubes as tall as Sam
- Mary and Joe painted pictures together at the easel
- Judy showed Jane what a C looked like on the alphabet chart.

Goodman, Smith, Meredith, and Goodman (1987, p. 6) suggest a double agenda for schools: "From the general perspective this is a thought and language-centered curriculum, but it is two curricula in one. It is a curriculum for the development of language and thinking, and it is a curriculum for learning through language and thinking." Halliday (1975, p. 138) discusses the functions of language and claims that we learn language as an interactive process that takes place in a social context. Vygotsky (1986) makes a strong case for the importance of social interaction in learning. Yetta Goodman (1985) suggests that our best assessment of what children are learning is by watching and listening to them in a social context.

In developing my beliefs about learning over the past six years, I have been particularly influenced by the work of Brian Cambourne and Don Holdaway, who applied what they observed about first language acquisition to classroom practice. The application of their work to my whole language classroom is discussed in the following chapter.

For Further Reading

Goodman, Kenneth. 1986. *What's Whole in Whole Language?* Portsmouth, NH: Heinemann.

Jaggar, Angela, and M. Trinka Smith-Burke, eds. 1985 *Observing the Language Learner*. Newark, DE: International Reading Association.

Smith, Frank. 1986. *Insult to Intelligence*. Portsmouth, NH: Heinemann.

Strickland, Dorothy, and Lesley Morrow, ed. 1989. *Emerging Literacy: Young Children Learn to Read and Write*. Newark, DE: International Reading Association.

Teale, William, and Elizabeth Sulzby. 1986. *Emergent Literacy: Writing and Reading*. Norwood, NJ: Ablex.

Wells, Gordon. 1986. *The Meaning Makers: Children Learning Language and Using Language to Learn*. Portsmouth, NH Heinemann.

2

Applying Whole Language Theories

Brian Cambourne: Conditions of Learning

Cambourne states that " . . . while the conditions for learning to talk cannot be precisely replicated for the written mode of language, the principles which they exemplify can" (1988, p. 45). These conditions are:

- Immersion
- Demonstration
- Engagement
- Expectation
- Responsibility
- Approximation
- Use
- Response

Immersion

Babies are immersed in the language that they are expected to learn. They hear family members conversing, the TV and radio, conversations in the grocery store, telephone conversations, and people talking to them.

There is a lot of print in my classroom. Songs, poems, charts, and big books in enlarged text are prominent throughout. A variety of trade books and writing materials, such as paper, pencils, and crayons, are available in all areas, not just the writing and library centers. Signs that indicate rules for a play area, how many children can be in an area at a time, and where materials are kept are purposefully placed around the room where children can see them. The children see me read and write for a variety of purposes as I communicate with parents through notes and newsletters, read notices from the office, and enjoy a book during reading time. I read to them throughout the day and provide time for them to read books of their own choice.

Demonstration

Immersion in language is not, by itself, sufficient to produce literate children. Learners need demonstrations. "Demonstrations are artifacts and/or actions from which we can learn" (Cambourne 1988, 47).

Babies continually receive demonstrations through artifacts and actions, usually accompanied by language. These demonstrations are whole, meaningful, functional. For example, we might ask (language) a baby, "Do you want a cookie?" (artifact) as we hand him or her one (action).

In my kindergarten I give demonstrations of language use throughout the day. I tell Katie how sorry I am that her cat is sick. I read what Sam's mom wrote in the guestbook we ask visitors to sign. I add Kevin and Ariana's name to the list of children who have taken out the cart and wagon so we can be sure everyone gets a turn. These demonstrations become concentrated during shared reading time and story time, when I read to the children, demonstrate print concepts and reading strategies by pointing to the print in enlarged texts, and engage in modeled writing in front of the class. On a given day, as we read the big book *Old MacDonald*, I might focus on where I start reading on each new page, discuss how the picture of the cow helps us know what animal is next, and write a group thank-you letter to the people at the Audubon Farm for giving us a hayride.

Engagement

Babies are given many demonstrations of language from the day they are born, but they only learn from these demonstrations if they become engaged with them. According to Cambourne, learners become engaged when the activity is personally meaningful and purposeful, when they feel they will have some success, and when the experience they emulate is positive.

I try to provide reading and writing demonstrations in an atmosphere that engages all the children. I frequently ask them to select their favorite poems and songs for shared reading and to write their own poems or charts. I encourage them when they want to make a sign telling the visiting hours of our class museum (see Chapter 12, "Dramatic Play Environments"), and I involve them in acting out a favorite big book, such as *The Teeny Tiny Woman*. By continually watching when the children are interested and when their involvement wanes, I can plan meaningful demonstrations.

Expectation

Stop parents in the supermarket and ask them if they expect their baby will learn to talk. They will look at you in disbelief at such a foolish question. Their expectation is high and their child responds.

I expect that all the children in my class are developing as readers and writers in kindergarten regardless of where they are on the reading continuum. I ask them to read and write every day, and I treat them as readers and writers.

Responsibility

According to Cambourne (1988, p. 37) children **"must** eventually learn to talk." They take the responsibility for choosing which demonstrations to engage in and which aspects of oral language to focus on at a given moment.

Although it is my responsibility to provide the best conditions I can for language learning in my classroom, it is the children's responsibility to engage in reading and writing activities that satisfy their developmental needs. For example, I repeatedly demonstrate several different ways for children to write a word, and they select the method that matches their development. They scribble, write random letters, write the letters they think are in the word, ask a friend, find the word in a chart and copy it, or come to me with their best attempt written out so we can discuss the word and its spelling.

Approximation

Parents accept and often celebrate their children's approximations, considering them natural and essential behaviors of language acquisition. Instead of correcting their child, parents usually will model standard usage in response to the meaning of the child's conversation. When Janie says "goo, goo," they rush over with a cookie and say, "Oh, here's a cookie." When Jake shouts, "I want what ball," they say, "Here's that ball," as they throw it to him.

In kindergarten I encourage approximations by creating an environment and atmosphere where children can take risks, approximate, self-monitor, and create meaning. In her ethnographic investigation of the literacy center at the Longfellow School in Cambridge, Massachusetts (which Holdaway developed), Shelley Midkiff-Borunda (1989) discovered that during shared reading each child was approximating at his or her developmental level within the group setting.

As we read *Greedy Cat*, I hear Michele say chips instead of potato chips. Andrew chimes in when we get to 'And that was the end of

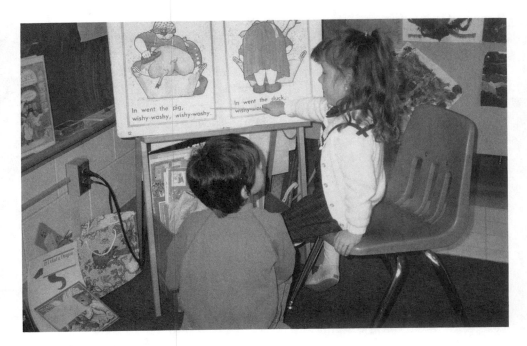

Figure 2-1 Role playing reading

that." Alissa reads word for word. During choice time I notice the children approximating as they read by themselves or with a friend (Figure 2-1). Wendy is role-playing as the teacher. She is pointing generally to the print of *The Enormous Watermelon*, but her eyes are on the pictures as she tells her story.

Approximating dominates learning, especially in the early stages of any developmental task (Holdaway 1984). Unfortunately, it is often difficult for schools to support approximations as legitimate because teachers have been trained and conditioned to correcting children and insisting on accuracy.

Use

Frank Smith (1983) says that one learns to read by reading and to write by writing. Parents of young children will tell you their children learned to talk by talking and that they find plenty of opportunities to use talk in meaningful ways.

In my kindergarten children have many opportunities to practice reading. They read every day during choice time, and they read and write as they play around the room. They read the signs that they write for their block constructions, read notes from friends, and read to each other while playing school.

Response

"Talking is a universal medium of communication," (Cambourne 1988, p. 41), and response is a natural part of talking. Parents give constant feedback in their conversations with their children. They answer children's questions, give them what they ask for, and tell them more about a subject of interest.

In my classroom children naturally receive responses to what they are learning from their peers and from me. They talk about their work at the writing table, hang up a painting on the sharing board, ask me to take a photograph of a skyscraper they made with blocks, offer to read to a visiting parent, and share their writing with the class at the end of choice time.

Don Holdaway: Natural Learning Classroom Model

Holdaway claims that "with some rather radical changes, the school environment also may embody the principles of natural learning to a significant degree" (Holdaway 1986, p. 62). In the early 1970s in New Zealand it was apparent to Holdaway and other members of the

Figure 2-2 Holdaway: Natural Learning Model

Department of Education that current traditional methods of teaching literacy were not successful in meeting the needs of their multicultural society. Holdaway was asked to explore alternative ways of teaching literacy in the schools. At the Richmond Road School near Auckland, he developed the shared book experience (usually referred to as shared reading in this country) as an essential strategy of natural learning classroom practice and began to apply the conditions of oral language acquisition to the school setting with children of diverse backgrounds and languages.

Holdaway has continued to analyze these natural learning conditions and developed a natural learning classroom model (Figure 2-2). The model includes Demonstration, Participation, Practice or Role-play, and Performance (Holdaway 1986), and supports children through the full cycle of natural learning. It gives them opportunities to become self-regulating learners, as both learner and teacher take dominant roles at different times, always in a social context, cooperating and collaborating in a noncompetitive environment.

Below is the model, adapted from Holdaway (1986, 1990), that I use to organize my classroom routine and to plan curriculum.

CLASSROOM ACTIVITIES	CLASSROOM ROUTINE	DOMINANT ROLE
1. Demonstration	Shared Reading	Teacher
2. Participation	Shared Reading	Teacher/Learner
3. Practice	Choice Time	Learner
4. Performance	Sharing Time	Learner

Demonstration and Participation

Shared reading is the time when the teacher demonstrates the reading and writing process and the entire class participates in a variety of language activities. I sit in a chair next to the teaching easel, and the children sit on the floor as a group facing me. We spend about a half hour enjoying, discussing, and dramatizing songs, poems, chants, and big books, which are all written in enlarged print so that the children can see the text as I point to it. The focus is always on meaning. Although I follow the cues, interests, and specific needs of the children and involve them in the planning, as teacher I play the dominant role in orchestrating and leading the session.

During Participation both teacher and learner are participants (Holdaway 1990). Midkiff-Borunda (1989, p. 138), in her study of the

Literacy Center at the Longfellow School in Cambridge, Massachusetts, discovered that "an overwhelming amount of interactions n
the Shared Book Experience were individual rather than group."
Each child participates at his or her own developmental level in this
noncompetitive group situation. Although the overall effect is one of
group singing or unison reading, each child is taking the responsibility for selecting what he or she needs to be successful.

As Holdaway observed, "The unison situation, properly controlled in a lively and meaningful spirit, allows for massive individual practice by every pupil in the teaching context" (1979, p 129).
When the children sing together, each one is approximating and self-
correcting to make sense of the text. Each is working toward becoming an independent, self-regulating reader.

Midkiff-Borunda (1989) identified three categories of interaction between teachers and students during shared reading: Reading
Participation, Textual Participation, and Non-Textual Participation.
Reading Participation involved oral reading of the text by the
teacher and students. Textual Participation "included comments by
teachers and students that related directly to the text" (p. 14). Non-
Textual Participation included comments and actions not specifically related to the text, such as comments about behavior and
social interactions by the teacher and students. She concluded:
"Overall, the teachers and students divided their time equally within
two major categories of interaction, Reading Participation and Textual Participation. Combining these two categories accounted for
over 80% of the data set. The category of Non-Textual Participation
was the least used in the SBE (Shared Book Experience). Text familiarity influenced these categories of interaction. When there was a
familiar text the teachers and students divided their interactions
equally between Reading Participation and Textual Participation.
When a story was unfamiliar there was less Reading Participation
and more Textual Participation" (p 155).

Practice or Role-playing

During choice time the children have opportunities to practice what
they need to learn without the teacher or demonstrator directly
involved. During this self-motivated, self-selected practice time
there is "no true audience except self" (Holdaway 1990, p. 5) In my
classroom most of the children are with their classmates or by
themselves, making choices about what, how, when, and where they
will learn. As they engage in activities that are meaningful to them,
they are self-monitoring and self-regulating, working toward the
automaticity in reading and writing that they have gained in talking.

I am not very visible at this time. I am working with individuals or a small group, or I am kid watching. I notice that the children like to do the same task over and over again.

Every day Tommy draws a picture of himself at the writing table. Until recently he avoided drawing because "I can't do it like Andrew."

I watch. It looks as if he is feeling success with the picture of a house that he draws day after day, needing to practice the same subject over and over again. When will he try a new subject? I'll keep watching.

Stephanie and Ryan spend a lot of time role-playing teacher and student with the pointer and big books in the reading area. I notice that they read the same three books every day. What is important about those books? I'll keep watching.

Allison usually chooses to create flower-like designs with pattern blocks at the math area. I notice that she starts with the same combination of blocks, but then varies her design a little each day. I wonder what her plan is? I'll keep watching.

Performance

During sharing time, as well as throughout the day, children have opportunities to share what they have learned with their peers and teacher. The traditional roles are reversed; the learner becomes the teacher and demonstrator, and the teacher becomes the learner and participator.

David proudly places his work in the sharing basket, which is in a common place in the writing area where children can place their work if they want to share it with the class at the end of Choice Time. Three boys are ready to put on a skit. Sari stuffs her drawing in her bag to show her mom.

Holdaway claims (Whole Language Teachers Association talk, 1990, Salem State College, Salem, Massachusetts) that we know learning has occurred when our students come to us and want to show us their work. They offer to share when they feel good about what they have done, when growth has occurred, when learning has taken place, and when they feel success. This is the most honest assessment because it encourages us, as teachers, to examine what the children indicate they can do as we become "a special, validating audience" (Holdaway 1990, p. 5) and a critic by invitation only.

For Further Reading

Cambourne, Brian. 1989. *The Whole Story: Natural Learning and the Acquisition of Literacy in the Classroom.* New York: Ashton Scholastic.

Holdaway, Don. 1984. *Stability and Change in Literacy Learning.* Portsmouth, NH: Heinemann.

————. 1986. "The Structure of Natural Learning as a Basis for Literacy Instruction." In M. Sampson, ed., *The Pursuit of Literacy: Early Reading and Writing.* Dubuque, IA: Kendall/Hunt.

Smith, Frank. 1988. *Joining the Literacy Club: Further Essays into Education.* Portsmouth, NH: Heinemann.

3

The Room

As I set up my classroom before the start of school and as the children and I change the appearance of the room throughout the year, it reflects what I believe about children and how they learn. I organize the room so that children can learn the classroom routine easily and can take care of themselves and their belongings independently. I keep wastebaskets, a tray for notes from home, writing supplies, and the daily attendance sign-in paper in the same place throughout the year.

A choice of materials that are easily accessible to the children is offered, and when appropriate, the shelves and materials are labeled. For example, several kinds of paper are available in the writing area, and each kind is labeled on the shelf (see Supplies and Materials for the Classroom).

Books, pictures, and writing materials are located in each area. In the block area I put books about buildings and building equipment. Prints of famous paintings hang in the art area. Paper and markers are available in the block area for children to make signs for their buildings, and note paper and telephone message pads are placed in the housekeeping area.

I start out with a limited amount of materials in each area, and during the year I gradually add new items as the children learn the classroom routines, show interest in various topics, and indicate a need for new challenges. For example, I start with measuring cups and spoons in the sand table, adding sifters and other equipment later.

Finally, I create areas where children can easily display and see their own work. I place a bulletin board with push pins in the writing area so children can hang up a picture or story they want to share.

The Main Permanent Areas

I start the year with five permanent learning areas—reading, writing, math, art, and dramatic play—plus a snack table, sharing area and

Figure 3-1 Room plan

sand table. These areas each accommodate between four and six children. As the year goes on a puppet theater, water table, and workbench are introduced, and specific curriculum-focus centers (such as magnets, insects, and hatching chickens) are set up (Figure 3–1).

Reading Area

The large carpeted reading area (Figure 3–2) is the focal point of my classroom because this is where demonstration and participation in literacy occurs during shared reading. It is also where children practice reading during choice time and where, at the day's end, the class returns as a group to share what they have done.

This area has a message board that lists our schedule for the day, a calendar, and the I CARE board (see Chapter 7), where children record the areas they have been to during choice time (Figure 3–3). There is a rocking chair, pillows for comfort, and materials for shared and independent reading. Big books, poems, chants, and songs (all in enlarged print) as well as a large, plastic writing board are permanent, and supplies such as pointers, letter and word masks, markers, and Post-its are easily accessible.

A teaching easel holds big books and blank paper for writing. I clip the poems, chants, and songs for the day on a teaching easel or

Figure 3-2 Reading area

Figure 3-3 A child fills in the I CARE Board

hang them from hangers on a large nail on the bulletin board. The bulletin board usually displays a pocket chart, posters, and pictures that focus on a theme we are studying, a class book we are working on, and examples of children's work.

Our supply of big books is stored standing up in a box under the easel and displayed along the wall. The poems and charts are stored on clip hangers from a metal clothing rack that is easily accessible to the children and me. Fiction and nonfiction trade books, predictable books (books with a simple pattern which support beginning reading), dictionaries, magazines, and the daily newspaper are available on library display shelves, regular shelves, plastic bins and crates, and on tables around the room. Throughout the year the children sort the books in different ways and rearrange the books on display.

A listening table that accommodates four people is always available. It includes a tape recorder, ear phones, story tapes, and multiple copies of text and song tapes.

Writing Area
This area has a table with chairs for six children, two desks for cooperative or quiet work, shelves for supplies, and a large plastic file

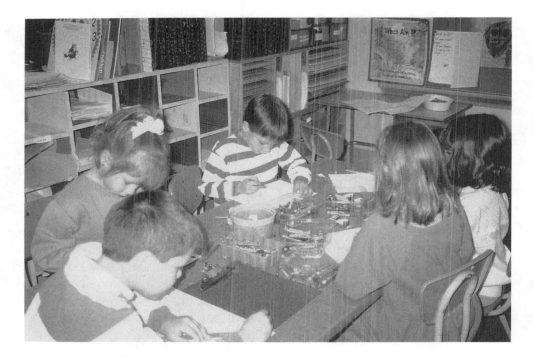

Figure 3-4 Writing Area

box for the children's work. Initially, I place lined and unlined paper, pencils, crayons, and a date stamp on the shelves. As the year goes on I add different kinds of writing paper, construction paper, a stapler, blank books, note paper, envelopes, and so on (Figure 3–4).

The alphabet, in upper- and lowercase letters cut from contact paper, is on a cupboard behind the writing table and placed at eye level for the children to see and touch easily. Wooden and plastic letters and copies of the alphabet are available. A plastic crate where the children file their work is in the area. Hanging colored files with the children's first names are placed in alphabetical order so they can file their own work and look at their writings and drawings throughout the year. A manila folder for finished work is in each file, and as the year goes on we add a colored folder that is labeled for unfinished work. The children are encouraged to keep the hanging file in the box so they will always know where their work is, and to take out the manila and colored folders as needed.

Math Area

At the math area the children work with a variety of math manipulatives. There are opportunities for free play and teacher-guided and teacher-directed activities, for individual challenges and cooperative games, and for discussion among peers and teacher. The area has a round table with six chairs, and shelves to store math materials such as Cuisinaire Rods, pattern blocks, color cubes, Unifix Cubes, attribute blocks, chip trading, dice, board games, puzzles, Lego, and other building sets. It also has a shelf with unit blocks and a large carpeted area for building. Big hollow blocks are located under the loft in the dramatic play environment area.

Art Area

In the art area the children have opportunities to express themselves through a variety of materials and processes. Tempera paints at two easels placed side by side, playdough, and recycled materials are always available for the children to select. Periodically, I introduce a process such as finger painting, printing, working with chalk, and paper tearing. Throughout the year we integrate art with the literature we read and with the dramatic play environment themes we develop. For example, the children might illustrate their own copy of *Fire! Fire! Said Mrs. Mcguire*, draw pictures for an innovation on *The Little Red Hen*, or make a class mural for an architect's office constructed in the dramatic play area.

Dramatic Play Environment Area

In the dramatic play environment area the children engage in a variety of play situations. A loft in my classroom provides added space for these activities. At the beginning of the year the upstairs is set up as a housekeeping area, and a set of big blocks and large trucks are kept underneath.

This dramatic play environment area, which is used for free play, cooperative learning experiences, and dramatic play themes, changes throughout the year. Sometimes the themes develop or generate from free play in this area, and one theme cycle often leads naturally to another. For example, one year the children built a bank, made money, and then built a supermarket. This led to a study about food and the farm. At other times I introduce curriculum units that correspond to the prescribed curriculum in my school Occasionally, the class community chooses a topic to pursue.

Snack Area

The snack area in my classroom is near the sink and consists of a small round table and four chairs. Cooking utensils hang on a pegboard behind the table. During choice time the children (four at a time) can choose to eat the snack they bring from home, and can plan when and with whom to eat. I encourage parents to give their children the responsibility for planning and preparing their snack. Some children bring a snack every day, while others only have snack

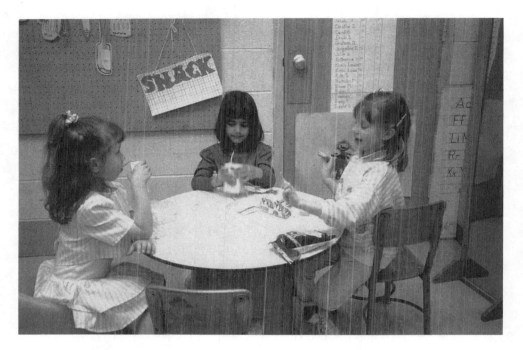

Figure 3-5 Snack table

if someone has brought something for the whole class or if the snack is the result of a class cooking project (Figure 3–5).

Learning takes place during snack time as the children socialize, share, and talk about what is meaningful and interesting to them. It was at the snack table that Andrew, who always started choice time there, learned how to initiate a conversation, listen to others, laugh at a joke, and be part of the group. I watched his confidence grow throughout the year as he made friends with the other children by sharing his snack and conversing with them in this informal setting.

Sharing Table and Bulletin Board

I always have a table and bulletin board available where the children can display things they've brought from home or that they've made at school and want to share with the class. Often these things become catalysts for reading topics during shared reading and story time, for special interest centers and for dramatic play environments. Also, through these sharing areas I can discover particular interests of the children.

Sand Table

A sand table is available during choice time. As the year goes by we add different materials and utensils, and sometimes it becomes an important part of our dramatic play environments. For example, it was part of the display when we made an aquarium, and it held plants when we built a greenhouse in the class.

Temporary Areas

Due to limited space, or because they need special materials, instructions, or supervision when introduced, the three temporary areas—water table, workbench, and puppet theater—are added as the year goes along and are sometimes available only on selected days or times of year.

Water Table

A large water table is filled and put outside on warm days in the fall and spring. During the winter a 2' x '4 x 3' transparent plastic tub fits on one end of the art table and is used as a water table.

Workbench

The workbench usually becomes a permanent work area after the children have learned the classroom routines. It is covered with a carpet to absorb the hammering noise and has a vice attached to the side. The supplies, such as wood, hammers, saws, screw drivers, nails with wide heads for safe hammering, and a variety of sizes of screws, are stored on a pegboard and shelf accessible to the children.

Puppet Theater

I have two puppet theaters. The large one can accommodate four people and also serves as a storefront. The other is small, portable, and easy to store and is adequate for two performers.

Although the physical set up of the classroom remains constant throughout the year, changes are made by the children and me as new curriculum interests develop. New materials are added and unneeded supplies removed so that everything in the room is purposeful and functional.

4

The Start Of The Day

A typical day in my kindergarten includes seven basic time segments, during which the children engage in meaningful activities as they interact in a noncompetitive community. (See Chapter 16, Question 1, for discussion of a longer kindergarten day and ways to make daily, weekly, and long-range plans.)

The start of the day includes settling-in time and community circle time. Although these take up a short amount of time in the daily schedule, they are very important because they set a positive tone for the day, and help us develop as a community of learners.

Daily Schedule

8:50–9:00	Settling-in Time
9:00–9:15	Community Circle Time
9:15–9:45	Shared Reading Time
9:45–10:40	Choice Time
10:40–10:50	Sharing Time
10:50–11:10	Clean-up & Outside
11:10–11:30	Preparation for Home & Story Time

Settling-in Time

The tone of the settling-in time is relaxed and informal. There is a quiet flow of activity and conversation as the children arrive in the classroom. We all need this settling-in time to help make a smooth transition from morning activities at home and the trip to school to the community learning environment in the classroom.

As she comes into the room Mariah puts a note in the basket telling me that she is going to day care after school, and Judd puts his home/school journal (a notebook for communication between parents and me), in the basket, too (see Chapter 14). Judy and Clare put their books in the library basket, ready to exchange at the school library during choice time. Amy always signs in first and then hangs up her coat and bag. Jake returns *When Goldilocks Went to the House of the Three Bears* to our classroom library and signs out a small copy of *The Gingerbread Man* to take home. Allison, Tommy, and Kevin are listening to *The Longest Journey in the World* on tape, and the other children build with pattern blocks, work on a puzzle, look at a book, or talk with their friends. Cara shows me a bird's nest that she found over the weekend. I encourage her to share what she has brought from home informally with her friends and me during this time, and then to put it on the sharing table. The leader for the day hangs the day's date on the calendar.

I talk with the children as they take care of these responsibilities for getting ready for the school day. Some help me select charts of favorite poems, chants, and songs (which are taped to hangers and hang on a wire coat rack) to include for shared reading that day. The tone of the settling-in time is relaxed and informal.

Sign-In

Harste, Woodward, and Burke, in *Language Stories and Literacy Lessons*, end a section in their book with the plea, "Let them 'sign in,' please!" (p. 22). I remember reading that plea three summers ago and starting school the following fall asking my kindergartners to write their names on 9" × 18" pieces of manila drawing paper every morning when they first come in. They have been signing in ever since, and I've adapted the process to fit the needs of the children, my goals, and the goals of my school system (Figure 4–1).

I write the date and day at the top of the paper, and put it on a table for the children to sign as they come into class. My assistant and I sign in, too. I like to have the entire class sign in on one paper because it shows our classroom community as a whole. When we gather for community circle time, I read the list to the class as a way of joining us together, and as a means of taking attendance. As the children show interest, they take over this activity.

Sign-In and Assessment

I find out what the children can do by watching them as they sign in and by evaluating their final product. In September, and periodically throughout the year, I use the sign-in procedure to assess each child's development and competencies. For example, I assess fine motor skills, spacial relationships, and letter knowledge. Some of the questions I specifically try to answer are:

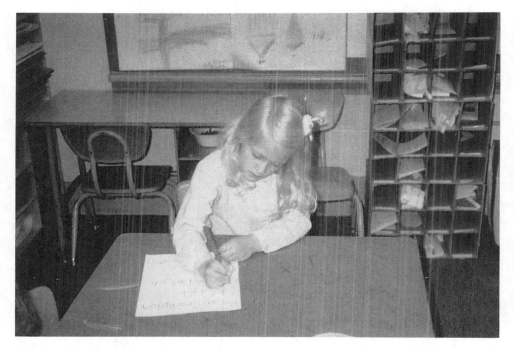

Figure 4-1 Sign-in

- Can they write their name? If they indicate they can't, I "teach" them so they can participate.
- Are they right- or left-handed? It is important to observe this periodically to note if the children have established dominance.
- How are they forming the letters?
- Is their letter size consistent?
- What upper- and lowercase letters do they write?
- Do they write their last name?

This procedure also gives me valuable information about the children as individuals and as members of the classroom community. For example, I notice who always manages to get to the table to sign in first, who cuts into the line, who elbows and pushes in line, who suggests that we need to form a line, who forgets to sign in, who signs in in huge letters, who crosses out other children's names, and the reactions of other children to their peers in this process.

Sometimes I use the sign-in list to validate a child's progress by commenting on what I notice he or she is doing, such as "I notice that you are using the lowercase *e* in your name, Kevin." I keep every sign-in sheet and use them to observe growth during the year. For example, Mandy and I looked at the sign-in papers from October to March and noticed that she now was writing her d's in the right direction.

Sign-In and Handwriting

Although I am continually demonstrating correct letter formation as I write class stories, thank-you letters, book lists, and so on in front of the class, in January I introduce a sign-in procedure that focuses specifically on handwriting, which I substitute for the regular procedure about three days a week. I write the names of four of the children on one piece of paper and leave a space underneath for each child to copy his or her name. Every day we use a new paper so they are always copying directly under my demonstration. As individual children show interest, I add their last name to the paper.

When I have a free minute during choice time, I sit with individual children and, using the current sign-in paper, we work together on their handwriting. First we look at how they signed in that day. Then we talk about what was successful and discuss what we will work on during this mini-lesson. For example, we might focus on forming a specific letter, writing a lowercase letter, or developing consistent letter size or spacing between letters.

This emphasis on handwriting eliminates some of the rich individualization and spirit of classroom community that the other sign-in form generates. However, using both procedures gives me the opportunity to observe any transfer of learning from the formal sign-in to the informal sign-in, and to personal writing. I notice that when the children are ready, they apply what they have learned during sign-in to their own writing.

Other Sign-In Procedures

Throughout the year the children are also signing their names in response to questions posed about a variety of topics. For example, in October we had a green pumpkin and I wrote on a piece of paper, "Will this pumpkin turn orange?" The children wrote their name in a "yes" or "no" column. Other questions ask for specific answers, such as "Which kind of fruit did you like best in the fruit salad we made?" The children wrote their name, followed by the name of the fruit. After a few demonstrations they begin to think of their own questions. Sign-up papers appear around the room and children take a clipboard and interview their classmates, using a class list to record their responses. They ask for favorite foods, colors, TV shows, cars, games, animals, etc. They also ask comparison questions: Which do you like best, pizza or spaghetti? music or gym? the book *Chicka,*

Chicka Boom Boom or *Good-night Owl*? and so on. Topics are often generated from the current dramatic play environment (see Chapter 12).

The natural-learning classroom model is in full use in these
activities. I start out as the demonstrator, posing my question, and
the children participate by responding. As they take over creating
the topics, interviewing friends and reporting their findings, they are
role-playing being teachers, and performing and sharing as profi-
cient users of the activity.

Community Circle Time

After settling in, we begin with community circle time, which sets the
tone for the day. We sit in a circle so we can all see one another and
participate as equal members of the group. During this time we
usually:

- Discuss the daily schedule
- Share "Headline News"
- Include sharing from home
- Read Mr. Bear's journal
- Talk about the calendar

Daily Schedule
Every morning before the children arrive I write the day's schedule
on the chalkboard. Since the daily routine is predictable, I always
use the same words to describe it so the children can begin to read
the schedule themselves. I also have these daily events written on 3"
× 6" oak tag cards, which the children arrange in a pocket chart
during settling-in time.

As we start community circle time we discuss the plans for the
day. We go over the daily routine, mention special events such as
gym, music, and school meeting, acknowledge anyone who is not in
school, and share anything we know about their absence. We also
greet visitors or parents who have come to help. Next we begin
"Headline News" and in January we include 'Children as Teachers."

Headline News
Knowing some of the things that are important in the lives of everyone in the classroom is essential in building our classroom community, so we often start community circle time with Headline News. At
the beginning of the year I model the procedure. As the year goes on,
the leader for the day directs Headline News by telling his or her
news first and then calling on each child in the circle to either tell his
or her news in a sentence, or "headline," or to pass. Limiting the

news to a headline gives everyone a chance to share and enables us to learn something about each other in a short amount of time. We learn that Mary's cat didn't come home last night, that Sam's grandmother is coming for a visit, that Steven is going to Sarah's house to play, that Ted's mom and dad are away on a trip, and that I am going to visit my mom for the weekend.

Sometimes someone asks a question for clarification, and if the news is of special importance to the children or me, we talk about it in greater depth. I try to relinquish my dominant role as much as possible during this time so that the children will have charge of the direction of the conversation. I participate as an equal member of the group and encourage the leader to direct the dialogue.

Sharing news in this formal way helps the children to understand, trust, and care about their classmates, and it helps each child realize that others have feelings and situations similar to their own. When John's mom was in a car accident and had to stay in bed for two months, the children had many questions for him. They understood what it was like not to have mom up and about, and had their own related stories. For the rest of the year they often asked John how his mom was doing, and she received a special welcome when she came to visit at the end of the year. These stories also help me understand what is important to the children so I can better respond to their needs.

Sharing from Home

By the second day of school, children are usually coming in with something to "show and tell." I want to encourage them to share their interests, and I want to build curriculum around those interests. Nevertheless, I find that show and tell, if left unstructured, can escalate very quickly into a time-consuming, self-centered activity, taking away from important components of the curriculum and detracting from the sense of classroom community

I have several strategies for making show and tell, which I call "sharing from home," an integrated and meaningful part of the kindergarten program. These are the "Sharing Table," "Children as Teachers" and the "Celebrating Me!" projects which are described in Chapter 12.

Sharing Table   My classroom has a sharing table where children display things they bring from home. As they settle in I encourage them to share informally with their peers and me what they have brought. This gives us the opportunity to look closely, to feel and touch, and to ask questions. As community circle time begins, the children place the items on the sharing table to be looked at further during choice time. Pictures and artifacts that children have made and special items agreed upon by the child and me are sometimes shared with the entire group.

Most items are acceptable. Stuffed animals are always welcome, as are trucks and cars for use at the block area. Transformers guns, war toys, and TV interactive toys are not allowed, and we discuss my reasons for excluding them from the classroom. I tell the kids that I want them to feel happy and safe in this room so that they can learn and have fun. I explain that I can't help them get along with each other and learn together if they are playing war (see Chapter 16).

Children as Teachers   In January I introduce a more formal sharing time called "children as teachers." The children take the role of teacher (or demonstrator) and I become one of the participants. The children are assigned one day a week when they can teach the class something that they have planned at home. This schedule continues for the rest of the school year. For example, they bring in books or art projects they have made, artifacts from another culture, collections or hobbies, something from nature, science experiments, magic tricks, a poem or song to teach the class, or a favorite book to read.

As they sit on the teacher's chair, they are encouraged to explain why they chose what they did, tell a few things about their sharing, and respond to questions from the audience. The procedure is flexible and changes as the year goes on. At the beginning of the year I usually act as scribe and write the information on a special form (Appendix A. 1), which is displayed with the item on the sharing table, but as the year goes on many children choose to write their own sharing description. The children draw a picture to accompany the writing. In getting to know the specific interests of their classmates, the children often choose one of the topics to write about at the writing table, and sometimes a particular interest acts as a catalyst for a dramatic play environment in the class.

Since I want parents to support their children in this activity, I send a letter home explaining the procedure and listing each child's sharing day. Depending on the size of the class, between four and five children are assigned each day, and if a child is absent, or there is no school, the children who miss their day can share the next day. Those who forget their day wait for the next week.

Some years this activity becomes an important part of the curriculum in my class, as the children have opportunities to introduce curriculum content and take responsibility for managing themselves as teachers in our community. They experience some of the considerations that go into planning and carrying out curriculum, such as, what topics are interesting to the group, what kinds of information the group wants to know, and how to speak in front of a group. As they experience the teacher's point of view, their understanding of themselves as pupils takes on a new perspective, the quality of their questions when they are participants changes, and their understanding of the importance of being a respectful audience grows. My role is to demonstrate and facilitate this growth.

Mr. Bear

Next we read Mr. Bear's journal and pass Mr. Bear (a stuffed animal) on to the child who will be taking him home for the upcoming night. (I got the idea for Mr. Bear from an article entitled "Oscar's Journal," by Susan Sinclair Durst, in *Understanding Writing*.) Mr. Bear travels in a bag, along with a composition book that serves as his journal, his toothbrush, and other artifacts that he has accumulated along the way. A letter written by Mr. Bear is at the front of the journal and explains where he came from and the general procedure for his visits. Parents, children, and other family members are encouraged to write and draw about Mr. Bear's visit to their house.

As the year goes on he makes repeated visits. When a journal is filled, he gets a new one and all the journals travel with him so families can read about his adventures in between stays at their house.

Mr. Bear's journal provides a meaningful way for the class to learn and care about each other, and involves the families in the classroom community. It lets me know about the home life of the children and gives the families a way to get to know me, since I take Mr. Bear home, too. For example, we have learned that Clare's grandmother lives with her, that Andrew's family says prayers every night, that Jake loves pizza, that Timmy watches TV when he comes home, and that I have a dog that barks a lot.

Calendar

Attention to the calendar in my kindergarten focuses on events that are meaningful to individual children and classroom happenings. For example, we talk about birthdays, holidays, school routines such as gym and music, and special school meetings and assemblies, marking them on the calendar with a marker or sticker.

Specific daily procedures with the calendar are brief. The leader of the day hangs the day's date on the calendar during settling-in time. Then, to celebrate the day, we count the number of days we have been in school as I point to a chart with the numbers to date As the days accumulate we begin to count by twos, fives, tens, and twenties, and the children can choose other numbers as well. About halfway through the year I make a weekly graph that guides us to count in different ways each day As we count the last number, the leader pops a balloon that I have pinned on the day's date on the calendar (Garland 1990).

My niece, a student in Elaine Nelson's kindergarten in Portland, Oregon, told me about Zero the Hero, a bear who helps children learn about numbers in her class. We now have a little bear in our class, whom I also named Zero the Hero Every day he holds the number from the calendar, and we talk about what we know about the day's date. For example, on March 15 the children shared the following: "there are two numbers," "my sister is 15," "the 15th letter of the alphabet is o," "the 1 only has straight lines and the 5 has straight and curved lines," and "if you turn 15 around you get 51 "

As the children make the transition from sitting in a circle facing each other during community circle time to sitting in a group focusing on the enlarged text in big books and on charts, we usually start with a favorite book, such as *Hush Little Baby* or *Where Does the Brown Bear Go?* and we start to chant or sing. We are ready for shared reading.

For Further Reading

Durst, Susan S. 1988. "Oscar's Journal." In Thomas Newkirk and Nancie Atwell, eds., *Understanding Writing: Ways of Observing, Learning, and Teaching*. Portsmouth, NH: Heinemann.

Harste, Jerome C., Virginia A. Woodward, and Carolyn L. Burke. 1984. *Language Stories and Literacy Lessons*. Portsmouth, NH: Heinemann.

5

Shared Reading: Theory

*"What a child can do in cooperation today,
he can do alone tomorrow."* VYGOTSKY

Shared reading is the time in the day when I demonstrate the reading and writing process and the entire class participates in a variety of language activities. Much of this half hour is spent enjoying, discussing, and dramatizing songs, poems, chants, and big books. Most of these books have enlarged print so that the children can see the text as I point. Usually, I sit in a chair next to the teaching easel and the children sit as a group facing me.

First we sing a few familiar songs and recite a favorite poem or chant. This joins us together as a classroom community and gives us the opportunity to engage in discussions about favorite texts as we become more familiar with them. Once or twice a week I introduce a new song, poem, or chant. Next we read one or two familiar big books, exploring the text more deeply with each reading, and about once a week we add a new big book to our repertoire. To vary the routine we sometimes have Community Sing Day, when we sing between fifteen and twenty favorite songs, or a Big Book Festival, when we read as many as eight favorite big books.

This chapter describes a typical shared reading session and discusses the theory behind the skills and strategies engaged in during this time which support children in their literacy development. Chapter 6 explains a typical shared reading planning schedule and describes some of the favorite texts and activities that the children and I enjoy.

A Typical Shared Reading Session

Six favorite songs and poems are hanging on the easel. We've just finished singing the first one, "Love Somebody," a favorite text I learned from Don Holdaway's *Foundations of Literacy* Hands go up, for the children know that they will have the opportunity to choose someone they love for us to sing about as we substitute their choice for "somebody." I take a post-it and begin to write Mandy's innovation, "my mom," asking questions, acknowledging responses, and demonstrating the spelling of the word.

"What does 'my' start with? What do you hear at the end? Yes, it sounds like an *i* but we write *y*. Remember, sometimes at the end of a word we hear *i* but we write *y*. The *y* is the vowel in the word." The children are also talking, each responding at his or her developmental level, and willing to take a risk because they know that no one will single them out as right or wrong. I continue writing the word "mom" and then stick the note on the text. I've just given a mini-lesson.

Tommy comments that if you write "mom" backwards it still spells "mom." This time I ask everyone to stop talking so we can all hear what Tommy has to say. He explains. Tommy has just given a mini-lesson.

We sing our newly created song and hands go up again. This time I encourage the children to "think what the innovation looks like because I'm not going to write it out. We'll just sing it." I want to keep the pace lively so everyone stays engaged. I want to keep the main focus of all our activities on meaning, not on spelling.

The next song, "Five Little Fishes," is one that Wendy requested when she came in that morning. The song is important to her because she had introduced it originally when we were studying the sea and setting up a classroom aquarium.

We sing the song twice and move on to "Pease-porridge Hot." I ask the leader to choose a letter to use in place of the P and he picks G. I write the letter on a post-it and ask the class whether we should use the sound of *g* as in "girl" or in "giraffe." The children seem interested in offering *g* words beginning with both sounds, and I write them on the board under the two headings. When someone suggests "jelly," we add a third column to accommodate the words beginning with *j*. After a lively discussion and sharing, we say the nursery rhyme with the *g* sound in "giraffe" and then repeat it with the *g* sound as in "girl." I don't point to the text for this one because I want to demonstrate the traditional hand-clapping actions that go with the text. I notice that Mark's approximations are getting closer to my demonstration and that Sari isn't participating at all. The hand actions have been difficult for her. Has she given up? I'll keep watching.

Cheers go up as I turn to "This Land is My Land." This has been an overwhelming favorite right from the first singing, and the class has already written an innovation, "This School is My School," which we will sing next. Before we get started Andrew shouts that he sees the word "my," and I invite him to come up and frame it so that everyone can focus on the word. All at once other children are asking to come up to mask or frame words they know, so Andrew calls on someone to be the next teacher. He gives them the choice of three sizes of masks, and they pick the one they think will best fit their word (See Appendix A. 2). Each time a new word is masked we begin singing from the beginning of the verse to discover or confirm what the word is. We are using the strategy of rereading part of the text, which successful readers use when they come to a word they don't know.

The next selection is the poem "Names," by Aubyn, one of the children in the class. We say it together as Aubyn points. A discussion ensues about the repetition of the word "names," a technique many poets use. We close this section of shared reading with a favorite song, "Mr. Sun" from a Raffi tape, which we sing joyously as we listen to it on tape, and then turn to a familiar big book.

The leader for the day picks *The Monsters' Party*, and we decide to act it out. During shared reading I usually point to the text because I want the children to have an accurate demonstration as they look at the print. However, when we act out a favorite book, I usually pick one child to point because I know that the attention of the audience and actors will be focused on the dramatic activity, not on the text. As I watch the children act out the parts of the various monsters, I know that they are into meaning!

We end the session reading *Who's in the Shed?* I've chosen this one because I have noticed that during choice time several children have been reading it on their own. Becoming more familiar with it in the safety of the group during shared reading will help them read it independently later. The class has been fascinated with question marks, and the children have started hooking their fingers in the shape of a question mark every time they notice one. With this reading someone starts counting the question marks by hooking a finger for each one seen, and very soon most of the children are joining in. I close by telling them I have a new big book for tomorrow, so they can anticipate.

Goals and Benefits of Shared Reading

I want the children to gain confidence in their ability to develop as language learners and users, so I try to keep the shared reading sessions lively, relaxed, non competitive, and always focused on meaning. This atmosphere allows all of the children to learn and participate.

As we sing or read, it often sounds like the group is singing or reading in unison, but as I watch what individual children are doing and listen to what they are saying, I notice that they are participating at their own developmental level and with their individual style. They seem to be taking the responsibility for selecting what they need to be successful. Each child is approximating and self-correcting to make sense of the text, and is working toward becoming an independent, self-regulating reader.

For example, during the third singing of *The Circus is in Town*, I notice that Mary is watching my lips, Judd is looking at the pictures as he mumbles most of the words, Stephanie is watching the text and singing most of the song, and Sarah just seems to be listening. As Holdaway has observed, "The unison situation, properly controlled in a lively and meaningful spirit, allows for massive individual practice by every pupil in the teaching context" (Holdaway 1979, p. 129).

Some of the benefits of shared reading that I believe support my kindergartners as learners are listed below. I believe that it:

- Develops a sense of community in the classroom, building upon the value of the group experience of culturally significant language that is transmitted through group participation.
- Promotes a community of learners where everyone has something to contribute and learn from one another.
- Acknowledges that language is social.
- Gives opportunities for all children to attend to what is personally meaningful, interesting, and functional and to share it with others.
- Engages all children in reading-like behavior.
- Enables children to share more of themselves by allowing for repeated opportunities to take risks, approximate, self-correct, and comprehend within the safety of the group in a non competitive atmosphere.
- Brings children in contact with the literary experience of books and the language of the outside world.
- Validates reading for meaning.
- Provides demonstrations of appropriate selection and use of the three cueing systems.
- Enables individuals to develop and internalize their own learning style.
- Gives opportunities for children at all stages on the reading continuum to be successful learners.

• Offers optimum quality and quantity time each day for teacher to demonstrate.

Skills and Strategies

Shared reading offers continuous opportunities for the development of reading skills and strategies. I think of reading skills as small units of knowledge. For example, knowing letters and sounds is a skill focused on in kindergarten. I can check children on their letter-sound knowledge by asking them to recognize each letter and to give me the sound for the letter.

I think of strategies as ways of establishing patterns of learning that will help the learner solve problems as they occur, while getting meaning from the text. For example, using the beginning letter and sound to predict and confirm the next word in a story is a strategy demonstrated to initial readers that will be used by them throughout their life. I can assess children's ability to use the skill of letter-sound knowledge strategically by watching what they do when they come to a word they don't know as they read to me.

Since successful readers apply skills as they predict, sample, and confirm or self-correct to get meaning from the text, I always demonstrate skills in support of strategies in context. During shared reading we focus on skills and strategies that the group has shown an interest in, or which an individual child has noticed during shared reading. We also focus on skills I have noticed the children exploring during independent reading and writing. For example, Brad was writing "az" for "is" at the writing table. During shared reading the next day, we focused on the word "is" in the book *Tails*. (I had written the text in enlarged print on a chart so we could all see it easily, a technique I often use with favorite, familiar books.)

The Literacy Set

Holdaway (1979, p. 62) suggests four factors of emergent literacy that four-, five- and six-year-olds display as the result of "the bedtime story," opportunities to practice reading on their own and experiences with literacy in their everyday lives. The factors that comprise what he terms "Literacy Set" are:

• Motivational Factors
• Linguistic Factors
• Operational Factors
• Orthographic Factors

Motivational factors refer to the children's enjoyment and appreciation of books, their interest in a variety of print (e.g., signs, labels, and advertisements), and their attempts at their own writing. Linguistic factors refer to the children's ability to become familiar with written dialect in oral form as they hear and manipulate the patterns of written language. Operational factors involve the essential strategies for handling written language, such as self-monitoring, predicting, understanding story structure, and creating images. Orthographic factors refer to print conventions: story comes from print, reading left to right, letter knowledge, and phonetic principles.

"Children who have developed a strong literacy set begin to operate immediately and automatically in appropriate ways whenever they are faced with print" (Holdaway 1979, p. 49). They begin to move toward "the 'early reading stage,' in which close attention to the visual detail of print in the final relating of cues brings about what we would recognize as 'true reading' " (Holdaway 1979, p. 57).

I find that as my kindergartners develop a strong literacy set, they begin to focus more specifically on print concepts, which I demonstrate and reinforce in context during shared reading. I use the following chart, which I have developed from Clay (1979), Holdaway (1979), and Reading in Junior Classes (1985), to plan shared reading lessons, to record the print concepts focused upon each day, and to assess and evaluate each child's progress toward application in their reading and writing.

Conventions of Print

---

1. Book knowledge

- Front of the book
- Back of the book
- Reading the left-hand page before the right-hand page
- Holding a book and turning the pages
- Distinction between pictures and print
- Title
- Author

2. Directionality

- Where to start reading on the page
- Reading left to right
- Return sweep
- Page sequence

3. Visual conventions

- Difference between a letter, word, and sentence
- Spaces between words
- Punctuation (period, question mark, exclamation mark, comma, quotation marks)
- Letter recognition (upper and lowercase)

4. Auditory conventions

- Sound-symbol relationship
- One-to-one correspondence
- Intonation (use of punctuation, emphasis of certain words, for example)

Schema and the Three Cueing Systems

Constance Weaver states that as children learn to read naturally, "it is abundantly clear that learning progresses from whole to part rather than vice versa; from heavy use of the reader's schemas to increasing use of the semantic/syntactic cueing systems, then to increasing use of the grapho–phonemic cueing system and finally to coordination of schemas with all the language cueing systems" (Weaver 1988, p. 207).

As we enjoy poems, songs, chants, and books during shared reading, we start by focusing on children's schema, or knowledge and experience of the subject of the text. We then move to participation and demonstration of ways that successful readers use the semantic, syntactic, and grapho-phonemic cueing systems.

The following are some questions I ask and strategies I use to help the children integrate the knowledge and experience they bring to the text with each of the cueing systems.

Integrating the Cueing Systems

1. Personal Schema. Our discussion starts with what the children know, focusing on the experiences and knowledge that they bring to the text.

- What do you know about the topic?
- What are some related experiences that have happened to you?

2. Semantic Cueing System. Our focus turns to the meaning of the text we are reading.

- What do you think the story is about?
- What do you think will happen next?

- What do the pictures tell us?
- Who would like to retell the story?
- What would make sense?
- What do you notice about the characters? (Character development)
- What are some of the important things that happened in the story? (Story structure)
- Does this book remind you of any other books? (Comparing texts, authors and illustrators)
- What other words could the author have used that would make sense?
- Can you finish the line with a word or phrase that would make sense? (Auditory cloze)

3. Syntactic Cueing System. Our focus is on the language, the grammar of the text.

- Does it sound right?
- What other words could the author use that would sound right?
- Can you finish the line with a word or phrase that would sound right? (Auditory cloze)

4. Grapho-phonemic Cueing System. The grapho (letters) phonemic (sounds) cues are a tool to predict and confirm a word in the text. Usually I demonstrate the strategy, the children participate and we discuss the strategy.

- I use the first letter to predict what the word might be.
- I use the first letter(s), last letter, length of word, configuration of word to confirm what the word is.
- While reading to the class I leave off the last word or words in a line, or say the first sound of a word in a text and ask the children to predict what it could be. (Auditory cloze)
- I show the first letter or letters of a word in a text, and ask the children to predict what it could be. (Visual cloze)

Although we may be focusing on one of the cueing systems at a given moment, the goal is for integration of children's schema and the three cueing systems. For example, one day I introduced the *Jigaree*. From their own schema, the children drew pictures of their predictions of what a Jigaree might be. Then, as they looked at the cover of the book, they predicted what a Jigaree might do and what might happen in the story. As we read the book the children took semantic cues from the pictures and the story as it developed, and syntactic cues from the rhythmic, repetitive text. The next to last page says, "Jigaree, Jigaree I will . . . " and before I could turn the page, the group chimed in, "take you home (or back) with me." It sounded right, and it made sense. We checked the first letter of home and confirmed that it had to be home. "If it said 'back home,'" claimed Amanda, "it would have to be a word that started with a *b*."

Predicting

As I demonstrate the integration of the cueing systems during shared reading, I am continually inviting the children to predict. "What do you think Greedy Cat will eat next?" "What do you think Greedy Cat will do after she eats the pepper?" "If this story continued, what would Greedy Cat do?"

Smith (1983) says that, "prediction means the elimination from contention of those possibilities that are highly unlikely and the examination first of those possibilities that are most likely. Such a procedure is highly efficient for making decisions involving language" (p. 28). Routman (1988) states that "good predicting means being able to use all available information—from print, from the story, and from experience—to make a carefully reasoned judgment" (p. 43). Predicting is a strategy that successful readers use all the time as they integrate the three cueing systems with their own schema.

When the children and I start looking at a new book we usually begin with the children's own knowledge or schema to predict what it will be about. We read the title and look at the picture on the cover. Then the children tell what they know about the topic and share some of their related experiences. As we read the text, we use the three language cueing systems to gain meaning. We are continually discussing if the text makes sense (using semantic cues), if it sounds right (using syntactic cues), and looking at words to confirm if we are right (grapho-phonemic cues).

Gaining Familiarity with the Text

During shared reading we read the same stories, poems, and songs many times. As one of my kindergartners said, "You hear it over and over and over and over again, and that's how you learn to read." We easily accept that babies learn to talk by "hearing it over and over and over and over again," and by participating in the language they are hearing. Early readers learn to read by hearing the same bedtime stories day after day and making connections between sound and print (Teale and Sulzby 1986). The goals for earning to talk and learning to read are the same: that children become independent, self-regulating talkers or readers, in control of their own learning.

Hearing the same story many times elicits deeper and deeper responses to the text, which supports children in their comprehension, develops skills and strategies for successful reading and writing, and gives confidence to the child as a reader and writer. The children call upon those familiar patterns of language as they develop as strategic readers, first gaining control over a familiar text and then becoming successful with new material.

Timmy often selects I *Was Walking Down the Road* for independent reading. This is a class favorite and we have read it many times during shared reading. Timmy has those familiar lines, which are repeated on each page, in his memory. As he points and reads, that memory supports him as he matches word for word. I ask him why he likes the story so much. "I'm little, just like the animals and little girl in the story, and they all are free," he answers. Timmy is becoming an independent reader through this book.

Benefits of Familiar Texts for Kindergartners

A major goal of shared reading is to support the children in their reading development through the use of familiar texts. The following list describes some of the benefits gained when the children are involved in stories, songs, poems and chants they know well.

Personal Schema

- Expands personal schema.
- Encourages personal response.
- Strengthens child's confidence as a reader.
- Gives opportunities to attend to individual interests and needs.
- Offers opportunities for successful independent reading.

Semantic and Syntactic Cueing System

- Establishes firm oral models for book language.
- Establishes strong memory models of written language.
- Establishes understanding of story structure.
- Deepens understanding and response.
- Expands vocabulary.

Grapho-phonemic Cueing System

- Strengthens grapho-phonemic cueing system as a predicting and confirming strategy.
- Enables the unlocking of print through the familiarity of hearing and seeing.
- Establishes eye-voice-ear link, one-to-one correspondence, and left-to-right processes.
- Strengthens knowledge and uses of concepts about print.

Integration of Systems

- Enables mastery of skills and strategies to become automatic.
- Offers opportunities for meaningful literary and artistic extensions.
- Develops freedom and familiarity in using language.
- Offers opportunities for self-monitoring, self-correcting.

For Further Reading

Department of Education, Wellington (New Zealand). 1985. *Reading in Junior Classes*. Katonah, NY: Richard C. Owen.

Holdaway, Don. 1979. *The Foundations of Literacy*. Portsmouth, NH: Heinemann.

Lynch, Priscilla. 1986. *Using Big Books and Predictable Books*. New York: Scholastic.

Routman, Regie. 1988. *Transitions: From Literature to Literacy*. Portsmouth, NH: Heinemann.

Weaver, Constance. 1988. *Reading Process and Practice: From Socio-Psycholinguistics to Whole Language*. Portsmouth, NH: Heinemann.

6

Shared Reading: Practice

This chapter describes the planning schedule I use for shared reading. It also describes some of the activities I have found successful in engaging the interests of my kindergartners and in helping them gain the skills and strategies to become successful readers and writers. My goal is to ignite and keep alive the children's love for reading.

Planning Schedule

1. Familiar songs, poems, and chants (between four and six each day)
Suggested language activities for: enjoyment, meaning, and integration of semantic, syntactic, and grapho-phonic cueing systems

- Discuss meaning of text, vocabulary etc.
- Include drama, dance, music, and rhythmic activities.
- Create innovations.
- Discuss concepts about print by engaging in masking and cloze strategies.

2. New song, poem, or chant (every two or three days)
Suggested language activities for: enjoyment, meaning, and predicting

- Predict what the piece is about.
- Sing or read two or three times for enjoyment.

3. Familiar big book (one or more)
Suggested language activities for: enjoyment, meaning, and integration of semantic, syntactic, and grapho-phonic cueing systems

- Oral retelling, collectively or individually.
- Group retelling written by the teacher, to be illustrated by children.

- Group retelling of important sequence of events. Written on chalkboard by teacher and confirmed by group reading.
- Innovation on the text to be made into a class book during independent choice time.
- Discussion of story structure, characters, setting, problem, resolution, favorite part, etc.
- Discussion of literary pattern of the book—repetitive, cumulative, interlocking, chronological, familiar cultural (for example, books about seasons, holidays, the alphabet), problem-solving, rhyme- rhythm, main character (Cochrane, Cochrane, Scalana, and Buchanan 1984).
- Language activities described above in familiar songs, poems and chants

4. New big book
Suggested language activities for: enjoyment, meaning, and predicting

- Predict what the story will be about—before and after hearing the title and seeing the cover.
- Group sharing of prior knowledge.
- Read the book for enjoyment and meaning, occasionally stopping to predict what will happen next and how the story is going to end.
- Reread the book immediately and/or reread it for the next few days until it becomes familiar.

Introducing a Big Book

Big books engage emergent and beginning readers in literacy activities and encourage children to learn in community. Adding a new big book to our classroom library is a big event in my kindergarten, and I take the opportunity to demonstrate many strategies and skills as I introduce one. I usually let the children know the day before that we will be getting a new book so they can anticipate. The session usually goes like this:

"Guess what the new big book might be about. A guess can be anything in the whole world. Raise your hand and I'll call on you so we can all hear what each other has to say."

"A rabbit running away from a fox," says Daniel who loves animals.

"A spring day," offers Mary, who draws houses, flowers, the sun, and a rainbow at the writing table most days.

"A birthday party," suggests Sara, who's birthday is tomorrow.

You can tell that it is spring. I never get guesses about bunnies at Halloween time. Even though I haven't given them any specific information about the book and have asked them to guess, they are already predicting from their own experience. They are bringing their prior knowledge and experience to the situation.

"We could be guessing all day," someone exclaims. "Give us some hints."

The children are beginning to realize that guessing takes a long time and isn't a very efficient way to find out what the story is about. I'm glad to see they are gaining an awareness that successful readers don't guess what they are going to read, but predict. Whenever we read a new book, I model strategies to help the children predict what the book is about and focus on the title the author has selected. I encourage them to call upon their prior knowledge, and I take the opportunity to demonstrate the integration of the semantic, syntactic, and grapho-phonic cueing systems in discovering the title.

Today in introducing *Dan the Flying Man* I have chosen to start with the grapho-phonic cueing system by writing a part of the first letter in the title on the chalkboard. The children call out the different letters it might be. As I write more of the letter, the predictions become more precise until the letter is almost finished and we all agree that it can only be a D. The letter generates possible first words for the title: Dog, Doll, Diane, Dip. etc. I write D A N on the board as I slowly say the sounds. I hardly begin to write TH for the next word before the children shout out "The." Most of them know it because we've talked about "the" as a handy word to know. The next letters F for "Flying" and M for "Man" generate many possibilities, and we keep checking them out to hear if they sound right and if they make sense.

I could stretch this activity out, but I sense the children are ready to move on so I finish writing the title. Before I go to the cupboard to get the book, the children predict what the story could be about. Seeing the cover gives more information, and the new and refined predictions come closer and closer to the author's intention. Our focus has returned to the semantics (meaning) and syntax (language) of the book.

Suddenly someone says, "Let's read the story!" And so we do, stopping occasionally for a quick prediction, but reading the text through for enjoyment and meaning. Usually the children want to hear it again right away, and this time they are "reading" along with confidence.

We will read this story each day for the next week until it becomes another familiar text. As it becomes familiar we will focus on some of the parts and details, while discussing skills and strategies in context. We follow this same general procedure with all the songs, poems, chants, and books we learn:

- Predict what the text is about.
- Enjoy the whole text.
- Become familiar with the whole text.
- Focus on skills and strategies in context.
- Return to the whole text.

Dramatizing a Text

The children like to act out *The Enormous Watermelon*, which has several Mother Goose characters (Figure 6-1). One day I wrote the names of the characters on strips of paper as the children told them to me. As I wrote we talked about the convention of using uppercase letters for the first letter of someone's name because that person is important. Since the characters in the story were indeed important, the convention began to have meaning.

I keep yarn necklaces and clothespins in a basket near my chair, and as children were picked to be a character, they put a necklace on and pinned the character sign to it. With the help of the audience

Figure 6-1 Acting out The Enormous Watermelon

they arranged themselves in order of the appearance of the characters, and the mini-play began.

The children act out a lot of stories during shared reading in my class. It is one of the surest ways I know to involve all the children, and it gives them appropriate opportunities to move around. Besides acting out favorite big books as we read the text, they dramatize favorite stories and make up their own words. Sometimes the children make up their own plays or puppet shows during choice time and perform for the class at sharing time.

Celeste Snowden claims that, 'Drama in education gives the child not only new skills but increased confidence and self-knowledge, so that he or she is able to more effectively communicate with others, to enter more fully into a social situation, and to grow as an individual being" (Snowden 1988, p 3). She goes on to say, 'Language is the key. And through increased ability in drama comes naturally a more effective, confident use of language, both verbal and non-verbal" (p. 6).

Using Children's Names

One of the most successful ways to engage children in literacy learning, especially at the beginning of the year, is to focus on their names. If they can recognize and write their own names they think of themselves as readers and writers. I make two sets of name cards, one with the child's first name and one with first and last name, which I laminate and use throughout the year. By focusing on children's names:

- The class draws together as a community.
- Children get to know their classmates.
- Each child personally engages in the text.
- Children learn to recognize and write their names and those of others for a variety of useful purposes in the classroom.
- Children develop as readers and writers.
- A familiar text is used to demonstrate grapho-phonic cues (I have picked someone's name that begins with a B, has the vowel *a* in it, has two syllables, etc.).

Since most of the children are familiar with nursery rhymes, we read many of them at the beginning of the year. The children tell me the ones they know, and I write them on charts. I pick my favorites, too.

I like to do an activity with "Jack Be Nimble" on the first day of school to learn about my new class. We read the enlarged text a few times and I explain that the candlestick referred to in the rhyme is a stick that held dipped candles while they were drying. I show them a set of dipped candles and a three-foot dowel that we use as a candlestick. One at a time I paperclip each child's name over Jack's name on the chart. As we all read the rhyme, each child comes up and jumps over the candlestick when his or her name is inserted.

This is an efficient way to assess a variety of competencies, such as:

- Who can read their own names or the names of their class-mates.
- How they go about the task.
- Who is willing to participate.
- How well each child jumps.
- Who jumps with confidence.
- Who adds drama to the part.

I give the children a copy of the nursery rhyme to take home and read to their families, validating that they are readers on the first day of school.

Later in the year some children found "Jack Be Nimble" in several nursery rhyme books and were surprised that some of the artists had drawn Jack jumping over a candle holder. Comparing nursery rhyme books became a favorite activity during shared reading and choice time.

Masking

We have just sung "I love New England Days" (Ippolito 1990). I hold up several different size masks (see Appendix A 2). The children will select the one that they think best fits the size of the word on the chart that they want to mask or frame.

"Who can come up and mask a word they know?" Joey picks one and masks the word "skiing" as we all confirm his response by reading the word in the context. Ellen comments that "ing" is in ski-ing and many of the other words in the text. We count how many we see as I point to the text.

Next Joey becomes the teacher and asks, "Who can find the word that is a season?" Joey knows the kinds of questions to ask because I have modeled them and because he has responded to questions asked by his peers. He calls on Stefanie, who picks a medium-sized frame for "fall." We confirm the response by rereading from the beginning of the verse. From Ellen's comment I know that she is focusing on details of print, and from Joey's question I know he is focusing on the meaning. I'll make notes of this later. I'll keep watching.

Masking letters, words, and phrases in a familiar text is a favorite activity during shared reading. I make several size masks for the children to encourage them to think about the sizes of words.

The purpose of masking is to focus on specific detail in print in context. Holdaway says, "It is vital that when we choose to talk about some detail of print, every eye is observing that detail at the same time as the accompanying sounds are uttered. Only then are we teaching that crucial eye-voice-ear link which makes print intelligible in the earliest stages of reading" (1979, p. 76).

We discuss the part being masked in the context of the whole word, phrase, sentence, and/or piece. We are continually asking (see Appendix B.2 for a list of masking questions I use):

- Does it make sense? (semantic cueing system)
- Does it sound right? (syntactic cueing system)
- Do the letters and sounds in the word confirm our prediction? (grapho-phonetic cueing system)

Alphabet, Letters, and Sounds

With gusto my children love to say "I'll fim-fam-fight'em" and "I'll crim-cram-crash'em" when we read *Hairy Bear*. Sometimes I put a self-sticking note over those words and as I slowly peel them off, the children read the text. This simple technique focuses on the beginning sound to predict and confirm, a strategy that good readers call upon all the time, and one that I notice the children begin to use as they work toward independence in reading.

I made a set of what we called our "fim-fam-fight'em strips," each with a different beginning consonant. Excluding the vowels, there were twenty-one strips. This prompted a lively discussion about the number of letters in the alphabet and about vowels and consonants.

To introduce the strips I paper-clipped them over the original text in the book, and we read them in place of the phrase that they covered (Figure 6-2). For example, "I'll crim-cram-crash 'em" was covered by "I'll tim-tam-tash 'em." Another time, the children organized themselves in alphabetical order as each child held a strip. This activity involved a lot of conversation, cooperation, and collaboration.

I'll mim-mam-mash'em.

I'll rim-ram-rash'em.

Figure 6-2 Hairy Bear: Consonant strips

The children kept looking at the alphabet hanging in the classroom and kept repeating it as they arranged and rearranged themselves. I just sat back and watched as they orchestrated and directed the activity. Later, during choice time, the "fim fam fight'em strips" were often used as the children read the book. They were a catalyst to get children to return to the text. (See Chapter 5 for a discussion of the benefits of becoming familiar with the text.)

Writing

It could be argued that shared reading ought to be called shared reading and writing. Butler and Turbill (1984), Cochrane, Cochrane, Scalena, and Buchanan (1984), Harste, Woodward, and Burke (1984), Hansen (1987), Harste and Short (1988), and Atwell (1989) have addressed the relationship between the two in classroom practice. As classroom practice begins to reflect a more integrated curriculum, I am sure that even more will be written on the subject.

I demonstrate writing during shared reading when I write the title of a new big book, list the important characters we can remember from a text, make signs when we dramatize a book, and write a thank-you note or class story. I also model writing in front of the children when, as a class, we write a group story, create an innovation on a favorite text, such as *Good Morning Sun* (from *Goodnight Moon*; see Chapter 8), or when I give a mini-lesson before the children begin to create their own books (see Chapter 9).

We discuss how to start a piece, how to write letters and spell words, why we cross out something that we have written and write it again another way. Through this demonstration and participation the children are seeing what writers do. They will experience themselves as writers during choice time when they will role-play or practice what they have learned, and when they share their writing with others.

Math

Math language and concepts are integrated throughout the shared reading experience. We are continually categorizing, comparing, ordering, numbering, and counting as we read a text and talk about it. Some specific examples of focusing on math language and concepts are:

- Observing page numbers.
- Comparing sizes in *The Billy Goats Gruff* (Scholastic).
- Using the table of contents in *What Am I?* (Rigby).
- Observing position in space in *Rosie's Walk*.
- Using ordinal number in poems such as "Five Little Monkeys" (Holt).

    Questions that focus on print concepts include counting

- the number of letters in the word _____,
- the number of words in a line,
- the number of words in the sentence _____,
- the number of times the word _____ is written on the chart, and
- the number of lines in a poem

Monday, Monday, I Like Monday

One big book that has lent itself to rich math discussions in my kindergarten is *Monday, Monday, I Like Monday*. Each page is filled with detailed illustrations of a group of children playing and working together throughout the week and during each season. I usually start with what I consider the best question to ask: "What do you notice?"

- It engages the children in what they know and what interests them.
- It joins the class in community as we observe what others have noticed.
- It validates every child, since all responses are received by the group without value judgment.
- It lets me know what the children know.
- It provides me with natural assessment.

Here are a few observations generated one day while we were looking at *Monday, Monday*. We came to a picture of the children in art class, and I asked "What do you notice?"

- There are six children.
- There are four girls and two boys.

- One of the boys is ripping up his picture.
- There is an easel for each person.
- One of the boys is drawing some fruit and looks like he wants to eat it.
- The same children are in the other pictures in the book.

Sometimes the children or I ask questions about a picture that the group answers collectively rather than individually. To eliminate competition for a right answer, I often ask the children to whisper their answer when I raise my pointer, and if it is a counting question, to show the number with their fingers. Once they get the idea they become expert questioners. For example, the following questions were generated by the class from another page in *Monday, Monday* (the children in the story are buying fruit from a fruit stand in the city):

- How much do the grapefruits cost?
- Are there more apples or oranges?
- How many children have hats?
- What is the lady weighing?

Do You Know the Muffin Man?

Do you know the Muffin Man? the Muffin Man? the Muffin Man?
Do you know the the Muffin Man,
Who lives on Drury Lane?
Yes, I know the Muffin Man, the Muffin Man, the Muffin Man.
Yes, I know the Muffin Man,
Who lives on Drury Lane.

Ben Forbes, a teacher in Cambridge, Massachusetts, gave me the idea for this activity. We sing this song substituting the children's names and addresses (for example, "Do you know Timmy? Who lives at 16 Concord Road"), which are written on two pre-cut strips of oak tag and hung on brass fastener hooks on the chart. The song is written on posterboard and laminated so it can stand the frequent changing of names during shared reading and choice time. This activity provides the children experiences in:

- Recognizing their names.
- Recognizing their addresses orally and visually.
- Reading numbers.

Some of the questions I might ask are:

- Whose street number has three numbers?
- Whose has one number?
- Whose has an 8 at the end?

Some group activities are:

- Lining up with our addresses in numerical order
- Getting in groups of those who live on streets, roads, lanes, etc.

Shared reading ends with planning for choice time. I have demonstrated skills and strategies in context and the children have participated in these demonstrations. During choice time they will have opportunities for meaningful practice and sharing as they develop as successful learners.

For Further Reading

Ippolito, Paul. *The Color Song*. (RFD 2, Box 128. North St., Chester, VT 05143).

Johnson, Terry D. and Daphne Louis. 1988. *Literacy Through Literature*. Portsmouth, NH: Heinemann.

Johnson, Terry D. and Daphne Louis. 1989. *Bringing It All Together: A Program for Literacy*. Portsmouth, NH: Heinemann.

Martin, Bill, and Peggy Brogan. 1972. *Sounds of Laughter* (Teacher's Ed.). New York: Holt.

Snowden, Celeste. 1985. *Developing Language through Drama*. Albany, NY: Delmar Publishers.

7

Organizing Choice Time

"What is your plan?" Hands go up as shared reading ends and we begin planning for choice time.

"To the writing area," says Ryan.

"Who else wants to start with writing?" I send four or five volunteers off to the green table.

"I want to be a veterinarian," says Amy. Three more children choose to start in the veterinarian office we have set up.

"I'm going to have a snack," claims Chris. Five other children want to join him, but since the snack table has only four chairs, two children have to make another choice. They will have their snack later when there is room. The rest choose to read, play a math game with me, or paint.

Everyone has left the rug area with a stated plan for starting choice time. Some will begin with a teacher choice, referred to as I CARES, while others will pursue an activity of their own choice.

Classroom Procedure

Choice time in my classroom—referred to by many teachers as work time, practice time, or independent time—lasts for about an hour each day. I call it choice time because the children and I are making choices about what we do.

The hour is planned so that about half the time is spent on the choices that I make for the children, which usually include reading, writing, and math. I call these teacher choices I CARES, and they are an important part of the classroom management system that I have developed over the years. I use the name I CARE because I want the children to know that these choices I made for them are what I especially care about and that I want them to care about these choices, too. I CARE substitutes for terms such as "Have To" or "Must Do," which imply teacher control and learner submission.

During the other half hour the children choose their own activities. For example, they paint, use the workbench, extend the time spent on I CARES, go to the school library, play at the sand table, eat snack, or play in the dramatic play area. I value their choices as much as my own choices for them, and encourage them to initiate their own activities. Since I have set up the environment with a workbench, puppet theater, big blocks, and so on, I have taken some control over the choices the children make. However, within these available opportunities, the children can choose the content of the activity and the use of materials. For example, when Mary chooses to paint, she selects what her painting will be about, how she will manipulate the brush, and which colors to use. She might also ask for a 12" x 18" paper instead of the usual 18' x 24" easel paper, or request violet-colored paper in place of the standard manila color.

My Role During Choice Time

In Holdaway's classroom model, choice time is the practice (role-playing) and performance time in the day. Children have opportunities to practice by themselves and with their peers what has been demonstrated during shared reading, and to share or perform what they have learned. Shared reading emphasizes demonstration by the teacher and participation by the child and teacher; choice time emphasizes self-selected practice and role playing by the child. My role during this time is that of " 'invisible' enabler/supporter" (Holdaway 1990).

As a teacher I have six primary functions during choice time: (1) to set up the environment, (2) to facilitate the routine, (3) to teach, (4) to act as audience, (5) to kid watch, and (6) to enjoy the children. During choice time, most of the children are practicing independently or with peers, and I work with individuals and small groups of students. I usually assume the role of demonstrator and the children become participants, as in shared reading, although sometimes my role is to be an audience while children are performing or sharing their work. During part of each day I watch children and conduct formal or informal assessments, and occasionally I sit down at the snack table and enjoy my snack as a member of the classroom community.

The I CARE System

The I CARE system is a management system that indicates to the children what I want them to do during the day, and keeps track of

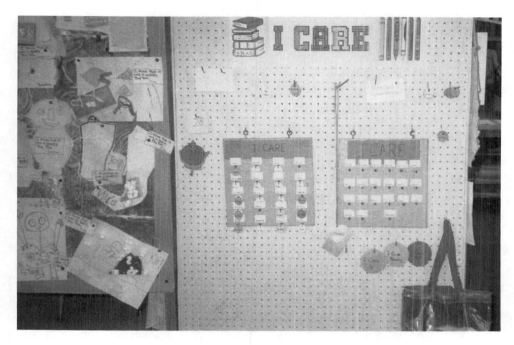

Figure 7-1 The I CARE Board

what they have done each day. It gives the children the responsibility
for completing the work I expect them to do, and at the same time
it helps them manage their time and make choices about when and
what they want to do.

Each of the main subject areas in the classroom is assigned a
color, and the tables in those areas are covered with craft paper in
the corresponding color. (If I don't have the paper or time to cover
the table, I put a piece of construction paper on the table to indicate
the color.) The color coding I use is:

Green—Writing
Yellow—Reading
Red—Math
Blue—Art
Orange—Science and Environmental Play Area

A 12" x 12" board, called the I CARE board, hangs on a 40" x 60"
pegboard shelf in the reading area (Figure 7–1). The children's
names are written on one-inch labels and arranged in alphabetical
order by first name on the board. A hook is under each name. Above
the board are six two-inch straight pegboard pieces, each of which
holds about thirty one-inch circles called I CARES (in white, green,

yellow, red, blue, and orange). Underneath the board are hooks for the three colored circles that we hang up each day to indicate the I CARES that are assigned for the day. For example, green, yellow and red, representing writing, reading and math, might be assigned on Monday.

When the children have finished working in an assigned area, such as math, they come to the I CARE board, take a matching colored (red) circle from above the board, and hang it on the hook under their name. This indicates to each of us that they have done the math I CARE. During clean-up the children take down the I CARES and return them to their pegboard hooks.

Getting Started

At the end of shared reading we plan for choice time. I explain the I CARES, and the class leader for the day hangs the large I CARE circles under the I CARE board to remind the children which areas I have chosen for them to go to that day. Since the instructions for reading, writing, and math are usually the same, I don't need to spend much time giving directions and answering questions after the children have learned the routine. If I need to give specific instructions for those areas or for the art, science, or thematic areas, I build them into my shared reading planning.

The children tell me their plans and choice time begins. I sometimes watch and note down what they choose to do first, because I believe it is an indication of what is particularly important to them. Some always get their I CARES done before they make their own choices. Others usually start with snack or a trip to the school library to exchange a book. Some almost always go to the blocks or dramatic play area first, while others vary the routine, depending on what is available and what they are interested in on a given day. I give the children this choice because I want them to have control over some of their time and to develop strategies for planning their time. This choice also minimizes their need to rush to "get through" and eliminates everyone ending up at the block or housekeeping area at the end of the day.

Choice Time in Action

Usually the reading, writing, and math I CARES are open-ended and allow for a range of pupil choice. For example, the children can choose their own book, writing topic, or math manipulative, and can work alone or with a friend. Most of the time they work in the specific area designated for the task, where appropriate materials are easily accessible, but they can also choose to work elsewhere in the room. Sometimes I plan an art or science activity in place of one of the regular I CARES, and often the I CARES are integrated into a dramatic play environment or into individual projects the children have chosen or initiated. For example, writing a sign for a puppet show is considered a writing I CARE.

If their first choice has been an I CARE, they hang the corresponding I CARE circle on the hook under their name when they have finished the work and then make another choice. I don't tell them when or where to go next, and they don't have to let me know. Halfway through choice time I ring a bell and signal the children to start or complete their I CARES if they haven't already done so.

Sometimes I check the I CARE board and discuss with certain children what they need to do next. Once in a while there are a few children who are not ready to take the responsibility for completing their I CARES independently. I work with them individually and perhaps offer them a choice of which I CARE to complete first, or ask that they get their I CARES done first for the next week. I offer broad choices to everyone, narrowing the options for certain individuals to support their development as the situation requires.

Some children get involved in what they are doing and want to stay in one area for the entire hour. It is important to respect this task commitment, so we talk about their desire for sticking with their special interest and may agree that tomorrow they will get to the other I CARE areas. If a child's interest is particularly intense and carries on from day to day, I help him or her integrate reading and writing into the project.

For example, for a week Chris became very involved in working with playdough. We saved his work each day, and when he had finished he made a sign for his work. He and I read *The New Baby Calf* together, which had pictures made from plasticine. Chris wanted to stick with the playdough, and I wanted him to include reading and writing. By kid watching and knowing Chris well and trusting him as a learner, he and I came up with a plan that met his needs and satisfied my goals, too.

For Further Reading

Hill, Susan and Tim. 1990. *The Collaborative Classroom: A Guide to Co-operative Learning.* Portsmouth, NH: Heinemann.

Johnson, Terry D., and Daphne R. Louis. 1987. *Literacy through Literature.* Portsmouth, NH: Heinemann.

Pappas, Christine C., Barbara Z. Kiefer, and Linda S. Levstik. 1990. *An Integrated Language Perspective in the Elementary School.* New York: Longman.

8

Reading During Choice Time

Every day the children are expected to read (yellow I CARE). The instructions are open-ended and offer a wide range of choices. They can choose what they want to read—trade books, big books, little predictable books, books published by other children, magazines, poems, or songs and chants written on charts around the room. They can also listen to the tape of a familiar story as they follow along in the book. Reading can be done alone, with a friend, with me, or with a visitor. At the end of the school year I interviewed my class about their reading. All the children said they were readers and that they learned to read by reading every day (Fisher 1990).

During choice time many children play school and role-play a shared reading session. They take turns being the teacher and using the pointer as they read big books and charts. They call on each other to frame words and point to letters. Others sit alone and read a book. Some look at a book together in the housekeeping area or the dramatic play environment.

Assessing Developmental Reading Stages

I am continually assessing the children's literacy development to learn more about them so I can support their growth appropriately. I observe them reading alone, with a friend, with me, and during shared reading. I want to know their interest and enjoyment in books and level of concentration while reading. I want to know if they can make up a story and retell a story. I also want to know how they handle a book, (for example, if they turn the pages from front to back) and their understanding of conventions of print (see Chapter 5). The formal and informal reading assessment procedures and organization that I use are described in Chapter 14 (also see Appendix A.7).

READING	Interest in Books	Retells a story	Watches text during Shared Reading	Recognizes name	Recognizes other's names	Recognizes upper case letters	Recognizes lower case letters	Sound/symbol Correspondence	School/class library	Reading stage
Pam	✗	yes	1	✗	✗	24/26	22/26	✗	3 times a week	P2
Peter	✗	detailed yes	2	✗	2	21/26	18/26	✓	✗	P1
Sam	2	?	3	2	3	15/26	10/26	0	2	I am a Reader

Figure 8-1 Class Assessment Profile for Reading

About once a month I assess each child's oral reading during choice time (Figure 8–1). I ask a child to pick a book, usually a big book he or she knows and likes, and to read it to me using the pointer. My role at this time is to listen, watch, wait, and then discuss with each reader what he or she did successfully. After each reading session I record the child's reading stage (Appendix A.3) and the strategies used so I have a record of the child's progress over the year and can plan appropriate instruction. Sometimes, as the year progresses and I get to know the children better, I can complete this assessment by watching them read independently, but I find it is most informative to spend individual time with each child.

I have developed, over the past five years, my own list of reading and writing stages and descriptors. Many of the terms and descriptive phrases are from Clay (1985), Cochrane, Cochrane, Scalena and Buchanan (1984), and Holdaway (1979, 1980), but I have also added some of my own. The descriptors I developed for specific reading stages match my understanding of what kindergarten children do as their competencies as readers and writers evolve. This list addresses the developmental reading stages of kindergarten children in the process of becoming independent readers only; I recommend that teachers be informed of the full spectrum of reading development as described by Holdaway and Cochrane, Cochrane, Scalena and Buchanan.

However the descriptors and stages are general indicators only. No child ever fits neatly into one stage at a time or exhibits all of the characteristics in a stage. Sometimes a child displays descriptors from several stages at the same time or appears to skip important characteristics in a stage. I agree with Weaver (1988, p. 205): "Seeing such stages helps us understand some of the natural phases that children may go through in learning to read and write, but of course day-to-day, child-by-child reality is much 'messier.' " In referring to the Cochrane stages, she adds that "the greater wealth of detail should give some sense of the potential variability among children."

Weaver, in her recent book, *Understanding Whole Language: From Principals to Practice*, continues to move away from stage theory. "Though there are developmental trends in children's emergent language and literacy, we shall see that these are by no means definite enough to justify a stage theory of development. There is pattern within the chaos of children's literacy development, and yet each child's development remains, in many respects quite idiosyncratic" (1990 p. 68).

I try to stay away from thinking of my students as reading at a particular stage. However, as a kindergarten teacher I need to keep track of the assessment of over forty children in a simple and organized way, so I can plan instruction and communicate with parents and school professionals. These general stages and informal descriptors help me to do this.

Stages of Reading Development

1. Introduction to books
Book awareness

- Displays interest in books.
- Likes to point out and name objects recognized in pictures.
- May look at books upside down and back to front.
- May mishandle them (e.g., rip them, color in them, throw them).
- Doesn't see meaning as connected to print.
- Begins to add scribble-like writing to drawings.

2. I am a reader!
Emphasis on meaning of the story and the sound of language (semantic and syntactic cueing systems)

- Acts like a reader and writer.
- Often reads alone or to stuffed animals.
- Loves to listen to stories.

- When looking at a new book, makes up a story from the pictures and uses book language, such as "once upon a time" and other phrases from stories previously heard.
- When reading a familiar story, uses much of the book language in retelling the story from memory.
- "Reads" story fluently and with a great deal of expression.
- May look around while reading.
- When looking at the book, often looks at the pictures while reading.
- Recognizes more and more letters.
- Begins to use letters in writing.
- Recognizes own name.
- Recognizes environmental print.
- Rhymes words and can give other words that begin with same sound.

3. Print Stage One
Begins to watch the print when reading

- Can point word for word with some accuracy with short texts that are very familiar.
- Moves back and forth from telling the story fluently (I am a reader stage) to trying to match the words to the print (Print Stage One), reading slowly, word for word.
- Can recognize most letters.
- Labels drawings phonetically and usually writes just beginning consonants.
- Can tell you the word the consonant stands for.

4. Print Stage Two:
Intense attention to print when reading

- Continued focus on and control of visual cueing system.
- Intense interest in watching the print when reading.
- Can point word for word with accuracy using texts that are familiar.
- Uses beginning consonant to help read an unfamiliar word.
- Begins to develop strategies to help with unfamiliar words (looks at the pictures, starts at the beginning and reads again, that is, reruns and self-corrects).
- Semantic and syntactic cues are often ignored because of intense focus on the print.
- Word for word reading.
- Reading is very slow, often in a monotone.

- Likes to read alone.
- Phonetic spelling with beginning, middle, and ending consonants and some vowels.
- Beginning of orthographic spelling.
- Less labeling and more attempts at strings of words in writing.
- Can read back own writing.

5. Becoming an independent reader

- Can read simple unfamiliar texts word for word.
- Fluency returns with familiar texts.
- Uses semantic, syntactic, and graphic-phonic cues.
- Often is aware when something doesn't make sense or sound right when reading.
- Wants to read to an adult often.
- Spelling shows more orthographic cues: sequence of letters, distribution, and word patterns.
- Writes sentences and leaves spaces between words.

I consider this descriptive list a draft. It will continue to change and never be complete because I am always learning as I observe children read and write and as I grow professionally through reading, attending conferences, talking with other teachers, presenting workshops, and reflecting. I encourage teachers to make their own list as they work with children in their classrooms.

"Doing Bedtime Story"

Sometimes I "do bedtime story" during choice time with children who, from my observations, have not developed a strong literacy set (Holdaway 1979). I refer to this as "doing bedtime story" because I try to replicate some of the conditions present during the bedtime story in the home which support successful literacy development. The children I read with in this way may not have been read to very much prior to coming to school and indicate a lack of experience enjoying and interacting with books. We read and discuss favorite stories that the children or I choose. (I often pick ABC books for children who need familiarity with letters and sounds.) I think of this time as an extension and reinforcement of the shared reading experience.

Weaver suspects that "a major reason why some children become stuck in the grapho/phonemic emphasis stage [in reading] is that they have not fully experienced the preceding stages, either at home or at school" (1988, p. 208). I have found Clay's approach to working with "slow" readers an appropriate direction to take with these children in my classroom, as well. In discussing early entrants in New Zealand schools, who correspond to kindergartners in this country, Clay says that "the teacher's task during that first year is to get the slow child responsive to instruction, happy to try and to discover for himself, steadily accumulating the early reading behaviors and not losing his buoyancy and bounce. Most slow learners, gaining confidence in this way are ready for book reading by the beginning of their second year at school" (1979, p. 43).

Responding to texts

Throughout the year I introduce activities that relate to the texts we have particularly enjoyed during shared reading. Sometimes the children come up with their own ideas, which they pursue at the writing table or introduce as a class activity. The integration of curriculum, both content and process, is inherent in literature extensions (adding onto the text and taking it further) and innovations (changing some of the words in the text), which encourage the children to return to a book to examine its text and pictures. Some of my favorite extensions are described below.

Extensions and Innovations of Texts

Goodnight Moon   I made a big book of *Goodnight Moon* by cutting up two paperbacks and pasting the pages on tagboard. Since I didn't want to separate the picture from the text, I kept the pages complete and enlarged the text under the picture. After reading the book many times, someone suggested that we write a *Good Morning Sun* book. Each day during shared reading we created about three pages of text, which I wrote on large paper. During choice time volunteers illustrated the new pages. We kept returning to the original text to follow the pattern of the book, placing the print in the same place and settling on the word opposites we wanted in our innovation.

Under the loft in our classroom we created the "great green room" by covering it with green paper. The children brought in artifacts mentioned in the book, and during choice time they would go in the room to read and spend quiet time together. Sometimes we would gather there for a story before going home. Up on the loft we made the "great yellow room," following our innovation of *Good Morning Sun*.

Brown Bear What Do You See?   Becky Eston, a kindergarten teacher in Lincoln, Massachusetts, shared this idea for an innovation on *Brown Bear* to help the children get to know their classmates early in the year. A parent volunteer cut out silhouettes of each child

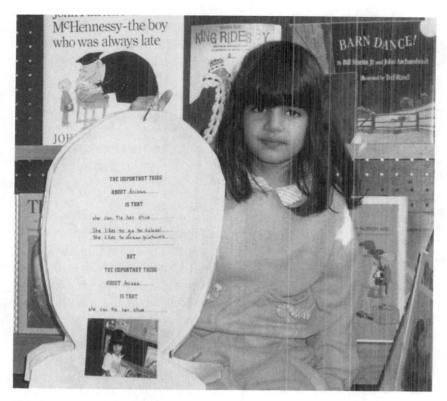

Figure 8-2 The Important Book

in the class. We made a class book and changed the text to the names of the children in the class. For example:

> Ellen, Ellen, who do you see? I see Andrew looking at me.
> Andrew, Andrew, who do you see? I see Joey looking at me.
> Joey, Joey, who do you see? I see Clare looking at me.

Important Book   Olga McLaren, a first-grade teacher in Dallas, Texas, gave me the idea for this innovation to use with *The Important Book* as a way of getting to know each other at the beginning of the year. After we were familiar with the book, I wrote the important things about me on a form during shared reading, following the pattern of the book (see Appendix A.4). During choice time children told me what was important about them, and I wrote it on their own form. Along with a photograph, which I took of each child, we pasted this form on one side of a 9" x 11" piece of white construction paper, cut out in the shape of a head and shoulders. On the other side the children drew their faces. We hung these up with a rope and clothespin so parents could see both sides on parents' night. Later, I laminated them and made them into a class book, which the children took home to share with their families (Figure 8–2).

It Didn't Frighten Me   The children loved this book (from Scholastic's Book Shelf Stage 2) right from the start. so I wrote the text on a chart for them to follow as I read the small book. When they began to make up their own characters for the text, I made a form that included the first part of the text and left blanks for innovations. I wrote their innovations on the forms, the children illustrated them, and someone designed a cover. Finally, we stapled the pages together, and gave the book to the school library for circulation. I made copies of the book for each child and for our classroom library.

Pop-up Books

In a Dark, Dark Wood   This is a favorite at the beginning of the year because the simple, interlocking text and illustrations help the children feel instantly successful as readers. After many readings of the story, I wrote the text on a chart, alternating the lines in green and brown marker. I wrote "In a dark, dark wood" in green and "there was a dark, dark house" in brown. This way we could see the visual pattern of the text, as well as hear it when we read. (Teachers who need to share big books with colleagues find this is a good way to keep an enlarged copy of the text in their classroom.)

We also made a pop-up book of the story We started from the end of the book, with the ghost, and added a page each day. On the back cover the children stapled a copy of the text so they could read it as they shared the book. Through the process the children learned how to use many writing and art materials.

Item	Skill	Material
Ghost	Spiral cutting	Black Line master of ghost
Box	Use of scotch tape	Square to tape over ghost
Cupboard	Use of brass fasteners	Brown construction paper, fasteners
Room	Paste	Paper, paste, and crayons
Stairs	Paper folding	2" x 12" paper strip, paste
House	Folding and pasting	Construction paper and paste
Path	Glue	Sand
Wood	Glue	Twigs
Text	Stapling	Copy of text

Murals

Dan, the Flying Man   While reading *Dan, the Flying Man*, the children noticed that the artist had drawn the people smaller to show them far away. I decided to capitalize on this observation and interest by guiding them in making a mural about the story. Each child was asked to paint a person trying to catch Dan and cut it out the next day. We decided to paste the people on our mural, from largest to smallest, to show where they were in relation to Dan. To arrange the people, the children held the person they had made and ordered themselves from biggest to smallest. They then went to the mural and added their character. The words from the text were added to the mural, and many of the children chose to read the mural for their reading I CARE.

Creating this mural involved a great deal of social interaction and cooperation, and it involved the integration of reading, writing, and math in an activity that was meaningful and interesting to the children.

Where the River Begins This book, written and illustrated by Thomas Locker, stimulated a discussion about where a river begins, which led to making a mural of the water cycle. On a big piece of white paper the children painted the background and used various recycled materials from the art area to represent different natural features on the mural. For example, they used silver paper for a lake, sand for the beach, and Styrofoam packing pieces for snow. We labeled the mural and it became one of the displays for visitors who came to our classroom aquarium (see Chapter 12).

Collaborative Drawings

Jigaree This activity introduced the book to the children and became an activity for a school-wide theme for the year called "Celebrating Differences." The children worked in pairs to draw a picture of what they thought a Jigaree was. I told them that it was alive, and that before they began, each team should decide if their Jigaree was a boy or girl, short or tall, fat or thin, and whether it had dark or light skin. As each team began, I wrote their choices on the back of the paper.

For this picture they made a crayon resist. First, they were encouraged to add a lot of color and press down very hard with their crayons to draw their pictures. Next, they painted over the entire picture with water-thinned paint. The paint colored the paper that was not protected by the crayon wax; the wax resisted the paint.

During sharing time the pairs held their pictures and grouped themselves according to the different attributes they had assigned to their Jigaree.

Taking Books Home

I believe that one of the most powerful ways I can help children love reading is by encouraging them to develop the habit of going to the library. Using the library regularly enables them to find books which meet their interests and learning needs. Many parents have told me that they are more apt to read to their child each night if he or she brings home a book from school.

Using the School Library

During choice time the children are allowed to go to the school library to return a book and take out a new one. Usually they take the book home. Some children go several times a week, most go at least once a week. I don't have a weekly library time when I take the entire class to exchange books, although sometimes we go as a group to see a film or hear a story, or a parent volunteer takes a small group to research a topic.

Using the Classroom Library

The children are also encouraged to sign out books to take home from our classroom library. After selecting a book, the children copy the title and stamp the day's date on an 8" x 11" tagboard signout form that is filed under the first letter of their first name in a special library file box. When they return the book, they put a check in the return column on the form, place the book back on the shelf, and check out another book.

For Further Reading

Cochrane, Orin, and Donna Sharen Scalena, and Ethel Buchanan. 1984. *Reading, Writing and Caring.* New York: Richard C. Owen.

Department of Education Wellington (New Zealand). 1985. *Reading in Junior Classes.* New York: Richard C. Owen.

Hornsby, David, and Deborah Sukarna, with Jo-Ann Parry. 1986. *Read On: A Conference Approach to Reading.* Portsmouth, NH: Heinemann.

Massam, Joanne, and Anne Kulik. 1986. *And What Else?* San Diego, CA: The Wright Group.

McCormick, Christine E., and Jana M. Mason. 1990. *Little Books.* Glenview, IL: Scott, Foresman.

Mooney , Margaret E. 1990. *Reading to, with, and by Children.* New York: Richard C. Owen.

9
Writing During Choice Time

The children write every day, usually at the green table in the writing area (green I CARE). Sometimes they write in another area of the room in connection with a project or theme they are pursuing. I find that when they write daily, they begin to think of themselves as writers and become engaged in the writing process for their own needs and interests. When given time they choose their own subject, genre, format, and how they want to share their work.

Much of the children's writing is story (narrative). However, Newkirk (1989, p. 24) presents a strong case that children can and will write "more than stories." He says that "as long as children have access to a variety of non-narrative forms, they will adopt them, just as they adopt other forms of adult behavior." In the classroom I demonstrate a wide variety of genres, such as lists, signs, letters, invitations, questionnaires, and notices, to encourage and validate many writing responses throughout the curriculum.

Daily Writing

Getting Started

On the second day of school I begin to establish the writing routine by presenting a mini-lesson during shared reading. Since most of the time the children will be both the author and illustrator of their work, I pick a colorful picture book with the same author and illustrator, such as *The Ant and the Elephant*, by Bill Peet, to read to the class, and we discuss the words and pictures used to tell the story.

Next, on a large piece of paper, I draw a picture of something that has happened to me recently and I write about it. For example, one day I told about the time I stepped on the dead bird that my cat had brought into the house. I talk as I write and draw, explaining what I am thinking about as I work. I tell the class that they are

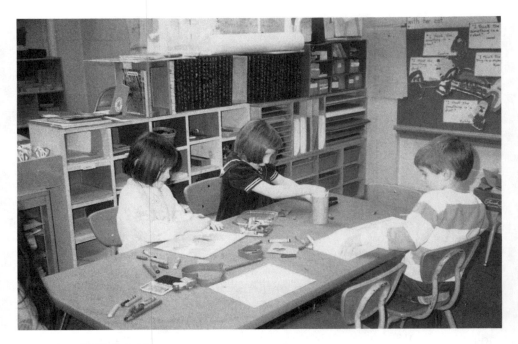

Figure 9-1 Writing table

authors and illustrators, too, and that I want them to draw and write about something that interests them. I explain the four general writing procedures for them to follow, which are written on a chart:

- Draw a picture.
- Write something about the picture.
- Write your name.
- Stamp the date with the date stamp.

We discuss the procedures: that putting their name on their papers means we will all know who the author is, that by dating each piece we will know when they were done, and that they will be saving their writings throughout the year.

"Raise your hand if you want to start choice time at the writing table" (Figure 9–1).

Cara states that she is going to draw a picture of her baby brother. I give her an unlined 8″ x 11″ piece of paper, and she goes to the writing table to begin. (As the year goes on the children will select from a large variety of paper on the shelves in the writing area.) Joey claims that he doesn't know what he is going to write about until he starts. He selects his paper and joins Cara. Several others choose to begin with writing, while the rest of the class makes other plans. During the morning, as space becomes available, they

Writing	Interest in writing	Elaboration of drawing	Drawing tells a story	Spelling stage	Reads back own writing	Writes a sentence	Writes first name	Writes last name	Pencil grip and direction	Uses some lower case letters
Peter	*	✓	2	2C	2	no	*	almost	OK ↑R	3
Sally	*	*	2	3VC	2	no	*	*	OK R	in name
Walter	*	*	1	2VC	1	2	*	*	watch ? ↑L	3

Figure 9-2 Class Assessment Profile for Writing

will come to the writing table. Since this is the beginning of the year and routines are being established, I remind children to come to the table and explain the procedure to them. As they become more responsible for classroom procedures. I will be less directive.

At the writing table I keep watching and help the children establish the routine of drawing, writing about their pictures, writing their name, and stamping the date. I begin my on-going assessment by using a Class Assessment Profile for Writing (Appendix A.8 and Figure 9.2), writing down what I notice the children doing and how they go about the task. For example, I record what they draw, what they say to each other as they work, their interest in drawing and writing, how deliberately they work, and how long they stay at the writing table. Today I ask them to put their pieces in the sharing basket on the paper shelf so I can look at them more closely at the end of the day.

After school I use these pieces of writing and the notes I took in class to record my observations of what each child can do as an illustrator and writer on the Class Assessment Profile for Writing (Figure 9–2) and on an Individual Assessment Profile (Appendix A.10). I notice that Ryan spent a long time at the area and that there is a lot of action in his picture about a warship. He has written a string of letters, mainly those in his name. I notice that Candace has drawn the sky, some grass, and a flower. She has spelled the word "SKI," written a G above the grass, and an F next to the flower (Figure 9–3). I notice that Billy has drawn something with yellow crayon. I can hardly see his drawing, and I don't know what he has drawn. As far as I can observe, he hasn't written any letters. I'll keep watching.

The next day we review the four-step procedure, and I tell the children that I will be at the writing area to help them set up a file

Figure 9-3 Candace's writing

folder so they can file their work. Yesterday I had put the pencils, date stamp, and crayons on the writing table, but today the children will take them off the shelves as they need them. Along with the 8 x 11 paper that everyone used yesterday, the children can also choose larger, recycled computer paper from the shelf.

The File
The children file their work in a plastic file crate that holds a hanging file for each child. At the beginning of the year, as they finish their writing, each child chooses a colored hanging file, and I write their name on the tab. Choosing their own color file helps the children find their files as they learn to recognize their names in a variety of contexts during the year. Adding a special sticker next to their name also helps. Hanging files always stay in the box so the files do not get out of alphabetical order. I also write each child's name on a manila folder that goes in the hanging file and holds their work. This manila file can be taken out as the need arises.

I feel that it is important for the children to be with me when we set up their file so they will understand the procedure and feel that the file is important and useful to them. I write their names because I want them to be legible for everyone to read.

Conferencing

For most kindergartners, their drawings and the oral stories that accompany them are the most important part of their work. When I conference with the children, the message I try to convey is that as authors, they write for an audience, and that they need to do everything they can to help the audience understand their ideas and what they have to say.

1. *Telling the story*   I usually start a conference by asking the children to tell me about their work. Some children tell a long story about their picture, while others give a short description of what they have drawn. I tell them what I have heard, share what I notice about their story and drawing, and ask questions for clarification.

2. *Adding detail*   Sometimes I encourage the children to add details to their drawings to tell their story, so that as they write stories they will add details in words to clarify and enrich their message. Sometimes they edit their work by adding to their drawing as they tell their story, and sometimes I ask what they could add to their drawing for clarification.

    Mary tells me about a walk she took with her mom. "Oh, I forgot to put our dog in the picture," she says as she picks up a crayon and begins to draw him. "He went with us and kept on barking."

    "I can tell that he was important to your story. I didn't know that until you drew him in. Tell me about the barking. Is it important for you to tell about that in your story?"

    Jerry tells me that he has drawn a house and a tree. When I ask him to tell me more, he says, "I am in the house watching a storm."

    I don't tell him what to add but ask, "Tell me more. What could you put in your picture so I would know your story?"

    "I could put me in the window, and make it really dark outside." He picks up his crayon and begins

3. *Attending to writing and print concepts*   Writing letters, words, and sentences and attending to print concepts is only one part of the writing process in kindergarten, and its development does not parallel the children's ability to tell a story orally and through drawing. I encourage everyone to write something about their piece (it might be a scribble or just one letter), and during our conference they read me what they have written. I comment on what I notice they can do, and sometimes encourage them to write a little more.

    Ryan has drawn a car on a road and has labeled "cr" for car and "rd" for road. I have noticed that he usually writes beginning and ending consonants and recently has added vowels to his words, so

I use the immediate moment to encourage him to say the word and listen for the *o* in road.

Candace has done several pieces with the sentence IMSBMS, meaning "I am standing by myself." She reads it to me and I read it back to her. Because she is displaying such confidence in herself as a writer and is willing to take risks, I celebrate her work by telling her what I notice she can do. I also remind myself to talk about leaving space between words next time in shared reading. When she is ready, she will incorporate that concept into her writing.

Sharing

When the children write for an audience it is important to provide opportunities for them to share their work. "For me, it is essential that children are deeply involved in writing, that they share their texts with others, and that they perceive themselves as authors" (Calkins 1986, p. 9). Holdaway refers to this sharing as "performance" in the natural-learning classroom model. The child, while sharing or performing, becomes the teacher, thus making a complete cycle.

Holdaway says that the best assessment for knowing if learning has taken place is when children come to us and want to show us their work. They share when they feel good about what they have done, when growth has occurred, and when learning has taken place. We should watch carefully what children have done when they offer to share (Salem 1989).

Kindergarten children share their work in many different ways, and I think it is important that the children, not me, choose *if* they want to share their work and *how* they want to share. It is their work, and I believe that writers need to be in charge of sharing in a way that satisfies them. In my kindergarten there are four main ways for children to share their writing: talking informally about it as they work, taking it home to share, displaying it on the sharing bulletin board, and sharing it from the author's chair (Hansen and Graves 1983).

1. Informally as they work   The children continually talk about their work as they sit at the writing table. Often this informal sharing is enough to satisfy them, and they file it or put it in their school bag to take home.

> They talk to themselves at the table. This may be a way of sharing with themselves and/or with the other children.
> They talk to someone else at the table, showing what they have drawn or asking questions. Often two children choose to sit together at a separate desk, which we call "the quiet

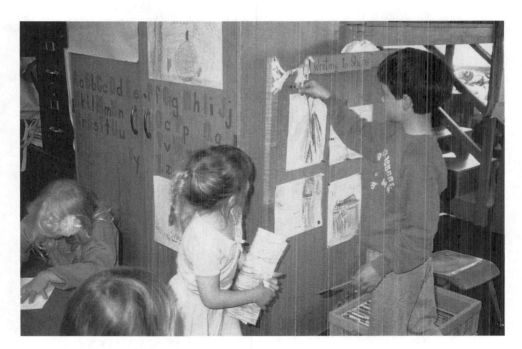

Figure 9-4   The Sharing Bulletin Board

table." Occasionally, they draw identical pictures or work on a picture together. They are learning from each other in a safe situation chosen by them.
- They show their work to me or another adult sitting at the table.

2. Taking work home to share   Sometimes children choose to take their work home to share. When I notice that this is a child's main choice of sharing I periodically ask the parents to send some of the work back so we can keep samples of the children's work throughout the year in the file at school.

3. Displaying work on the sharing bulletin board   Some children choose to hang their pieces on the sharing bulletin board in the writing area above the file box. After they have been displayed for a week or so, the children file them. They also use this bulletin board to share work they have done at home (Figure 9–4).

4. Author's chair   Children can choose to put their work in the sharing basket if they want to sit in the author's chair and share with the class at the end of choice time. Usually we have time for two or three authors to share each day, so I keep a checklist to ensure that everyone who wants to share gets a turn at least every other week.

The author sits in the author's chair and tells about the piece. Then he or she calls on three or four children to ask questions or tell what they notice about the piece. I also participate as one of the audience.

"I notice that you colored the sun red and orange."

"I notice that you drew different kinds of flowers."

"I notice that the swimmer looks like he s moving very fast."

"I notice that you left spaces between your words."

Starting with the phrase "I notice" helps the audience focus on the author as writer, and helps the author focus on the audience as reader. The author expands upon the comments, and an informal discussion between the author and the audience may develop. The piece is filed, displayed on the bulletin board, or taken home.

Sometimes our time is limited. As a way of acknowledging the work of the children who want to share but who do not get the opportunity to sit in the author's chair on a particular day, I hold up the pieces from the sharing basket for what we call a "quick share," and each child tells one or two important things about the work.

Writing Books

We read books and talk about authors all the time in my class, so it seems only natural that the children also write their own books. They staple some pages together, draw and write, and add a cover. Sometimes I make blank books and leave them in the writing area. However, about three times a year I introduce "formal" bookmaking and everyone writes a book.

Getting Started
When the children start making books on their own at the writing table, I introduce bookmaking to the entire class. I have observed that if children can choose their own paper and topic for their daily writing, and if a stapler is available, bookmaking usually begins by October or November. At this point I introduce bookmaking in a mini-lesson and ask every child to participate. The procedure I use is modeled after that described by Mary Ellen Giacobbe (talk given for the Whole Language Teachers Association, 1986, Haynes School, Sudbury, MA), and follows the general steps listed below.

Mini-Lesson
I demonstrate the general procedure for bookmaking by giving a mini-lesson during shared reading. I start by telling the class that I am going to make a book about the time that a skunk was asleep in my cellar, and that I think it will take about five pages. Then I

quickly sketch out each incident on a piece of paper and write a sentence about each picture.

Next, I ask the children to think about an idea for a book they will make, then call on someone who is ready to share his or her idea. Robert says his book is going to be about digging for treasure. We talk about his story and I ask him how many pieces of paper he thinks he will need to tell it. He says six, and I staple the pages together and send him to the writing table with his blank book. Marie says that she doesn't know what her book will be about until she begins. She decides on seven pages, but knows that she can add more or take some away as she works. Four other children follow a similar procedure, and the remaining children make their first choice for the morning. As space becomes available they will come to the writing table, and I will help them get started.

At the Writing Table

I spend the day at the writing table, listening and encouraging the children. Although my mini-lesson demonstrated writing a story, I notice that many of the children do not tell a story in their books. Jackie has drawn four different pictures of rainbows, Ellen is making a book about opposites, and Sam "just drew a picture book." The children choose topics and a structure that is meaningful to them.

I notice that Andrew decides to number the pages in his space book, and several others follow along. Clare adds a cover to her book about cats, and several of her friends think this is a good idea and do the same. I purposely don't give many suggestions because I trust that the children will come up with their own ideas as they gain ownership and take responsibility for their learning. Throughout the process I have set some parameters. The children work within them but are free to change and modify them. They become their own teachers at the writing table.

Unfinished Work

Some finish their book in one day, while others take several days to complete it. I find that this is a good time to introduce a folder for unfinished work to help the children organize their papers. Each child selects a colored file folder with pockets, and I write their name and "Unfinished Writing" on each one. They put the pages to their unfinished book in it and file it in their hanging file along with their regular writing folder. Just like the authors whose books they read, these kindergarten authors are beginning to experience writing as an on-going process. As Jessie commented, 'You don't expect an author to write a book in one day, do you?' The unfinished work folder underscores this concept to the children.

Figure 9-5 Sharing books

Sharing

Many children want to sit in the author's chair and share their books, so I set aside extra time for this. Sometimes they share their books in small groups or read them to another class (Figure 9–5). Many of the children want to take them home as soon as they are finished to share with their families. I encourage them to do so, and also to bring them back for the classroom library until the end of the year, when they can again take them home. These books, which become part of the classroom library, are often selected during reading choice time and are signed out to take home overnight.

A few children immediately start another book, while many return to the predictable routine of drawing and writing on a single piece of paper, or writing in connection with their play in the block or dramatic play environment.

Publishing a Book with an Editor

I find that kindergartners are usually satisfied with producing their own books as described above. They know when their books are finished. They are very confident with their invented spelling and don't want to draw the pictures again for an edited book. No looking back!

However, a few children do become interested in publishing a more formal book. I find that these are usually the children who spend a lot of time at the writing table. They often make books and their drawings tell a story. They are advanced phonetic spellers (Buchanan 1989), able to write sentences and leave spaces between words.

When I notice individual children displaying some of these behaviors, I ask them if they would like to have their story printed on a computer and "bound" like the books in our library. If they say yes, I act as their editor. We sit together with their draft and they read me what they have written while I write each page in conventional spelling on another paper. We talk about where they want the print to be on each page and what the title page will look like. I send the edited pages to a parent who has agreed to be the "typesetter," and when the pages are returned, the children add the illustrations and draw a cover on a piece of tagboard. I bind the pages with cloth tape, and the book is ready to go on the bookshelf.

Some years this formal book publishing takes off in my class as children see an edited book shared by a classmate, and the classroom becomes a mini-publishing house.

The writing process described in this chapter is part of the everyday routine in my classroom. In addition to this process the children are also writing for a variety of purposes as they engage in activities at other areas, such as the sand and water tables, the block area, and the dramatic play environments. In fact, their writing at the writing table often relates to these other areas. For example, they make signs for the zoo animals at the sand table, write road signs for the block city, and fill out appointment cards at the veterinarian's office. Typically, the children write often during the day and throughout the room.

For Further Reading

Buchanan, Ethel. 1989. *Spelling for Whole Language Classrooms.* Katohah, NY: Richard C. Owen.

Butler, Andrea, and Jan Turbill. 1984. *Towards a Reading-Writing Classroom.* Portsmouth, NH: Heinemann.

Calkins, Lucy M. 1986. *The Art of Teaching Writing.* Portsmouth, NH: Heinemann.

Cambourne, Brian, and Jan Turbill. 1987. *Coping with Chaos.* Portsmouth, NH: Heinemann.

Clay, Marie. 1975. *What Did I Write?* Portsmouth, NH: Heinemann.

Hubbard, Ruth. 1989. *Authors of Pictures, Draughtsmen of Words.* Portsmouth, NH: Heinemann.

Newkirk, Thomas. 1989. *More Than Stories: The Range of Children's Writing.* Portsmouth, NH: Heinemann.

10

Math and Physical Science During Choice Time

Math

During shared reading and throughout the day the children are exposed to math language and math concepts, and have numerous opportunities to count and work with numerals. They work daily with math manipulatives and then hang up a red I CARE to indicate they have been to the math area.

Getting Started

During the first month of school I want the children to become familiar with some of the math manipulatives that we will be using during the year. These include Cuisenaire Rods, Unifix Cubes, pattern blocks, color cubes, dice, and geoboards. I put the same manipulative on the table for about three days in a row and ask the children to build with it during free play activity. During this introductory period I spend some time sitting at the table, building things myself, and listening to the conversations. I write down how long the children stay at the table, what and how they build, how they interact with their peers, and the number concepts they demonstrate.

As I kid watch at the math table and in other areas of the room throughout the day, I take notes on the Class Assessment Profile for Math (Appendix A.9) and a Class Grid (Appendix A.12). Along with this on-going informal assessment, I conduct a formal math assessment with each child at the beginning of the year (see Chapter 14). I tell them I want to find out what they know about math so that as their teacher I can help them learn. This assessment helps me plan activities for the group and for individual children that support the children's evolving competency in math

Types of Activities

After the children have been introduced to the different manipulatives and have had time to become familiar with them, the focus of the math I CARE varies from day to day, but falls into three general categories (Bergen 1988). These categories—free play, directed play, and guided play—form the framework for the math activities during choice time.

In applying Holdaway's natural-learning classroom model of demonstration, participation, practice, and performance, I relate directed play to demonstration and participation and free and guided play to practice and performance. However, for math, in which the children learn by touching and manipulating the materials, I begin by letting the children practice (free play) with the materials before I demonstrate. I find that they need to become familiar with the materials through free play before they can participate in a teacher-directed demonstration.

Free Play   Free play, or free exploration (Baratta-Lorton 1976), is the most open-ended type of activity because it lets the children make choices about what they do with the materials. They either select their own materials or work with the manipulative I have chosen for the day. I encourage free play throughout the year and build in time for the children to return to the same materials again and again. I believe that free play offers the best opportunity for the children to work and learn at their own developmental level because they are directing what they do. The conditions of natural learning are present as the children approximate, self-correct, and share with their peers what they have discovered.

One day, during free play with pattern blocks (teacher choice), Trevor was building a tower, Alison was making a flower pattern, Anissa and Kevin were sorting the blocks into shapes and counting how many in each pile, and David and Marisa were making identical structures. Another day during free play (student choice), five children chose to build a zoo with the unit blocks, four played a dice game, several built with rods, a group constructed a tower with bristle blocks, and several linked Unifix Cubes across the room. In listening to their conversations, I heard children estimating, counting, comparing, categorizing, and measuring. They were learning how to negotiate, share, cooperate, and collaborate, teaching themselves and each other.

Frequent free play also encourages children to get to know the attributes and qualities of the materials and make new discoveries about them. For example, after many days building with Cuisenaire

Rods, several children started building staircases. They were thrilled at this discovery, and I was glad that I had given them time to discover this basic construction on their own. Staircases became very popular in the class, and children started building multiple staircases and staircase designs. One day they used all the rods and linked the many staircases together. The children were learning in community, and I didn't need to "teach" one child how to make a staircase.

Free play does not need or warrant teacher direction. It is primarily a time when the children practice with the materials without the teacher (demonstrator) present. During those days when the math I CARE is free play, I usually work in a directed way in another area. I might have writing conferences, read with children, facilitate finger painting, or direct a water-play activity. However, I do observe and record informally what the children are doing in the math area. I can then build upon their interests and competencies and act as a scaffold for further learning during guided and directed play.

Directed Play   During directed play I facilitate a game for five or six children, or direct cooperative or individual tasks. Some examples of group games are:

- Attribute block games
- Banking game with dice and white and orange Cuisenaire Rods
- A commercial or teacher-made board game
- Chip trading

Some examples of cooperative or individual tasks are:

- Copying pegboard or bead designs
- Making patterns with Unifix Cubes
- Making trains with Cuisenaire Rods
- Dice games
- Geoboard designs
- Task cards for pattern blocks, tangrams, geoboards, Cuisenaire Rods, Unifix Cubes, color cubes, beads, pegboards

My beginning of the year assessment, along with daily on-going informal assessment, helps me to know how to work with individual children during directed play. This continual kid-watching supports me in the questions I ask children, in the challenges I present to them, and in the materials that I offer them. I can interact with children at their "zone of proximal development." "With assistance, every child can do more than he can by himself—though only within

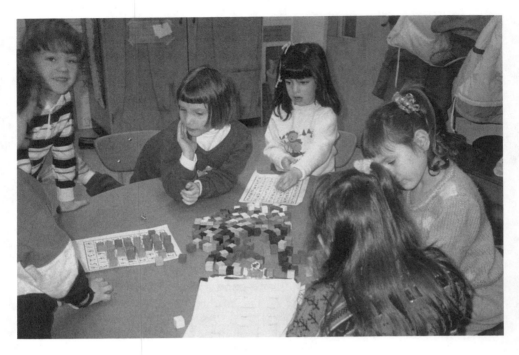

Figure 10-1 Guided play

the limits set by the state of his development" (Vygotsky 1986, p. 187).

Guided Play   During guided play the children are given some direction from me. Often they play a game or continue a task that I have introduced during directed play. They might choose their own banker and play chip trading. I might ask them to complete some of the task cards that I introduced during a prev ous directed lesson. Although I check in periodically to see how things are going, I don't stay at the table. The children need to practice and role play without the demonstrator, using what is meaningful to them at their developmental level. The rules for the activity will change as the children make choices about what they want to learn (Figure 10–1).

Helping Individual Children

I also work informally with individual children whose assessment indicates they cannot recognize numerals, don't have one-to-one correspondence, and/or don't demonstrate general math language. I "do bedtime story" with them as we enjoy counting books together. I engage them in authentic activities that give them experiences with numbers, counting, and patterns. For example, I ask them to help me count the notices going home, the paint brushes we need for four painters at the art table, and the number of children at the writing table.

Cooperative Learning

Whenever possible the children work in pairs or teams. When chip trading, two children share a till. I encourage them to act as teachers by checking each other's work. When making patterns with Unifix Cubes, the children read their patterns to each other. They are always willing to help each other. If one child is stuck on a tangram pattern, a friend will join the task.

Unit Blocks

Unit blocks are placed in a prominent place in my classroom and are often chosen when the math I CARE is free choice or during the children's free-choice time. I want the boys and girls to become engaged in building with unit blocks, and I have developed a few strategies that encourage everyone in the class to spend time building with them (Figure 10–2).

Some weeks I announce that everyone has to build with the unit blocks during the week and to indicate after they have done so by signing their name on a clipboard or checking off their name on

Figure 10-2 Unit blocks

the class list posted in the area. At the beginning of choice time each day, I ask for about four volunteers to start in the area, and by Friday everyone in the class has participated.

At other times I ask the children to work in teams of three or four at the block area to plan and build something, and to share their construction with the class by making a presentation at the end of choice time. Sometimes I form the groups and other times the children make their own. I check in with them periodically to hear how they are doing and help them solve any problems. At the beginning of the year I help them plan their presentation to the class (with practice they can do it on their own). We discuss the speaking order of presenters, what each presenter is going to say, and how questions are going to be answered. Afterward the group talks about what they did to work together successfully and if there are things they could do next time to work more cooperatively.

Sally Wilson, a kindergarten teacher in Boulder, Colorado, hangs a set of enlarged photographs of important local buildings in her block area for the children to use as models while building. She also makes available a school floor plan. These models invite the children to expand on what they know as they work together through interactive play to learn more about their community.

Workbench

In November, after the children have settled into the classroom routine, I introduce the workbench. The children generate most of the safety rules that need to be followed, and I add my own if they have not been mentioned by the children. Here are the rules that one of my classes made, which I recorded on a chart.

1.   No hitting.
2.   Always use a vice when sawing.
3.   Keep the tools at the workbench.
4.   Only use the tools for building.
5.   Only two people can work at the workbench at a time.
6.   Write your name on your unfinished pieces.

In the beginning we start out with wood, nails, two hammers, and a saw. During the year we add drills, screwdrivers, screws, and different size nails and recycled materials.

Physical Science

Throughout the year the children and I develop "science focus studies." During shared reading and story time we read and talk about the topic, and during choice time the children engage in related activities. The three focus studies described in this chapter—magnets, sand, and water—are offered as suggestions of approaches teachers can take in developing their own studies. Sand and water are two topics in the prescribed science curriculum in our school system, while magnets is a topic I choose to introduce. Sometimes a science focus study (usually one of the natural sciences) develops into an in-depth study and becomes a dramatic play environment, as described in Chapter 12.

Sand Table

The sand table is available throughout the year in my classroom for free play during choice time. Periodically, I add different artifacts to encourage renewed and varied play and to introduce or expand on a science or thematic unit. Then the sand table becomes the focal point of a curriculum focus, and I direct or guide the play.

Some guided and directed activities encourage the children to explore the properties of sand. For example, they sort it examine and compare different kinds of sand, weigh it, and experiment with sand and water. Using different size measuring containers, they estimate and measure quantities of sand. One year the children made a science lab book to record their observations as scientists.

The sand table is often used in the play environment we set up as part of a thematic unit, and books and poems relating to the topic are included during shared reading. When we set up a farm in our class, we put plastic farm animals in the sand table. Later we added woodland and jungle animals and read about different kinds of animals. When we developed our aquarium, the sand table became a beach to display shells. As part of a school-wide study entitled "Westward Ho," I sprayed small pebbles with gold spray paint and the children "panned for gold" with different size sifters.

Water Table

I have a 12" x 18" x 4" water table, which I put outside my classroom door in the fall and spring. During the winter I use a transparent plastic 12" x 18" tub that the children are able to set up independently. They place a plastic cloth and newspapers on the art table, put the tub on one end (leaving room for art activities at the other end), and fill it.

Usually the children fill the water table using buckets and plastic milk cartons. Sometimes I set parameters or pose questions about filling it. For example, I might ask the children to write down their estimate of how many gallons (quarts, cups, etc.) it will take to

Figure 10-3 Water table

fill the tub half full, and then record the actual number. This suggestion often encourages the children to take a clipboard and class list, make their own choice of container, and get estimates from everyone in the class. One day two children decided to see if it took the same number of cups to empty the table as fil it. A lively discussion followed.

I introduce other water activities that illustrate physical science concepts we're studying, such as:

- Sink and Float
- Conservation of liquid—pouring from and filling different size and shape containers
- Bubbles
- Properties of water: liquid, solid, gas

Before I initiate guided and directed activities at the water table, we establish appropriate water-play routines and give ample opportunities for free play. As the year goes on I give plenty of chances for the children to return to free play so they can practice what has been demonstrated during the teacher-directed and -guided activities (Figure 10–3).

Magnets

This science focus unit has the children working as scientists, recording their observations. We set up a science laboratory with the store front/puppet theater, and add three chairs, white shirts for lab coats, clipboards, pencils, a date stamp, and a variety of magnets. The activities with the magnets are an orange I CARE.

I introduce the study by recording on a chart what the children know about magnets. The first day they experiment and explore with the magnets, and are encouraged to move about the room testing them on everything available. At sharing time they share their discoveries.

I read *Micky's Magnet* to introduce other I CARE activities. These include discovering and recording three things that adhere to the magnet and three things that don't, recording what pieces of metal have iron in them, working in teams to discover things around the school that contain iron, and experimenting with the north and south poles of magnets.

Reading, writing, math, and physical and natural science are integrated with a variety of art processes.

For Further Reading

Baker, Ann and Johnny. 1990. *Mathematics in Process*. Portsmouth, NH: Heinemann.

Baratta-Lorton, Mary 1976. *Mathematics Their Way*. Reading, MA: Addison-Wesley.

Beaty, Seddon, and Karen De Rusha. 1987. *Sand and Water*. Lexington, MA: Early Education Curriculum.

Bergen, Doris, ed. 1987. *Play as a Medium for Learning and Development*. Portsmouth, NH: Heinemann.

Hirsch, Elisabeth S., ed. 1984. *The Block Book*. Washington, DC: National Association for the Education of Young Children.

Renner, John W., and Edmund A. Marek. 1990. *The Learning Cycle and Elementary School Science Teaching*. Portsmouth, NH: Heinemann.

Whitin, David J., Heidi Mills, and Timothy O'Keefe. 1990. *Living and Learning Mathematics: Stories and Strategies for Supporting Mathematical Literacy*. Portsmouth, NH: Heinemann.

11

Art During Choice Time

Art is related to almost everything the children do throughout the day. During shared reading we talk about the illustrations in a book and discuss the artist's style and technique. During choice time the children apply what they have learned as they paint scenery for a dramatic play environment, draw a picture for an innovation on a big book, or draw as part of the writing process. Several processes and techniques are often used together on one project.

The art table is available every day during choice time, usually as a free-choice activity, but sometimes as an art I CARE (blue). The I CARE introduces the children to the processes of painting, printing, collage, and construction, and skills such as cutting, pasting, and stapling. They can then choose to pursue these activities as a free choice another day, develop them in book or writing extensions, or incorporate them into the current dramatic play environment in the classroom. Occasionally I ask the children to choose any art activity for an I CARE. They might paint at the easel, use watercolors, work with playdough, or make a construction with recycled materials (Figure 11–1).

Taking Care of Materials

Free-choice activities are ones that the children can undertake without adult supervision. In the beginning of the year I show the children where the materials are kept and how to take care of them so they will be able to use them on their own as the year goes on. I teach them how to put the plastic cover on the table, how to use a paper clip to open up the glue bottles, how to refill the paint and hang easel paper, how to change the jar of water for the next person after watercolor painting, how to put their names on their constructions, and where to put finished work.

The children are responsible for wearing smocks when they paint. We keep a supply of men's shirts available, shortsleeved or

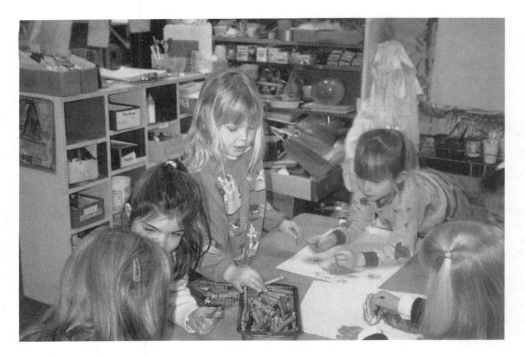

Figure 11-1 Art table

with the sleeves cut off, and the children are encouraged to help each other button them. The Sudbury Extended Day teachers gave me this idea for making a smock: cut open the bottom of a plastic supermarket bag and use the two handles for arm holes.

Crayons

Crayons are used almost every day in my classroom and are the primary medium for drawing in the writing area. I provide both the thick primary crayons and the thin standard crayons. These are stored separately in several large margarine tubs on the shelves in the writing and art areas, and are taken to different areas in the room as needed.

The children use crayons in many ways and for many purposes. For example, they crayon on white paper, colored paper, fabric, wood, and recycled materials. They also use crayons for rubbings, printing, stenciling, and crayon resist.

Paints

Tempera Paints   Tempera paints are always available at the side-by-side easels in the art area during choice time. I put the paint (about four colors to an easel) in eight-ounce yogurt containers, which fit easily and securely into the paint tray. To prevent the paint from drying out during the week, I place a sandwich baggie over the container, cutting a hole in it for the paint brush. Every Friday the children and I clean the brushes. I change the paint color and the size and color of the paper from time to time, and encourage the children to suggest the colors and paper that they want.

Watercolors   Sometimes I assign watercolor painting as an I CARE. I set up six paint trays and water in baby food jars, and the children can work without adult supervision. When they finish, they change the water for the next person and put their painting in a designated area to dry. Watercolors are also available on the shelves for the children to get out as a free choice.

Finger paints   I find that finger painting needs direct adult supervision and that parent volunteers can help with this activity, freeing me to work in other areas during choice time. Sometimes finger painting is an I CARE, and I like to have it available for a choice once a month. To prepare for finger painting, I place several layers of newspaper over a plastic cloth on the table. The children write their names on the back of the finger paint paper before we wet it and add the paint. After a painting is finished I remove it, along with a layer of the newspaper. This leaves a clean surface for the next worker.

To flatten out finger paintings I iron them on the back after they have dried. This was especially effective for one class project, when we used finger paintings as background for a class mural of *Jump, Frog, Jump*. The morning class used blue finger paint for the water, and the afternoon class made the land with green finger paint. The children drew and cut out the different characters from the story and glued them to the background.

Finger painting seems to invite children to mix colors, and one day we focused on primary colors. The children each chose two of the primary colors for their finger painting. We made a chart of what colors they picked and what color the mixture made. I read *Color Dance*, by Ann Jonas, which led us to further experimenting by adding black and white to the primary colors.

Printing

Periodically, I introduce different kinds of printing materials at the art table as demonstrations of techniques and processes that the children can then incorporate in their work throughout the year. The children use various objects from the environment, such as blocks and recycled materials from the classroom, and leaves twigs, and seeds from outside. Sometimes clothespins are clipped on shapes cut out of sponges or other materials for easy, less messy printing. Thumbprints and other printing using stamp pads are also favorites with the class.

Construction with Recycled Materials

One of the favorite free-choice activities in the art area is making things with recycled materials, often referred to as "junk." Most of the materials are organized in labeled shoe boxes on a shelf in the area. Some of the categories are labeled by property (metal, wood, paper) or by function (lids, tubes, yarn, buttons). Larger materials, such as large tubes, coffee cans, cardboard, and paper scraps, are stored in boxes on the floor.

In order to keep the area replenished, the children and I bring in things from home. I keep a bag for recycled materials in my kitchen, and when it is full I bring it in and show the class. For example, I collect plastic yogurt and butter containers, coffee scoops, and pieces of string. The children help me sort it according to properties and uses, and place most of it in labeled shoe boxes in the art area. This demonstration encourages the children to bring in their own bags of "junk." At the beginning of the year I send home a list of materials we need (Appendix B.8), and write a reminder in my weekly newsletter when supplies need replenishing.

Other Processes

Modeling   Playdough and plasticine are always available at the art table. The children often use assessories such as cookie cutters and utensils, and sometimes bring in their own trucks to make roads and tracks in the plasticine.

Papier-Mâché   We made papier-mâché fish for our aquarium and fruit for our supermarket.

Cutting and tearing paper   Several children looked at *Frederick*, and other books by Leo Lioni, and tried his technique of tearing construction paper and pasting the shapes on paper to create pictures.

Weaving   *Charlie's New Cloak*, by Tomie dePaolo, was the catalyst for the children's attempts at weaving with paper strips.

Sewing   After reading *Corduroy*, by Don Freeman, the children made a sleeping bag for a favorite stuffed animal. Parents helped them use big needles and heavy thread.

One of the purposes in introducing the children to various art media and techniques is to demonstrate a variety of processes that they can use when they want to express their feelings, or their reactions to books or events. For example, using bright paint and increasing page sizes (modeled after Eric Carle's *The Hungry Caterpillar*), several children made books about what they like to eat each day of the week, while others made a game about a jungle, using fingerprints to mark the spaces where the animals should move.

The art area is also used extensively in conjunction with the dramatic play environments. Meagan and Adam modeled plasticine dog bones to feed the animals in the veterinarian office. David made a check-out machine for the supermarket out of recycled "junk." Almost everyone participated in painting posters to sell at the aquarium. Art in its many forms is a powerful means of expression for children and, in my classroom, is an important contributor to the whole learning process.

For Further Reading

Clay, Marie M. (1986) "Constructive Processes: Talking, Reading, Writing, Art and Craft. *The Reading Teacher*, vol. 39 (April), pp. 764–770.

Devonshire, Hilary. "Fresh Start." New York: Franklin Watts.

————Drawing, 1990.

————Moving Art, 1990.

————Printing, 1988.

Pluckrose, Henry. "Fresh Start". New York: Franklin Watts.

————Crayons, 1987.

————Paints, 1987.

12

Dramatic Play Environments

"Can we go play now?"

Kindergarten children love to play. Play serves an important function in the cognitive, creative, language, social, and physical development of young children (Saracho 1986). "Play, which allows children to choose their learning focus and which fosters a broad range of developmental goals, should be included as an essential learning element" (Bergen 1988, p. 1). The works of Altwerger (1988), Carlsson-Paige and Levin (1987), Katz (1989), and Piaget have also influenced my understanding of the value of play in the kindergarten.

In my classroom many kinds of play are present throughout the day. During shared reading we play with words as we sing, read, and act out favorite stories. During choice time children play at the sand and water tables, and are involved with free, guided, or directed play when building with blocks at the math area. And, of course, there is free play on the playground.

Dramatic play is the medium for learning in the dramatic play environments, which the children and I set up throughout the year. Through these dramatic play environments we create the conditions where process and content are woven together, as they are in our everyday lives. The process areas of language (reading, writing, speaking, listening), drama, art, music, movement, and mathematics are naturally integrated as the children focus on the content areas of social studies and science in a social situation. The basic developmental issues that children work on to understand life and their place in the world arise from their needs and interests. Certain developmental issues are addressed as they work together and take on the various roles in the environment. Nancy Carlsson-Paige and Diane Levin (1987, p. 18) define them as: control and power, separation and autonomy, fantasy and reality, and gender identification.

Through the process of generating a dramatic play environment (farm, hospital, greenhouse, bank), the children focus on social studies and science themes (animals, the human body, plants, money). They experience many learning processes as they explore the developmental themes in their lives, and they build upon what they know through science and social studies themes that are authentic, meaningful, and interesting to them.

All my beliefs about how children learn are present as the themes of content and development are integrated in dramatic play environments. The conditions for natural learning are present as the children make choices in noncompetitive play situations. They use what they know about literacy, and they expand that knowledge as they talk and play in a social context that is whole, meaningful, interesting, and functional to them.

Choosing A Dramatic Play Environment

We usually create six dramatic play environments a year, with each one lasting five or six weeks. They begin with the selection of a theme or content area and develop as we learn about the subject, set up the environment, and play in it. They culminate with the class sharing what we have learned. (See Appendix B.3 for a list of suggested dramatic play environments.)

Holdaway uses the terms "developmental" or "generative curriculum" to describe a curriculum that most closely parallels the natural-learning model. In my classroom dramatic play environments are generated in four major ways:

- From free play and/or child interest.
- One dramatic play environment generates another.
- The whole class chooses a topic.
- Teacher choice.

Regardless of how the dramatic play environment is chosen, the selection always involves collaboration between the children and me, and is an important part of the process. I guide the process and contribute to the discussion to assure that the theme fits certain criteria:

- It directly relates to the life situation and interests of the children.
- A dramatic play environment can be set up in the classroom.
- It allows children to gain information by one or several of the following: (1) taking a related field trip (2) talking with an expert in the field at school, or (3) using audiovisual material and books.

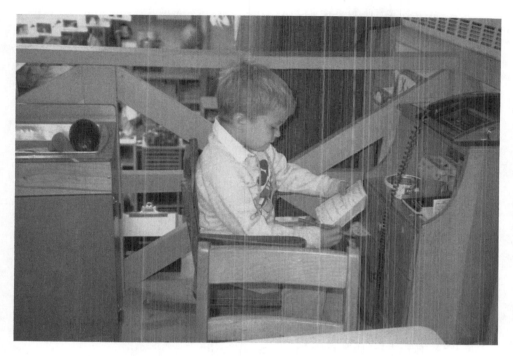

Figure 12-1   The office

• It lends itself to opportunities to expand children's interests, experiences, and concepts.

• It offers opportunities for discussion and problem solving of social situations as a means of fostering personal growth and community building.

Dramatic Play Environments Generated from Free Play

When the children come to school in September, a housekeeping area is arranged in the loft and big blocks are available underneath. During choice time they have opportunities for free play in the areas. Some years free play continues into October; other years the children have focused on a theme and begin a dramatic play environment right away. I know this is happening when day after day they build the same kind of structure, when they bring specific props into the area, and when they ask if they can leave it up overnight.

The year we created an aquarium, the children had shown interest in building an office early in the year. Every day pencils and paper appeared in the structures they were building, and they asked for a telephone, chairs, and notebooks (Figure 12–1). At clean-up time we would put the props away and stack the blocks. The next day another group would rebuild the office. Capitalizing on this interest, I initiated a discussion about different kinds of offices, their purposes, and the jobs of office workers. We interviewed the school secretary and took a field trip down the hall to her office. Children began bringing in recycled envelopes, stationary, memo pads, stamp pads, carbon paper, pencils, and so on. They interviewed their parents about their jobs and the place an office played in their work, and the parents wrote their responses on an interview form (Appendix A.5).

One Dramatic Play Environment Leads to Another

A few weeks later, after one of the children in the class invited us to see his new house under construction, the office became an architect's office on top of the loft and a building site was created under the loft. A student teacher made arrangements for us to visit the Acorn Homes factory, and a father came in to tell us about his job as an architect.

This office-theme cycle continued throughout the year as one dramatic play environment generated another. We set up a reception office for the aquarium, made a post office in February, and created a veterinarian's office in the spring.

The Whole Class Chooses a Topic

"What are we going to build next?" is a question often asked after we have experienced a few dramatic play environments. If a new theme cycle does not develop naturally, we decide as a class what our next theme will be. This was the procedure we used to settle on the veterinarian theme.

First we brainstormed all the topics we were interested in studying and I wrote them on the blackboard. Topics included jungle animals, cats, hospitals, trucks, space, bees, and pets. A show of hands indicating favorite topics, eliminated some that were of limited interest. Hospitals, cats, and pets emerged as popular ideas. After we grouped them into a single theme, we came to consensus on a veterinarian office.

Teacher Choice

Sometimes I choose a theme that interests me, or because I have materials and ideas that will contribute to a successful environment, or because it is part of our system or school curriculum. Even though I have selected the theme, the children are involved in its planning and development from the start.

A Dramatic Play Environment: Celebrating Me!

One year I introduced a sharing project called "Celebrating Me!" as part of a school-wide theme on celebrating diversity. I didn't intend for this project to generate a dramatic play environment but as we got going it seemed a very natural result.

To start off the project I shared with the class a one-page form, entitled "Celebrating Me!" (Appendix A.6), and a shoe box filled with examples of my favorite things. The form asked who was in my family, what was my favorite animal, food, TV show, etc. It asked what I like to do inside and outside, how I am like other people, how I am different from other people, and what I thought was special about me. The shoe box contained pictures of my family and examples of my favorite things: a small glass hedgehog, the book *Gifts from the Sea*, the label from a Wheaties box, and so on. The children then took home a form and a letter explaining the project. The letter asked parents to fill out the form with their children as they filled a shoe box and talked together about their children's favorite and important things.

The boxes were brought to school over the next three weeks, and usually two children shared theirs in front of the class each day. As needed, I helped them tell what was on the form while they showed what they had selected for their box. Hands went up as I asked how the children were alike and different from their classmates.

"Raise your hand if you are like Anna because you have dark hair. Raise your hand if you are different from Anna because you don't have dark hair."

"Raise your hand if you are like Anna because you like to play tag. Raise your hand if you are different from Anna because you don't like to play tag."

"Raise your hand if you are like Anna because you like to laugh."

The purpose was for us to get to know one another better and to appreciate that we can be like someone in some ways and different in others.

This project developed into a dramatic play environment as we turned the play area of our room into a museum to share our boxes. The children were responsible for choosing a space to arrange their things, and as more boxes came in we discussed ways to provide enough spaces for everyone. We made shelves with the big blocks, borrowed a table from the teacher across the hall, temporarily gave up the use of the quiet table in the writing area, used one of the bookshelves in the library area, and put a board on top of the sand table.

As a group we created an announcement, which we sent home to parents, placed in school staff mailboxes, and hung on the announcement board in the school lobby. It advertised the museum, listed the two days that it would be open, and the hour during choice time when people could visit. (These hours could be expanded to before school, during dinner, and in the evening to accommodate parents who do not have a flexible work schedule.)

The children made tickets to give to visitors, money to buy them, and a work schedule for the main museum jobs. The two ticket sellers sat in a booth at the door and gave out tickets. The ticket collectors wore aprons with pockets from a lumber store for the collected tickets and asked visitors to sign in on a clipboard. The four guides/guards used rhythm sticks as pointers to direct people through the museum. Everyone with a job wore a sign clipped to their clothes with a clothespin. When the children didn't have a job, they chose something else to do, such as build with blocks, draw or paint, play at the water table, listen to a tape, or read.

Two hundred sixty-nine people registered at the museum. Teachers usually sent small groups of children. Parents, grandparents, home caregivers, and younger siblings had the opportunity to get to know their children's classmates. After visiting the museum, visitors from home were encouraged to explore the rest of the room with their child. We made a list of the areas they might enjoy and hung it on a notice board for them to see as they entered the room. The list included big books, writing files and folders, snack table, blocks, the library, and the notice basket holding books and notes from home. Marisa's mom read her daughter a story. Nicky's younger brother joined in and drew a picture at the writing table, and Mary's sister enjoyed the water table. I had the chance to chat briefly with many of the parents about their child's growth in kindergarten.

Applying The Natural-Learning Classroom Model

Once we generate a dramatic play environment, I apply Holdaway's natural-learning classroom model to plan and guide its development. The four aspects of the developmental learning sequence—demonstration, participation, practice, and performance—are areas of focus that we return to throughout the theme cycle.

Demonstration   The children gain new information and expand their schema from various demonstrations. They go on field trips; listen to speakers; observe artifacts; see filmstrips, movies, and videos; work with computer programs; read books, magazines, and newspapers; and hear songs, poems, and chants.

Participation   Children interact with the demonstration in a variety of ways. They ask questions, participate in discussions, explore and investigate the artifacts, and discuss extend, and innovate on texts.

Role-playing or Practice The main focus for role-playing or practice is through play in the environment we set up. Sometimes the children take the role of a character or animal related to the environment, as they did in our veterinarian's office when they became the vet or an animal. At other times they play themselves, as they did when they brought their "pet" to be treated. The roles are not clearly defined by adult standards, but are continually changing as the children move back and forth in different roles. Children also have time to practice through art projects, math application, music, reading, writing, and science investigations that are related to the dramatic play theme.

Performance Finally, the children want to share what they know. I have found that the most meaningful and authentic way to share play environments is to invite people to visit the environment. Some other ways include displaying art work in the room, around the school, and in town buildings such as the library; publishing books, pamphlets, or newspapers; giving demonstrations to other classes; putting on plays; and creating a video show.

Throughout a dramatic play environment I refer to a Planning Guide (see Appendix B.4) to be sure that the four conditions of natural learning are being met, and to remind myself of activities I might introduce.

A Dramatic Play Environment: The Aquarium

We didn't decide ahead of time to build an aquarium, it just began to happen. Perhaps it started when I read *Where the River Begins*, by Thomas Locker. Over several readings, spanning several days, we discussed the illustrations and the thunderstorm, and we generated questions and information about where a river ends. We wrote Mr. Locker, telling him how much we enjoyed the book and suggested that he write a story about where a river ends. (He sent back a postcard telling us that another of his books, *Sailing with the Wind*, is about where a river ends.)

Next, I read the class *The Beginning of a Brook*, and the following day we started painting a mural about the water cycle: where water comes from, how it forms into a pond, develops from a brook to a river, and finally flows into the ocean. First the children painted large areas of blue and green for the water and land. Then they added

Styrofoam for snow, clear cellophane with black mark for rain, blue cellophane with cut-out whales under it for the turbulent ocean, and different materials from the "junk" area for fish, trees, and shrubs.

We labeled the important parts of the mural, and during shared reading I pointed to the words as we discussed the water cycle (Demonstration and Participation). During choice time children took a pointer and told the story to themselves or a friend (Role-playing or Practice). Later, when visitors came to the aquarium, the children explained the water cycle to them (Performance).

We set up an aquarium in the classroom, and I brought in a few fish to get us started. We named each fish and discovered we had a responsibility to take care of them, to feed them, to keep the tank clean and the water temperature steady. We discussed how the fish are independent in the tank but dependent on us, too, and the ways we are all independent yet dependent on one another. Throughout the rest of the year many children brought in fish to contribute to the tank. We kept a list of the kind of fish and the date we got them, and when one died we recorded that date too.

From then on the children started building a fish tank under the loft with the big blocks. They brought books and magazines from home and the library. Meagan proudly displayed a necklace with a fish on it. Bryson suggested that we get a recording of the sea and play it under the loft. Children drew fish on the chalkboard, and fish and sea themes began appearing in their daily writing. During group time they had opportunities to tell about their related experiences. Children took on the roles of fish, workers, and visitors. Adam reported that he and six of his classmates had gone through the aquarium that day. The children were engaged.

I would have liked to have taken the children on a field trip to the New England Aquarium, but couldn't arrange a visit. However, many of the children had been there with their families, and we used their experiences, as well as books and magazines, for information (demonstration) as we created the aquarium. During shared reading we read many fiction and nonfiction books and learned several related songs and poems.

I decided to initiate a class discussion to plan and focus this dramatic play environment (participation). We decided that the aquarium tank would be under the loft, the work area where the workers tended the fish and repaired the equipment would be up on the loft, and the rest of the area would be a museum (Role-Playing or Practice). We would open the aquarium to visitors (Performance).

From then on both the children and I initiated various activities and projects (Role-Playing or Practice). Each child posed one question he or she would like to answer about fish and the sea. I wrote them on a chart, and as we shared many fiction and nonfiction books and magazines, we kept the questions in mind. Before the aquarium was opened to visitors, the children made a 'report" (usually a picture and some writing) to hang in the museum that answered their question.

We created a library of related books in the aquarium for reference as we painted and stuffed big fish to hang in the tank, drew many paintings and pictures, and set up the sand table as a beach to display fish and shells. We made fish prints of a flounder, which was then washed, frozen each night, and displayed on the museum table along with other related artifacts that the children made or brought in. Children wrote about the fish at the writing area, created related artifacts at the art table to display in the aquarium, and made posters to "sell" to the visitors.

When a disagreement arose that the children couldn't work out themselves, I would gather the group together to problem-solve. If it involved a few children, we would meet as a small group. If it involved many children or seemed like an issue that would affect the entire group, I would call the class together at the rug area for a discussion.

One day there was disagreement between two children about whether the aquarium was open or not. I sat with the two of them, and after each gave his/her point of view, they agreed on when to open. Another time when there was a lot of noise in the area, we met as a class to talk about the situation. Through class discussion the children decided to limit the number of people that could play a given role at one time. They decided there could be two ticket sellers, four guides or workers, and three fish. To eliminate confusion, they decided to wear signs pinned to color yarn necklaces that indicated their roles (for example, the guides wore orange yarn, the fish, blue yarn and the ticket sellers, red yarn).

Since the children are eager to resolve the problems so they can continue their play, these situations are opportunities for them to learn how to effectively resolve conflict in a positive way. I often notice that the conflict resolution strategies learned during dramatic play are used throughout the day, as the children collaborate in the block area, share crayons at the writing area, or take turns on the tire swing on the playground.

The office theme, which had started at the beginning of the year, continued. Several children set up an information booth and ticket counter at the entrance to the aquarium. They added a telephone, paper, pencils, and made money and tickets. When we began planning for visitors, everything was ready to go.

Since the children were expected to be museum guides, they practiced ahead of time and helped each other. When ready, they would take a pointer and guide me through the aquarium, telling me what they would say and how they would act as a guide. At first only a few children were interested in this process, but the rest of them watched their classmates, and soon everyone became engaged.

The aquarium, which was open to visitors for three days, followed a procedure similar to the one described earlier in this chapter for "Celebrating Me." By the third day, I noticed that the children were less involved in the aquarium and were becoming engaged again in routine activities in the room—painting, building, their own writing and drawing.

The next day during community circle time we shared what we liked about the aquarium and agreed it was time to take it down. When I asked what we should do next in the area, the consensus was to "just have the big blocks and housekeeping for a while."

Throughout the time we had the aquarium play environment, the conditions of natural learning were present. Demonstration, Participation, Role-playing or Practice, and Performance flowed naturally back and forth as the children and I orchestrated the experience. The children were engaged in a meaningful, authentic, and interesting project. They determined the extent of their involvement in it, its direction, how they shared what they had learned from it, and when to bring it to closure.

For Further Reading

Bergen, Doris ed. 1988. *Play as a Medium for Learning and Development*. Portsmouth, NH: Heinemann.

Davidson, Evelyn, ed. 1986. *Interaction: Teacher's Resource Book*. Crystal Lake, IL: Rigby.

DeRusha, Karen. 1990. *Dramatic Play*. Lexington, MA: Early Education Curriculum.

Gamberg, Ruth, Winniefred Kwak, Meredith Hutchings, and Judy Altheim. 1988. *Learning and Loving It: Theme Studies in the Classroom*. Portsmouth, NH: Heinemann.

Katz, Lillian G., and Sylvia C. Chard. 1989. *Engaging Children's Minds: The Project Approach*. Norwood, NJ: Ablex.

Levin, Diane, and Nancy Carlsson-Paige. 1987. *The War Play Dilemma: Balancing Needs and Values in the Early Childhood Classroom*. New York: Teachers College Press.

13

The End of the Day

Sharing Time

At the end of choice time we all come together again as a classroom community to share what we have done. Children share their writing, paintings, constructions made at the art area, or ask the class to move to the block area to see a building they have made. Sometimes they share what they liked during choice time, or acknowledge something positive they notice their classmates have done. We might enjoy a class book just completed, or I might read a familiar story to settle us down before cleanup. Holdaway emphasizes sharing (Performance) as the fourth part of the natural learning classroom model. Many of the ways that sharing occurs during the day are discussed throughout this book.

Cleanup

Although children are expected to clean up individual spills and messes, clean-up after choice time is a cooperative endeavor in my classroom. Adults and children work together to pick up the room after choice time. At the beginning of the year I ask for volunteers or assign children each day to an area. I work along with them, demonstrating where the blocks go, how to organize the crayons, ways to hang up the dress-up clothes, how to wipe the snack table, and how to stack the chairs. I note the children who seem to know how to pick up, the ones who stick to the task, the ones that wander off, the ones who don't volunteer, and the ones who continue to play.

In early October I divide the number of children in the class into six permanent clean-up groups, which last throughout the year. I put considerable thought into forming these groups because I consider clean-up time an opportunity for cooperative learning, not just an efficient way to get the room in order. For example, I don't usually place a natural leader in each group, because I have found that they

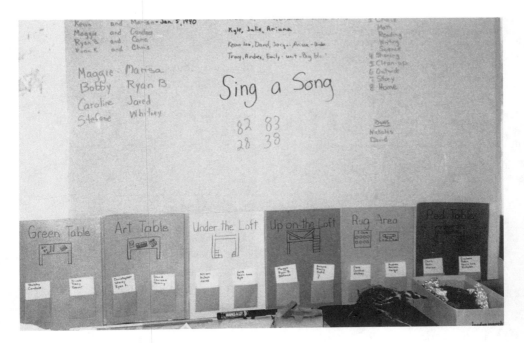

Figure 13-1 Clean-up assignments

do most of the work while the others remain followers. Therefore, I
might put several leaders in one group so they can learn to work
together. Sometimes I put the children whom I've noticed tend to
play or wander during cleanup in the same group so they can learn
to clean up and take responsibility. I often put a child who has
trouble becoming part of the group with a class leader, and put a
child who has behavior issues with a positive role model.

Each group is responsible for cleaning up one of the six areas
in the room for the week: math (red), reading (yellow), writing
(green), art (blue), up in the loft (orange), and under the loft (white).
A color-coded pocket chart indicates the six areas. The members of
each group are written on a card that goes in the pocket chart,
indicating the cleanup area for that week. Every Monday we change
cleanup jobs, and I rotate the group card to the next pocket on the
chart and read the children's names and new cleanup area (Figure 13–1).

The responsibility of each group is to work together to clean up
its area. As the children work together throughout the year, they
develop ways that work best for them. For example, some groups
divide the tasks at the area and each member works independently.
Others work more cooperatively. Some groups work very efficiently
and finish promptly. Others spend time discussing, arguing, and

negotiating. If one member of the group isn't doing his or her share, the group has to work out the problem. I try to stay out of the process, expecting that they can work it out among themselves, but sometimes I am asked to act as a mediator.

As each group finishes and is dismissed by me or the class leader, the children go outside to play.

Outside Play

I am committed to getting the class out to play every day if possible. Aside from the need to expend physical energy and be involved in gross motor activities, outside play gives opportunities for children to develop socially and for the class to grow as a community of learners. It lends itself to free play more than inside play, which tends to be more directed or guided.

Our playground has a grassy area, black top with hopscotch and four square, swings, slides, seesaws, and two wooden forts. We have a cart and wagon big enough for two riders. Children can choose to take out a box of sand toys, a ball, or a book. They are free to develop their own games and select the equipment they want to use. My role is to observe and help individuals or small groups work out problems, and to act as a facilitator for developing playground rules for groups when needed.

Preparation for Home

We come in as the rest of the school goes out for recess. The children get a drink of water, pick up their school bags and any notices to go home, and gather at the rug for the last fifteen minutes of school. I place notices from the classroom and the school office on a table, and the children are expected to pick them up and put them in their school bags. At the beginning of the year I demonstrate this procedure, and throughout the year I support children in getting the notices into their bags. If a notice is particularly important, I write each child's name on it and hand them out individually. The children are encouraged to bring a bag each day. They bring backpacks, tote bags, or recycled bags from the grocery store.

Ending the Day: A "Bedtime" Story

I like to end the day as it started, with all of us together as a classroom community. We discuss what went well during the day, share plans for tomorrow, and enjoy a story. Unlike shared reading, when the children actively participate in lively demonstrations of predictable, rhythmic stories, at this time we just relax with a good "bedtime story" that I read.

14

Assessment

Throughout this book I have described how I assess the children's evolving competencies when they sign in, participate in shared reading, and practice during choice time. I have also described how I watch kids during independent reading, writing workshop, math time, sharing time, and throughout dramatic play. I am continually assessing reading comprehension and reading patterns, and monitoring the reading, writing, and math skills and strategies that children are using. I find that planning appropriate instruction, both immediate and long range, becomes easier when assessment is an integral part of the curriculum.

In addition, I employ a formal system to record these observations to assist me in being accountable to all of the involved stakeholders: the children; parents, other family members and care givers; school staff, administration, and committee; and state and national officials. Throughout the year I use a child's assessment folder to evaluate his or her progress for my own planning, in preparation for a parent conference or a special needs evaluation, or to discuss my program with administrators and fellow teachers. At the end of the year I will use the information in those folders to aid in placement decisions for the next grade and to evaluate my program.

This chapter describes the assessment checklists, profiles, and procedures that I have developed over the years to accurately and comprehensively demonstrate the growth the children in my classes have made in reading, writing, and math. I suggest that teachers use these, as well as others, to develop their own set of assessment procedures that address their needs, those of their children, and their school system.

Assessment Recording Forms

I use several different forms to record the assessments I make during the year: Class Assessment Profiles, an Individual Assessment

Profile, a Class Checklist, an Anecdotal Class Grid, blank paper for anecdotal records, various questionnaires, and specific recording forms (see Appendix A.7-14).

Class Assessment Profile and Individual Assessment Profile

I have developed a separate Class Assessment Profile for reading (Appendix A.7), writing (Appendix A.8), and math (Appendix A.9). Each lists all the children's names and descriptors for the specific subject. I also have developed an Individual Assessment Profile (Appendix A.10) for each child that lists the descriptors for reading, writing, and math found on the Individual Assessment Profiles. Usually it is easiest for me to use the Class Assessment Profile during the school day, especially if I am focusing on a specific area, and then transfer the information to the Individual Assessment Profiles after school.

I find that a flexible coding system—using words, a number system, and symbols—allows me to describe most accurately what I have observed.

Number System	Symbol System
1 Most of the time	* Has full command
2 Some of the time	+ In control
3 Not noticed yet	0 Needs time

Class Checklist and Anecdotal Class Grid

The Class Checklist (Appendix A.11) lists all the children's names in the left-hand column, with ten columns to the right for recording specific information. I record information that isn't on the Class Assessment Profiles, such as the child's birthday, who usually reads with a friend, who reads alone, and who volunteers during shared reading. I also use the checklist to record who has shared in the author's chair, who has taken out the wagon, and whose turn it is to take Mr. Bear home.

The Anecdotal Class Grid (Appendix A.12) has a 2″ × 1½″ box with each child's name where I write short notes (Fig. 14–1). I start each week with a blank grid and add notes throughout the week concerning individuals and groups of children at the writing, math, art, science, or environmental play areas. I jot down specific incidents as they occur or record them at the end of the day. I try to observe objectively and quote the children verbatim. This week-by-week record becomes an important summary of what I have noticed over the year and provides a detailed record of the child's work.

Ellen 10/11 Wrote a book with Kevin. 10/12 Recognizes dice without counting	**Nick** 10/11 Sat on edge of group. 10/13 Read book with Ryan - 10 minutes.	**Sandy** 10/12 Built tall castle with unit blocks 10/13 Blocks again. Wrote signs to tell about it.
Taisha 10/11 Shared magic markers at writing table 10/15 wrote her last name when signing in.	**Timmy** 10/12 Held pencil correctly without a reminder. 10/13 wanted to share his writing ☆ a first	**Tom** 10/12 stayed at math table - Attribute Blocks for 2 games. 10/15 Direct A Block game on his own.

Figure 14-1 Anecdotal Class Grid

Some of the things I record on a weekly basis are:

- What a child selects to do first at choice time.
- A child's writing topic.
- The book a child chooses for independent reading.
- Who spends time at the unit block area, at the sand table painting at the easel, etc.

Questionnaires and Specific Recording Forms

I use questionnaires to interview the children about reading, writing, and math. Usually I tape record the interview and write the responses on a printed form. Specific recording forms allow me to get more detailed information about a particular learning area. For example, the letter recognition form I use enables me to record every letter a child can recognize. On the Class Assessment Profiles and Individual Assessment Profiles, I just record the total of letters recognized.

Organizational System

I keep the check lists and profiles on two clipboards. One clipboard holds the Class Assessment Profiles for reading, writing, and math, and an Anecdotal Class Grid to record monthly reading observations. The other holds a weekly Anecdotal Class Grid and Class Check List to record specific observations in reading, writing math, science, art, social interactions, and so on. When I see a need, I take a new form, date and label it, and begin recording. For example, if the children are involved in making pegboard designs at the math table, I might want to record my observations of how they go about the task, which designs they can do, and how I want to support their development. If I notice that at the dramatic play environment the children are turning to me to solve their disagreements before trying to work it out among themselves, I might record the incidents and how I interact in the situation.

I keep a file for each child in the class. It contains their Individual Assessment Profile, interview and assessment forms, a monthly copy of a piece of writing, a Parents' Goals form (Appendix A.15), notes from parents, anecdotal records, and any other information. About every other week after school I transfer the information from the Class Assessment Profiles to Individual Assessment Profiles. This procedure allows me to observe the growth of each child and plan for individual and group instruction.

My assessment framework is organized into three categories— "beginning of the year assessment," "on-going assessment," and "summary assessment." I continue to refine, modify, and change it as I learn from the children in my classroom, from conversations with colleagues, from participation in workshops and conferences, and by reading professional books and articles.

Beginning of the Year Assessment

During the first two months of school I conduct a series of assessments in reading, writing, and math with each child. I use them throughout the year to plan large-group instruction and to give specific support for individual children.

Reading and Writing

Literacy interview   I start by interviewing each child about reading and writing (See Appendix A.13). The interview questions fall into six categories:

- General warm-up questions: for example, "What are some of the things you like to do?"
- Being read to at home: "Are you read stories at home?"
- General reading knowledge: "What is reading?"
- The child's reading: "Can you read? Tell me about it."
- General writing knowledge: "What is writing?"
- The child's writing: "Can you write? Tell me about it."

Reading   I observe children reading during choice time and/or ask them to pick a book and read to me. On the Class Assessment Profile for Reading I record:

- General observations: interest, enjoyment and concentration.
- Sense of story: telling a story from pictures and retelling a familiar story.

- Conventions of print: book handling and awareness of and attention to print.
- Developmental reading stage.

Writing   I observe and record writing behavior during sign-in and writing workshop; confer with the children about something they have drawn and written; and assess their drawing, sense of story. and spelling development in a piece of writing. On the Class Assessment Profile for Writing, I record:

- General observations: interest, sharing with others and concentration.
- Sense of story in their picture and oral telling.
- Mechanics: handedness, directionality, pencil grip.
- Spelling development.

Letter, sound, and word-sound identification   I use the "letter identification" procedure developed by Marie Clay (1985, pp. 23, 24) and record the children's responses to:

- Letter recognition: upper- and lowercase letters.
- Sound identification: beginning consonant sounds. (I get a sampling response to assess their understanding of sound-symbol relationship.)
- Word-sound identification: words that begin with a certain letter. (Again, I ask for just a few words.)

Math

During the first month of school I spend time watching the children at the math area and recording my observations on the Class Assessment Profile for Math (Figure 14–2).

	Interest in math	Develops own ideas	Counts to	Recognizes numbers	Writes numbers	One-to-one correspondence	Conserves number	Uses math language	Creates patterns	Classifies
Rosie	*	2	29 (40)	1-20	3	*	*		+	A B abs $\not{7}$
Tammy	? o	watches peers copies	9,11,18	1-9 no tens	3	to 7	no		2	2
Victoria	rushes	3	1-15	confuses 6 9	3	to 8	no		0	3
Math										

Figure 14-2 Math Assessment Profile

One-to-one correspondence   I line up twelve identical chips and ask the children to count. I record what they do: for example, if they point when they count, if they just count with their eyes, if they count out loud. If I am not certain what they are doing, I ask them to touch the chips and count.

Conservation of number   Next I move the chips apart and ask how many there are. Children who conserve (understand that the number stays the same, or constant) tell me the number without recounting. When I then ask them to tell me how they knew there were the same number, they usually tell me that I didn't take any chips away, so there has to be the same number.

Rote counting   I ask the children to count as far as they can go or until they want to stop. If they skip some numbers, I record the omissions. I also ask them if they can count any other ways.

Numeral recognition   I show the children flash cards with the numerals 1 to 20 and record which ones they recognize.

On-Going Assessment

The beginning of the year assessment outlined above serves as a framework for the assessment I conduct throughout the year. I observe, assess, and monitor the children in a wide range of contexts, and adapt instruction to meet their immediate needs. I continually assess their reading and writing development and keep informed of their growth as I update their Individual Assessment Profiles and monthly self-portraits.

Developmental Reading Category
About once a month I read individually with the children in my class. (This procedure, along with my list of the descriptors of the Developmental Reading Stages, is described in Chapter 8.) On an Anecdotal Class Grid I record the book each child chose to read and my assessment of his or her current reading stage. I note strategies each child used successfully, what we talked about after the reading, the child's retelling of the story, the child's interest and enthusiasm, and any other observations.

Writing Development
In Chapter 9 I described the assessment procedures I use during daily writing. Every month I make a photocopy of a piece of each child's writing to add to his or her individual file.

Three times a year, before parent conferences in November and April and at the end of the year in June, I go over the children's writing folders with them. I regard this review primarily as a celebration of what each child can do and a way of validating their progress. After they tell me about their work, I write what we have noticed on the inside of their writing folder and record the information on the Individual Assessment Profiles for Writing. Sara's folder looked like this:

11/8/89
We noticed Sara likes to draw

- rainbows
- hearts
- pictures of her cat and her family

We noticed that Sara can

- write the first letter in many words
- write most of the uppercase letters
- write lowercase m and f
- write lowercase a in her name

We notice that Sara

- usually draws with crayons and writes letters with a pencil
- uses lots of colors in her drawings
- usually remembers to date her work

I put her work in an envelope and give it to her parents at conference time, asking them to return it after they have enjoyed it with Sara at home. I file the returned work in another file and her writing file starts to fill up with her new work. Sara and I follow the same procedure in March, looking at her work going back to September and updating her folder with comments.

3/3/90
We notice that Sara

- still draws rainbows, hearts, cats, and pictures of her family
- draws about different kinds of weather

We notice that Sara can

- write the first and last letter of many words
- write her last name
- write lowercase h and i

We notice that Sara

- sometimes makes books
- draws people who look like they are really moving

In June we will look at all her writings and describe the growth Sara has made during the year. Sara will select her favorite pieces to put into a loose-leaf portfolio. I will put in a few of my choices of her work, too. The rest of her work will go home in an envelope.

Individual Assessment Profile and File

In January I update the Individual Assessment Profiles. I take a new Class Assessment Profile for reading, writing, and math and record what children can do as I kid watch and work with them throughout the month. As I transfer the information to the Individual Assessment Profiles, I make a list of specific information missing on any children and spend the next few days watching and filling it in. Since I know the children better, this assessment does not take as long as at the beginning of the year.

Monthly Self-Portraits

At the beginning of each month I ask the children to draw a self-portrait. They write their name and copy the month and year on the paper. We hang these up with pushpins on the bulletin board in the classroom, placing the current portrait on top. This gives me a record of the children's drawing and handwriting throughout the year which I share with parents at conference time. At the end of the year the children organize their portraits into a book to take home, along with a record of the height and weight that they have gained during kindergarten.

End of the Year Assessment

This assessment is similar to the initial formal assessment and follows the same general procedures. I begin some of these assessments in March in preparation for parent conferences in April, and complete other parts by the middle of May for class placement and program evaluation.

Reading and Writing Interview

This interview (see Appendix A.14) focuses on what the children can tell me about themselves as readers and writers, and what parts of the reading and writing program have been important to them during the year. For example, one of the questions I ask is, "Did you learn more by reading with a friend or by yourself?" (Fisher, 1990).

Reading

My on-going assessment records give me most of the information I need to complete this section. However, I fill in any missing or incomplete information, and administer the "Concepts about Print" test (Clay 1985) to children for whom I need more information. This gives specific information such as the child's awareness of letters and words, that print gives the message and that reading starts at the top left.

Writing

In addition to relying on the assessment records I have kept through-out the year I do the following:

- Go over individual writing folders with each child. We sort the pieces according to month, pick favorites for a special portfolio, and celebrate growth made over the year.
- Complete a written assessment of a writing sample.
- Ask each child to write a list of all the words they can spell.

Letter, sound, and word-sound identification

- Oral assessment: repeat letter knowledge test; assess for sound and word-sound identification.
- Written assessment: children write their full name on a blank piece of paper; they identify a simple picture ("bike" for *b*), and if they can, write the upper and lowercase letter with which the picture begins; they write the numerals from 1 to 10.

These assessment recording procedures, along with the children's work over a period of time, help me to organize my under-standing of what the children can do. I believe that assessment is most effective when it is conducted during the routine of the day, when the children are engaged in meaningful, interesting, and authentic tasks.

For Further Reading

Clay, Marie. 1985, 1979. *The Early Detection of Reading Difficulties.* Portsmouth, NH: Heinemann.

Cochrane, Orin, and Donna Cochrane, Sharen Scalena, and Ethel Buchanan. 1984. *Reading, Writing and Caring.* New York: Richard C. Owen.

Fisher, Bobbi. 1990. "Children as Author ties of Their Own Reading." In Nancie Atwell, ed., *Workshop* 2. Portsmouth, NH: Heinemann.

Goodman, Kenneth and Yetta, and Wendy Hood. 1989. *The Whole Language Evaluation Book*. Portsmouth, NH: Heinemann.

Holdaway, Don. 1979. *The Foundations of Literacy*. Portsmouth, NH: Heinemann.

15

Communicating With Parents

Throughout the school year I am in contact with the parents of my kindergarten children in a variety of ways because I believe that parents, teachers, and children all benefit when they work as a community. In this context "parents" include all interested parties in the children's lives, such as grandparents, older siblings, aunts, uncles, and other relatives; day care providers; and foster parents

Positive communication with the school enables parents to support their child's social, emotional, and academic growth at home. I find that when parents are informed and understand what is happening at school, minor concerns can be handled easily and major concerns can be addressed cooperatively. Additionally, informed and involved parents become rich resources as helpers and role models in the classroom.

Starting The Year

Letter to Parents and Children
The first contact I have with the parents and children sets the tone for the entire year. I mail them each a letter in August, introducing myself, describing what will happen on orientation day when they come to school together, and explaining some of the routine procedures, such as snack policy and bus notes, that are important to parents and children on the first day. Teachers who cannot mail a letter prior to opening day could send a letter home with the child on the first day (see Appendix B.5 and B.6).

Parents' Night
During the third week in September, parents are invited to an evening meeting at my school to visit their child's classroom and meet the teacher. I take this opportunity to discuss my goals for the year

by describing a typical day, answering questions, and making certain that I meet each parent. Although I want the room to look as it does every day when the children come in, I also want to use the opportunity to inform parents about whole language theory and curriculum. Therefore, I display many of the big books, trade books, charts with favorite poems and songs, art materials, and math manipulatives that we will be using throughout the year. Sand and water tables, blocks and trucks, and the dramatic play areas are set up. The room is immersed in children's work.

Parent's Packet

At the orientation meeting on the first day of school, or on parents' night, I give each parent an information packet that includes a Parents' Goals form, suggestions of ways that parents can help, a list of recycled materials we need from home, a Bibliography of Professional Books for parents from my lending library, an article about reading and writing, and notices from the school office. I discuss the forms and request that parents return them within a week.

Parents' Goals   This form (Appendix A.15) gives parents the opportunity to tell me about their child and helps me to get to know them both at the beginning of the year. It provides space for the parents to write what they believe are their child's intellectual and social strengths and the areas where growth is needed, as well as their goals for their child in these areas. It also asks for the most convenient times for a parent conference. It lets parents know that I believe they are important, that I am willing to listen, and that I am sensitive to their work schedules. I use the forms as I prepare for parent conferences in the fall and as a guide to summing each child's progress at the end of the year.

Parents as Helpers   This list of suggestions (Appendix B.7) provides parents with ways they can help in the classroom or at home. For example, they can plan an activity for a small group of children, follow an activity that I plan for them, act as scribes for class books, read with children, and/or share their jobs or hobbies. A sign-up sheet is available for them to schedule a day to visit the class. Parents who find it difficult to help in school can bake for class parties, mend dress-up clothes, arrange for field trips, and help make books for children's published stories.

Contributions from Home   This list of things we need in the classroom (Appendix B.8) are items that parents and children can contribute from home, such as recycled materials, wood for the workbench, dress-up clothes, and large appliance boxes.

Lending Library of Professional Books   These are categorized under the following topics: learning theory, early literacy, reading and writing, parenting, and social issues. At parents' night I hand out the Bibliography of Professional Books for Parents (see page 213), a letter explaining the procedure, and upon request I send books to them at home.

On-going Communication

I maintain many avenues of communication with parents during the year, some of which I initiate at the orientation meeting and at the school open house. I keep a monthly checklist, noting the personal contact I have with each parent. For example, on a Class Checklist (Appendix A.11), I record when I talk with parents when they come to help, when they stop by to deliver food for a class party, when they pick up their child after school, when we communicate through our home/school journals, and when I talk with them on the telephone. At the end of the month I review the list and write a positive note about their child to any parents with whom I haven't communicated.

Parent Helping Day
On the days parents are scheduled to help in the class, I encourage them to arrive with their child so they can see how the day begins and participate in shared reading. During choice time they can facil-itate a project they have planned with their child, help with an activity I have planned, or read with the children. I ask that younger siblings not come for this special time between parent and child. Later in the year we will invite younger brothers and sisters to visit our aquarium or to participate in a sing-along.

Weekly Newsletter
Sending home a weekly newsletter (see Figure 15–1 and Appendix A.16) is one of the most successful ways I know of keeping parents informed about what is happening. Our "Kindergarten News" is divided into six boxes, one for each day of the week and one for general notices. At the end of each day, sometimes with the chil-dren's help, I write what we did during the day. For example I record something important we did in shared reading ("we acted out *Hairy Bear*"), the books we read, the leader of the day, an exciting happen-ing ("Matthew and Sara built a tower that was taller than the book-shelf") and special choice time activities.

For each day I indicate that the children read, write, and work with math manipulatives. The section for notices tells about upcom-ing events (e.g., field trips, when school pictures will be taken),

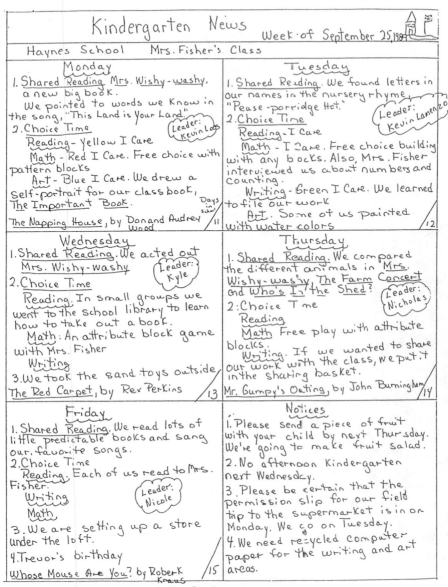

Figure 15-1 Weekly Newsletter for Parents

makes specific requests (e.g., we need more recycled materials for the art area or a parent to help the children make a sleeping bag for a stuffed animal), and explains in greater detail the daily activities (e.g., the importance of rereading favorite stories).

Nancy Hildreth and the children in her kindergarten in Framingham, Massachusetts, publish a newspaper about every six weeks. It features the children's drawings and writings; favorite poems, songs, and chants they have enjoyed and learned in class; classroom and school news; and news from home.

Home/School Journals

On parents' night I introduce personal Home/School Journals (Fisher 1988) as a way for parents and I to maintain a dialogue about their child. In a 7″ x 8½″ school composition notebook addressed to each parent I write a brief note, indicating something positive about their child. I might write that Billy seems to enjoy painting and puts a lot of details in his pictures. Sometimes I describe a situation where I am supporting a child for success. For example, if a child sits in the back and has a difficult time focusing during group time, I might write that I am encouraging him or her to sit in front during shared reading.

I encourage parents to share things that the child has done at home, and to have the children and other family members write in them, too. One parent wrote, "Mary went right to her room after school yesterday and came out an hour later with her version of *Mrs. Wishy-washy.*" Brad's brother wrote, "Have you read *Dan the Flying Man* to the class yet? It was my favorite big book when I was in kindergarten."

The journals also offer an opportunity for parents to ask me questions about their child and about the program. Billy's dad wanted to know if his son was writing in school; he hadn't seen any work coming home. I responded to the question and made a renewed effort to get more work home with all the children. I have found that the expressed concern of one parent is often the unexpressed concern of other parents.

Parents also use the journals to request a conference, ask if they can come in and help, set up a time to bring visiting grandparents to the class, and so on. Some parents send them in regularly, others use them occasionally, and some not at all.

These journals do not take a lot of time to answer. I usually find time to reply with a short note sometime during the school day, unless there is a question or comment that requires more thought or a longer response. When I introduce the journals on parents' night, I explain to the parents that I will try to respond within a day or two and that, due to limitations on my time, my replies will be short. I find that parents would rather receive short, frequent responses than longer, less frequent ones.

Writing Folders

I send the children's writing pieces home in a large manila envelope at least three times a year: after conferences in the fall, at the end of January, after conferences in the spring, and any other time at the parents' request. The pieces are returned to school, and at the end of the year the children select their favorites for a special portfolio (see Chapter 14).

Additional Contacts

- Encourage relatives who are visiting a child to come to school.
- Send home a note or make a telephone call describing something positive the child has done.
- Invite parents to a sing-along or class sharing.
- Plan a story hour for younger siblings.
- Invite older siblings to read to the class.
- Send home articles of current interest.

Parent Conferences

In my school we are required to have two formal parent conferences a year, one in November and another in April or May. Since I have kept the parents informed about classroom curriculum and procedures, the conferences focus primarily on the social and intellectual growth and development of the children. In planning for each parent conference, I write down the main points I want to cover during the conference on a Parent Conference Planning Form (Appendix A.17), and I make sure that I have available samples of the child's work and the assessment forms and records I need.

I start the conference by giving positive examples of the child's social and intellectual development. For example, I might focus on David's willingness to include everyone while playing, by describing how the other day he moved over and made space for a new student to join a game. As we look over the child's writing folder, I might comment that since David has started to leave spaces between his words, I notice that he is writing longer stories. I then encourage the parents to tell me what they have noticed and what is important to them.

Using the Parents' Goals form, my assessment forms, the child's writing and drawings, and other work, we discuss growth since the beginning of the year. We also consider the next steps we want to take to support continued development. I share my immediate and long-range plans for the child, and ask the parents for their input. In conclusion I ask each parent if there is anything else they want to discuss or share, and emphasize that we are partners in supporting their child.

The end of the year conference follows the same form as the earlier conference, although more emphasis is placed on the child's growth throughout the year. We look at samples of the child's work, and I review my assessment data. We discuss the parents' goals again and talk about next year. I inform them that we will be visiting all the first grades in June, and that on the last day of kindergarten the children will go with me to meet their teacher for next year.

Closing Celebration

On the next to last day of school, the children and I give a party for parents, younger siblings, and relatives to celebrate our year together. We present a shared reading program of some of the songs, poems, and chants we have enjoyed, read a book made by the class, and share a favorite big book. Each of us tells something important we remember about the year. The party ends with refreshments, and provides me the opportunity to say good-bye personally to the parents.

16

Questions Teachers Ask

1. *I have a full-day kindergarten. What changes would you make if you had a longer or full day?*

I would love more time with the children. Essentially, I would extend the time periods that I now use, giving the children more time to engage in what interests them and offering me more time to get to know them and support their development.

- Have a longer settling-in time, with a free-choice time as the children arrive. This is especially successful if the children don't arrive at the same time and if parents drop them off at the door. It's a time for the children to talk with each other, and it gives you time to kid watch and chat informally with the parents.
- Have a longer choice time. (I often feel that just as the children become involved in an activity, choice time is over.) This would provide more opportunities to work with children who could benefit from "bedtime stories," experiences with numbers and counting, and conversations with an adult.
- Have a special time for math, when everyone is working on a variety of directed, guided and free-play activities.
- Provide more time for music and drama.
- Schedule another group time during which the children could share their work, read to the class, act out stories, become involved with musical instruments, play games, and work with math manipulatives. Include more "children as teachers" activities and read more fiction and nonfiction to the class.
- Spend more time playing outside and take equipment, such as trucks and sand toys, out more often.
- Have a consistent time every day, probably after outside play, for sustained "silent" reading.

2. *Do you have any specialists? My children leave the room for music, art, and gym once a week, and I am supposed to take them to the library, too. This leaves us only one day without interruptions. I feel I don't have enough time with my kids.*

Many teachers with a half-day kindergarten express this same frustration, even though they appreciate the time to make phone calls to parents, organize paperwork, keep up their assessment records, plan with teaching colleagues, copy a new song on a chart, and so on. Most teachers with a full day kindergarten have told me that they have enough classroom time with their children. They too, appreciate planning time, and feel that the change of pace that specialists offer is beneficial to them and the children. However, where more time with the children is desired, some of the following suggestions might be helpful.

In my school the children go to gym and music. Some years I have been successful in having both of those specialists scheduled on the same day, which leaves the rest of the week free for our own planning. For example, on Tuesday we would start the day with community circle time. The children would go to music from 9:15–9:50, and return to the class for snack and a short free-choice time until 10:25, when they would go to gym. We would end the day with sharing and a story. The afternoon class would have a similar schedule on another day. We called this "our different kind of day."

I've eliminated a regular weekly library time by arranging for the children to go to the library by themselves during choice time if they want to get a book to read in class or take home. After all, that's why one goes to the library, and I want them to develop the habit. Some go several times a week and often take out books I have read in class. At the beginning of the year I ask a parent to take small groups of children to the library to show them how to use it. From then on they go on their own unless we go as a class to do research or hear a story. I am aware that in some schools children can only take out books when they go on a weekly scheduled visit with their teacher. I suggest that teachers advocate for changing that policy, if possible.

In order to gain more uninterrupted time in the classroom, what about having the art teacher come to your room and work with small groups during choice time? How about inviting the music teacher to work with you and the children during shared reading? As we work toward an integrated curriculum, I think that classroom teachers can act as catalysts in restructuring school schedules to meet the needs of the children.

3. *How do you make long-range plans, as well as weekly and daily plans?*

In September, on a monthly calendar, I block out long-range plans for the year. I highlight holidays, school events, and evaluation focus times that I want to be sure to include in my plans. I also mark curriculum areas that I want to introduce, such as bookmaking, workbench, and dramatic play environments. I change and add to the calendar throughout the year as I get to know the interests of the children and the ways that they function as a group.

I also work with weekly and daily planning sheets. At the beginning of the week, on the Weekly Planning Sheet (Appendix A.18), I write down special notes and plans for the week, including specialists, school events and assemblies, parent helpers, special celebrations, and current plans for the dramatic play environment. I note my focus for shared reading and choice time for each day.

Before each day, on the Daily Planning Sheet (Appendix A.19), I write down what I plan to do the following day. This daily planning is more specific than the weekly because it more directly relates to what has happened on the previous day. Aside from noting specialists and any special plans for the day, I indicate if there will be a special focus at community circle time and write down the opening story for the day. I record the texts, strategies, skills, and artifacts (i.e., a puppet for a story, masks for framing words, or musical instruments for a chant) that I plan to use during shared reading. I include specific plans for the day's I CARES, the student choices, and the dramatic play environment. I note if we will have a formal sharing time, if we will go outside to play, and what the end of the day "bedtime story" will be.

Although these planning sheets are useful to me in planning for the day ahead, they are especially valuable as a springboard in planning for the next day (and week). Therefore, at the end of each day I add to that day's planning sheet what we actually did during the day. For example, community circle time often takes a different focus because something important has happened to one of the children. One day Daniel reported that his father had been taken to the hospital during the night, so we spent time talking about that. During shared reading Marisa made a connection between the text we were reading and another familiar text. While reading *Mrs Wishy-washy*, she commented that the same animals in that story are also in *The Farm Concert*. This led to comparing the animals in the two books and starting a graph depicting the animals in different farm stories.

4. *What do you do about leaving plans for substitutes? A lot of subs aren't used to the activity, talk, and independence that we encourage.*

I think that once substitutes get used to working in whole-language classrooms they will find it easier and more enjoyable because the children are engaged and can manage the classroom routine themselves.

Aside from leaving the Daily Planning Sheet for the next day, I leave a folder for substitutes. On the cover I highlight "Ask the children, they know what to do!" The folder ncludes information especially written for the substitute: the daily schedule, general time frames, specialists, routines, specific suggestions, and a list of the things the children can do during choice time. It describes the general procedure for shared reading and suggests that he or she ask the children to pick the big books to read and songs to sing. It indicates that the children will know what to do for the reading, writing, and math I CARES.

5. *How do you keep the two daily sessions separate for your own organizational purposes?*

I assign each class a color for the year. The morning class is the Blue Class, and the afternoon class, the Red Class. When the classes switch times halfway through the year, they keep their same colors. I use the colors to code name cards, class books, weekly newsletters home, and the bear that goes home every night.

6. *I have thirty children in my kindergarter. How can I possibly give them the choices and responsibility that you suggest? How can I manage when I don't have an assistant?*

I believe that the larger the class, the more essential it is that the children are given choices and responsibility freeing you to work with individuals and small groups instead of directing and disciplining all day. You may have to organize cho ce time differently, perhaps having the children complete an I CARE every other day instead of daily.

Shared reading is successful with a large group of children. It builds community as each child participates at his or her developmental level. In New Zealand, classes often have forty or more children successfully participating in shared reading and choice time.

Consider asking a parent to organize parent volunteers to come in on a regular basis. Aside from having them work with children, leave a box, with instructions, of things that they can do to help. For example, items to be duplicated, charts to be copied, permission forms to be checked off, and books to be mended.

If you have a large class and/or no assistant, try to accomplish in two days what you would normally cover in one day. Keep simple checklists to record your conferences and interactions with individual children to be certain that you have reached each child every other day. Set your priorities and accept that you cannot accomplish everything.

7. *Do you have the same dramatic play environment for both classes? What if one class chooses a different theme than the other?*

The children are aware that they are part of a larger community that includes the other kindergarten session, and that from time to time they have to consider the interests of that other class. They know that next year they will be in first grade with these children, and that they will have shared a common kindergarten experience.

For organizational purposes I have decided that both classes have to focus on the same dramatic play theme. Sometimes one class starts creating an environment and the other class adds to it. However, both groups become involved in its development and are interested in seeing what changes the other class has made. When the whole class chooses a topic, I share the suggestions of each class with the other. Through discussion we come to consensus on a theme that includes some of what is important to each group.

8. *What do you do about guns, war play, and interactive TV toys?*

This is one of the most complex issues that teachers currently face. I do not allow the children to bring in guns or most interactive TV toys, and I do not allow war play in the classroom. I want the curriculum in my kindergarten to be built upon positive relationships, and I don't think I can help create a community of learners within an atmosphere of war play.

However, I realize that the children's lives are touched by danger and violence from TV and real life, and that they need to work out the developmental issue of control and power (Carlsson-Paige and Levin 1987). Therefore, I try to offer opportunities for the children to talk about these issues during community circle time, when conflict arises during play, and as they express their feelings in their writing and drawing. I want them to feel powerful and in control through the inventions that they create at the art table, through building with blocks, through success in sliding down the pole on the outdoor jungle gym, by going to the library by themselves or reading to another class, through working out a disagreement with a peer to the satisfaction of both, and through the satisfaction in helping another classmate.

9. *What do you say to parents who feel there is not enough work going home or who want to see worksheets?*

Often when parents express these concerns, they are asking for assurance that their children are learning, and their child's teacher is aware of how to help their child continue to learn. I believe that it is important to discuss these concerns with parents. I help them to see the limits and shortcomings of worksheets, which are not authentic texts but which focus on skills in isolation. I ask them to come in to help during class time and to talk with me after class. I show them my assessment records, which indicate their child's progress over time. I make sure that their child's writing goes home regularly.

10. *Do you "do letter of the week"?*

No. Letter of the week, in which the teacher and children focus on a different letter (and corresponding sound) throughout the year, has been an important part of the culture, lore, and curriculum of kindergarten for many years. But it's losing its prominence as teachers become knowledgeable about whole-language theory and as they observe children engaged in the reading and writing process.

I don't "do letter of the week" because I want the primary curriculum focus in my classroom to be on authentic and meaningful activities that meet the interests of the children, not on letters and sounds. I believe that "doing letter of the week" suggests that the central focus of the curriculum is knowing letters and sounds, not meaning, and that writing is labeling, not conveying meaning. I also find that the children already know some letters and sounds, and that they learn most of the remaining in context, as they need them to read and write.

11. *What do you do about children who pick the same thing or activity every day? I have a boy in my class who always wants to play at the block area, a girl who draws rainbows every day, and several children who select the same book to read for independent reading.*

I let them go to the block area, draw their rainbows, and read that favorite book, and I watch carefully what they do. My assumption is that important learning is going on with these children and I trust them as authorities of their own learning. I also trust myself as an effective kid watcher and an insightful teacher who knows when to step in and help expand the children's knowledge.

By kid watching I have discovered that children often don't do the same thing even when they have picked the same activity, materials, or subject. Buildings take different forms, become more complicated, and tell different stories. Rainbows are drawn in a variety of sizes and shapes, embellished with detail, and become parts of different stories. The children who read the same story over and over again, read the book differently as they work through early reading stages. This special book, which can have deep emotional meaning for them, is often the one that supports them as they gain mastery of the reading process. I had a child in my class who told me that she learned to read by reading *The Birthday Cake* every day (Fisher 1990).

Throughout the year I pose new challenges in the block area. I form building groups and suggest that the children build something that relates to our dramatic play environments. I ask them to build the tallest or longest building they can. I involve the children, especially that block builder, to pose challenges to the group.

I bring in books with pictures of rainbows, and during shared reading we discuss how the illustrator has drawn the rainbow and how it enhances the story being told. We talk about how rainbows are formed and how they relate to the weather. What better way to integrate reading, writing, math, social studies, and science than through the special interests (such as rainbows) of the children as demonstrated in their own work.

Periodically, I listen to the children read their favorite book, and I record their reading stage and strategies. Each child can become an expert on a certain book and read it to individual children or to the class.

I structure choice time so that children *can* return again and again to activities and projects that are meaningful to them. I feel comfortable allowing for this choice because I know that they are spending some time each day reading, writing, and doing math as part of the expectations (I CARES) I have for them.

12. *What do you do about a child who doesn't seem to be engaged?*

First, I give both of us time to get to know each other. Sometimes the child just needs to get used to the class environment, the

other children, and me. I am also aware that children often are involved, even though they don't show it.

Mainly, I ask some of the following questions in an effort to discover the best approaches to successfully engage a child.

- When are the times he/she is involved? During community
  circle? During shared reading? During choice time? During
  outside play? When I am reading a story?
- What are the activities that do engage the child?
- What are the things that the child does well?
- In what areas does the child show confidence?
- What are the child's interests, and how can I encourage
  engagement through those interests?
- Who are the child's friends, and how can I build upon that?
- What are some of the personal issues in the child's life that
  may be getting in his/her way, and what can I do to support
  the child in school?

13. *I have ESL children in my class. Is whole language appropriate for these kids?*

Yes. Whole-language practice has its roots in New Zealand,
where there was a need to work with children coming to school with
English as a second language. Today many ESL classrooms throughout the continent are applying a whole language philosophy.

The natural learning classroom model and the shared book
experience, based on the conditions of natural language acquisition,
were developed in New Zealand by Don Holdaway and his colleagues
in response to an influx into the cities of children from diverse backgrounds, speaking many different languages. According to Holdaway,
an approach was required that would not immediately misinform
children who were insecure in English that they were inferior. No
traditional methodology could meet this requirement. He goes on to
say that what they were doing was applying conditions of natural
language acquisition to the school setting.

14. *I don't have many big books, and I have to share with the other teacher's in my building. Do you have any suggestions for making the most of what I have?*

You don't need to have many big books. In fact, you don't need
to have any as long as during shared reading you are providing demonstrations with enlarged text, and reading predictable texts which
support emergent and beginning readers.

Poems, songs and chants can be written in enlarged print on butcher paper or brown paper bags. If you don't have predictable texts in big book form, the short predictable books from The Story Box, The Sunshine Series and TWIG Books (Wright Group), Century 2000 (Rigby), Ready to Read (Richard C. Owen), and many trade books have print that is large enough for children to see as you point to it during shared reading.

I suggest that if you have to share big books with other teachers in your building or system, keep a book for at least a month. The children will become very familiar with it and will have the opportunity for extensions and innovations before you have to send it on. Try to obtain a small version of the book so everyone can continue to enjoy it and plan to get that big book back later in the year.

17

Classroom Management and Organization

Since the first edition of *Joyful Learning* was published I have had many opportunities to talk with kindergarten teachers about classroom management, particularly about choice time and I CARES and full- and extended-day kindergarten. The first section of this chapter describes in more detail the I CARE procedure introduced in Chapter 7 and responds to some of the questions teachers have asked me about I CARES (teacher requirements or assignments during choice time) and choice time. I have also included some of the successful variations and adaptations that teachers have shared with me. The next section explores in more detail the suggestions found in Chapter 16 "Questions Teachers Ask" regarding the differences in organizing and managing a full-day kindergarten versus a half-day schedule.

Teachers agree that a workable management system is essential for a successful program that engages children in meaningful learning. We all have "wonderful" ideas, strategies, and activities, but without an organized classroom structure and schedule, the children's potential is never fully realized. Teachers and students need a predictable daily routine, procedures for moving from one area or activity to another, a relaxed atmosphere in which to take risks, a clear understanding of expectations, and meaningful methods for accountability.

Regardless of the length of the school day, I believe that Holdaway's Natural Learning Classroom Model provides a sound theoretical framework and a practical planning model for kindergarten. Every day I want to have a shared literacy time when I demonstrate and the children participate in literacy events, a choice time when children practice what they are learning, and a presentation time when children share or perform their new learning. These components, demonstration, participation, practice/role-play, and performance, can be included in a half-day kindergarten schedule as well as a full-day kindergarten program.

Choice Time and I CARES

General Procedure

My classroom is divided into five major areas that are color coded and correspond to the I CARES: writing (green), reading (yellow), math (red), art (blue), science (orange). I either cover the tables in each area with craft paper, or place a piece of construction paper in the center of the table. The sixth major area, the dramatic play area (not an I CARE), includes a loft with spaces underneath and above for play (see Figure 17-1).

Each day the children are required to go to the designated I CARE areas sometime during choice time. After completing their work in each area they hang up a one-inch colored circle (which corresponds to the I CARE area) on a hook under their name on the class I CARE board in the meeting area. This acknowledges to both of us that they have done their I CARES. For example, after writing in the green area, they hang up a green circle or I CARE, and after reading they hang up a yellow I CARE.

The I CARE System in Action

"Let's do our reading and then have snack."

"After we do our math, let's go to the library and then come back and play in the loft."

- Writing—Green—Write something, draw something, put your name and date on your paper.

- Reading—Yellow—Read a little book, big book, chart, listen to a story tape. Read by yourself, with a friend, or with an adult.

- Math—Red—Through free or guided play or direct instruction build with math manipulatives, play a math game, or solve a problem.

- Art—Blue—Create by painting, building with recycled materials, making a craft, modeling with clay, and so forth.

- Science—Orange—Perform experiments and/or explore at the science table.

Figure 17-1 I CARE areas

"Mrs. Fisher, can we keep building this city and tomorrow start with our writing I CARE?"

"I'm going to make a label for my painting and then hang it on the sharing board."

"I've been practicing reading A *Long, Long Tail* (Cowley) every day and I'm almost ready to read it to the class."

These comments indicate the ownership and control that the children feel about their learning. I call this part of choice time I CARES because I care that the children are challenged to grow as learners, and I want them to care about their own learning, too. I CARES are those activities or projects that I require the children to do. Generally they have three I CARES to complete every day, reading, writing, and math. Sometimes I substitute or add an art or science I CARE. When they are not working on I CARES they are choosing from a variety of possibilities in the room: sand and water table, environmental play area, artwork, science experiments, and block building. Sometimes it is difficult to tell where the I CARES leave off and other choices begin.

As a general rule I think of I CARES as taking up half of choice time and student choices making up the other half. I've seen children spend almost the whole time at the writing area for several months, and then devote more of their time to a play environment. Over the year these patterns change. For example, in the fall Sara often spent over half of choice time reading books, and then in January started putting in great lengths of time at the writing area

The children don't consider the I CARES as assignments to get completed for the teacher, but rather as opportunities to express themselves, take on new challenges, and feel satisfaction as learners. There is a lot of flexibility in the system. If someone is very engaged in a project one day, he doesn't have to stop just to get his I CARES done. We negotiate an alternative plan. If children become engaged in a dramatic play environment and don't get to their I CARES, their work is celebrated and they are encouraged to start with I CARES the next day.

In order to achieve this atmosphere, in which the children are committed to taking responsibility for managing their own learning, I continually have to include them in active participation in the management of the system. I spend a lot of time at the beginning of the year helping them learn how the I CARES work. They learn the general instructions for each I CARE, which I keep simple and consistent so they can learn the procedures quickly, and so I don't need to take up a lot of shared literacy time giving directions.

Every day before choice time we talk about which I CARES they are required to do that day, and we review the directions. During choice time I help individual children hang up the appropriate I CARE when they have completed their work at an area, and I acknowledge them when they have gained independence in this. Halfway through choice time I remind the children to start their I CARES if they haven't already done so. At the end of choice time we review how things went that day. As we check the I CARE board, children may admit that they forgot to hang up an I CARE or didn't get to one and I ask them to hang it up now or remember to do it tomorrow.

Although I need to spend less time on these procedures as the year goes on, we review them from time to time throughout the year. Usually this review consists of quick reminders so the children are continually aware that I CARES are an important part of our learning community.

Questions Teachers Ask About I CARES

1. What about the children who don't do their I CARES?
The system works easily and satisfactorily for the majority of children in my class. But there are always a few who need special attention at various times throughout the year. In order to help them I begin by watching what they do during choice time and look for answers to some of the following questions: Do they seem to know what to do? When *do* they demonstrate direction, purpose, and engagement? Is there any I CARE that particularly seems to interest them? Do they have friends? Do they work alone or with others? How do they interact in a group? Sometimes I take anecdotal notes to help me understand. Some don't understand the system and need more time or explicit instruction to learn how it works. Some get very involved in one activity and may need my support to help them organize their time. Next I talk to the children and find out what they have to say about their I CARES and together we work out a plan.

The plans we develop together vary with the individual children. Ideally, I want them to come up with the plan and they often do, such as "I will do my I CARES first" or "I'll start with writing for the next two days." At other times I give them limited choices: "I want you to start with I CARES for the rest of the week. Which do you want to do first, your reading or your writing?" Regardless, I want them to understand that reading, writing, and math are important.

2. What do you do about the children who hardly get to "play" because they're just able to finish the I CARES?
I start with kid watching and then talk with the individual children about how choice time is going for them. For example, I want to

know if they feel frustrated that they don't have time to play or if they have chosen to spend most of choice time on their I CARES. If they need help, we work on a plan together so they feel satisfied that they have a chance to play. They need to know that I value their play and free choices as much as I do their I CARES.

I believe it is essential for children to be in charge of managing their time during choice time. In deciding the order in which they will do their I CARES and individual choices, how much time they will spend at a specific area, and with whom they will work. they are developing study skills that will continue to evolve throughout their lives and they are expressing the kinds of learning patterns that fit their personality. For example, do they prefer to work alone or in partnership? Do they like to get their I CARES done first? Do they like to spend a long time at one project or can they move success-fully from one to another? The better they understand themselves as learners, the more successful they will be as productive lifelong learners.

3. What do you do about the children who regularly rush through their I CARES ?

I usually spend several weeks observing the children who appear to get through their I CARES quickly without apparent interest or in-volvement. Given time, I notice they often work quickly in one area but conscientiously in another. This is especially true at the begin-ning of the year when they are learning the procedures. Then throughout the year, as the children receive literacy demonstra-tions, observe each other, and start working together, the classroom learning community grows and both individually and as a group they become more conscientious and begin spending more time with each I CARE. As the classroom learning club develops, even the learners who were most reluctant at first want to join.

I have some specific strategies for children who don't appear to be engaged, usually in the areas of reading and writing, which are more abstract than math. (Most children like to work with math ma-nipulatives.) *The key is to be interested in the children's interests.* For example, if a child is interested in insects and bugs, I gather some fiction and nonfiction books on the subject and we spend time reading them to-gether. We might make a text set and place the books in a specially labeled box. Perhaps the child will share them with the class or with a small group of children. Sometimes a project or writing topic is generated from the experience. I find that when I do this with one child, other children gather and pretty soon they are learning from each other and I can move away and let the children take control.

I follow a similar procedure with writing. During a writing conference I ask the children to tell me about their drawings and we talk about them. I might ask them what they could add to their picture to show what they have told me. Often, over time, as other children share from the author's chair, the reluctant writer begins to see the possibilities for his/her own writing.

One of the advantages in having children read, write, and do math every day is that repeated opportunities focus on the quality of their work as the process develops. For example, if children are not satisfied with their work one day, they have the opportunity to try again the next day. We learn to read by reading (Smith 1983) and children benefit from daily practice. If they write only once or twice a week, they don't get as involved in their own writing life, and as teachers we begin to overfocus on product, and try to control their process. Children also need daily experiences over time to develop mathematical understandings.

4. What do you do when too many children want to be in one area at the same time?

Throughout the entire choice time children are working in all the areas of the room, and there is a natural flow as they move from choice to choice. Since the children don't have to do their I CARES before making their own choices, they don't feel the need to rush through their I CARES in order to get to the play environment or the blocks, and this eliminates everyone wanting to play in these areas at the same time.

For the most part the physical area defines how many people can work successfully in one place. For example there are six chairs at the art table, two painting easels, and four places at the snack table. The writing table has six chairs and several desks nearby for children who want to work quietly or in pairs. Sometimes children sit on the floor and write with a clipboard. Six chairs fit at the math table, and the block area accommodates four or five children comfortably. There is unlimited space in the reading area. As one teacher commented to me, "Children don't need to be told how many are allowed at a center. Given the opportunity, they can make choices as to where they will work. If there are more people at a center than they are comfortable with, they will choose another center. This also helps them become confident in problem solving, creative thinking, and peer interaction."

Sometimes specific situations arise and we have to develop some procedures so that everyone will have a turn, especially in the dramatic play loft. For example, when we set up the veterinarian's office, I kept a list of who had a turn to be the vet and the secretary. We discovered that four people can play successfully up in the loft and four under the loft. These numbers are flexible. Sometimes five children will play well in an area, and at other times three seems to work better. I've had some classes in which we hardly ever had to set specific numbers. In other classes we've had to spend a lot of time discussing how things are going in the area. One teacher wrote, "As for limiting the numbers in the different areas, the children will do that themselves after a while. You don't always have to get involved.'

Another procedure is for the children to wear a piece of colored yarn around their necks to indicate they are playing in the area. This eliminates misunderstandings when a child leaves for a moment and it clearly indicates who is playing there. We hang these pieces of yarn on a hook near the area.

5. *What are you doing during choice time?*

My job is to help the children grow in their literacy and mathematical development as they learn to work together in a community. Each day I decide what I am going to do during choice time. At the beginning of the year I am available to help children establish the general procedures: hang up I CARES, file their writing, use art materials appropriately, clean up after their snack, and share and include all their classmates.

Since my job is to teach, it is essential that the children take responsibility for managing their behavior and learning so I don't have to spend all my time facilitating routines and directing procedures. As soon as they demonstrate this control, I begin to focus on specific learning areas or experiences during choice time. These include

- Conducting writing conferences
- Reading with individual children
- Conducting a guided reading group
- Interviewing children
- Directing an art activity
- Working with a small group in science
- Teaching a math game

I find that if I am not available to direct all the classroom procedures, the children are more apt to help each other and figure them out themselves. For example, stationing myself at the math table to play an attribute block game reduces my involvement in management and enables the children to develop some of their own procedures.

Students' responsibility for their own behavior and management routines supports learning and is especially essential if the class is large or if there is no classroom aide. It is very difficult to teach in a holistic way if you have to control twenty or thirty children, but when

they take over some of the responsibility for their own time management and curriculum choices, you are free to teach. This doesn't
mean that the procedures are perfect. Throughout the year we talk
about them, refine them, change them. One teacher commented, "I
liked the idea of positioning yourself in one center and allowing the
other students to be independent in other parts of the room."

Teacher Adaptations to I CARES

The following are some variations of the I CARE system that teachers have shared with me after discovering what works best in their
classrooms.

- Record which center a child is using by providing a duplicated sheet of photos of everyone in the class. When a
  child goes to a center he circles his pictures. This can be
  used to assess the activities that the children have done
  during the week.
- Adapt the I CARE board to allow the teacher to see at a
  glance what each child has done (see Figure 17-2).
- Use pictures of the areas as well as colors to help the children find their clean-up area.
- Use key tags (bought in bulk at a hardware store) and color
  code them using sticky dots.
- Divide the room into seven areas: playhouse, blocks and
  toys, math, writing, art, books and charts, and science.
  Variation: eight areas—reading, writing, math, building,
  art, puzzles, playhouse, and science.
- Call the I CARES "Teacher and Student Choices." Leave a
  check-off sheet at each of the teacher-choice centers that
  the children mark by their names to show that they did the
  activity.
- Have two children make an announcement that choice
  time will end in five minutes, and ask them then to pick
  two clock-watchers who announce the end of choice time
  and dismiss for clean-up.
- Use "Buzz Groups" to help the children plan, do, and review for choice time. First they get into small groups and
  tell one another what they plan to do. At the end of choice
  time they talk about what they did.

Summary

I believe that teachers and students need a consistent management
system in their classrooms and that teachers should create one

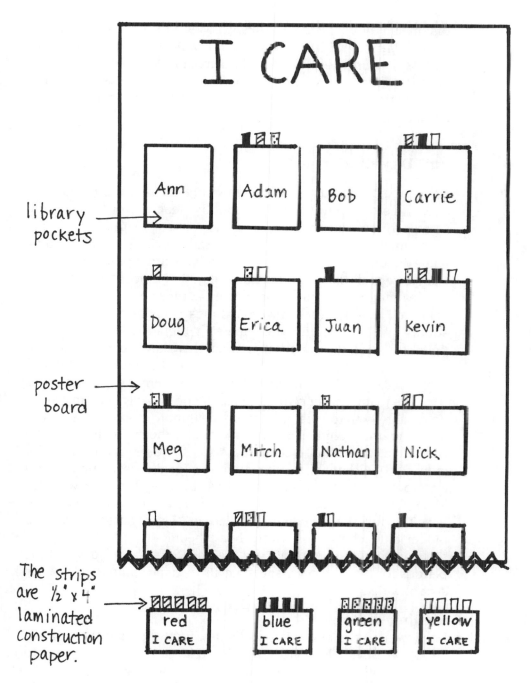

Figure 17-2 I CARE board variation

that meets their individual teaching styles and specific school situations. The I CARE system worked for me and my students in my half-day kindergarten. It allowed for accountability but offered flexibility. I did not assess children on how many I CARES they did or whether they completed them every day. *Learning, not the* I CARES, *was at the heart of choice time.*

Full-Day Kindergarten

Full- or extended-day kindergartens are slowly being added in school districts throughout the country. Teachers of full-day programs have told me that they have been able to adapt much of what I described in the original edition of *Joyful Learning* simply by adding and extending the schedules, because the learning theories do not change regardless of the length of day. An atmosphere of caring and learning in community permeates as they apply the conditions of natural learning. There are group times when the teacher demonstrates and the children participate in literacy events; there are times for independent practice; and there are opportunities for sharing. Teachers with ESL students especially welcome a full-day program to give children more literacy opportunities.

The main difference between half- and full-day kindergarten is time: more time to meet as a group, hear more stories, pursue topics of inquiry, extend, elaborate, and add to the curriculum, and focus on a particular discipline. Also, there is more time for individual teacher/child interaction and for the development of a classroom community. Full-day gives us time to review what we learned during the day and anticipate and plan for tomorrow.

The full-day schedule included in this chapter provides a model for teachers to use to create a schedule that fits the length of their school day and specifics of their school system, such as time periods for lunch, recess, and specialists, and requirements of the school-wide curriculum (see Figure 17-3).

Settling-in Time

I believe that the beginning of the day, from the time the children cross the threshold (Peterson 1992) and enter the classroom to when we gather as a group for shared literacy, sets the tone for the caring and learning that continues throughout the day. Both children and teachers need time to make the transition between life at home and life in school. Full-day kindergarten allows for a calm, relaxed settling-in time during which we all can socialize, get ready for the day, and go about our learning.

When the children enter Carol Fitzpatrick's extended-day

8:00–8:30	Settle-in
8:30–9:15	Shared Literacy (See Chapters 5 and 6)
9:15–10:30	Choice Time
10:30–10:50	Sharing Clean-up
10:50–11:20	Outside Recess
11:20–12:00	Workshop (Writing. Reading, Social Studies, or Science)
12:00–1:00	Lunch Rest and Independent Reading Story
1:00–1:45	Math Workshop
1:45–2:35	Specialist (or Outside Recess, Workshop)
2:35–3:00	Review of the Day/Planning for Tomorrow Story

Figure 17-3 Full-day schedule

kindergarten in Westwood, Massachusetts, they put their folders from home, which contain notes from parents, in a basket, sign in, and make a "wise choice" from the materials in the room. On the day I visited, one boy was drawing, two girls were making snowflakes, several children were in the reading area and at the puppet theater, and the rest of the group was building with blocks. This relaxed time went on for about a half hour before Carol told them that they had five minutes to clean up. Slowly the children put away their materials and gathered at the rug area for shared literacy. While the children were involved in their wise choices, Carol took the lunch count and quietly conversed with individual children.

Sign-in
Sign-in includes all the ways that children write or mark that they are present in the class on a given day. It is their way of taking attendance. All children can sign in if they can make a mark or scribble on a piece of paper, even if they don't know how to write their name in letters. (If teachers use the sign-in for the official school attendance they must be certain that the records they turn in are accurate.) When all the children sign their names on one piece of paper we have an ongoing

document of the class as a community, as well as an individual record of various literacy understandings of each child.

Full-day kindergarten gives time to develop a variety of sign-in procedures that offer opportunities to integrate the curriculum. For example, children can answer a question and sign in under a yes or no column (see Figure 17-4), also taking the responsibility for tallying and reporting the results to the class. They can be encouraged as well to come up with questions and to generate new ways to sign in.

Committee work

In first grade I organized the children into five committees: math, reading, science, social studies, and writing. Each committee was in charge of organizing and managing the supplies and plans for each of these school academic disciplines. In a full-day kindergarten I would have the social studies committee be in charge of the dramatic play area, and I would add a sixth committee, the caring committee, which would help with class meetings and hospitality for visitors to the classroom.

Schedule for the day

Every day I write the schedule for the day on the teaching easel by my chair at the rug area. For the first part of the year I keep the words constant so the children can learn to find the information they need and "read" them in context. Justin used to come in every

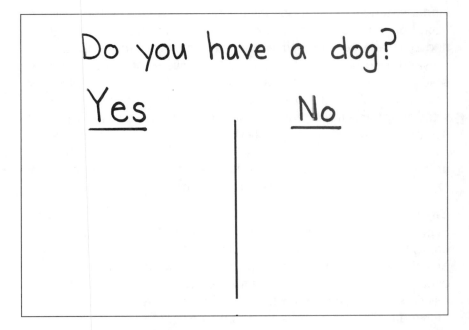

Figure 17-4 Sign-in: Yes/No Question

day and ask if we were going outside. Initially I would tell him to look at the schedule as I pointed to the word "outside." After a while, he didn't need to ask me, but would go to the easel and read for himself. Justin was not an independent reader but he was able to find the information (in this case a word) that he needed. Later in the year we talked about other words that meant about the same as "outside" and I varied the words on the schedule. The children came up with conventional synonyms such as recess, as well as creative, poetic phrases, such as "beautiful sun time."

Morning message

I like to write a daily message to the children under the schedule on the easel. The children can count on finding a note telling them something that is going to happen during the day or posing a question that we will discuss during our meeting time. Teachers have done a variety of things with these messages: save them and put them into a book, add to the message with the children as a record of the day; make a copy and send it home at the end of the week.

Calendar

There are a variety of ways that teachers include the calendar in their morning ritual. Many focus on experiences with numbers such as counting (by ones twos, fives, tens, etc.) the number of days school has been in session or by grouping the days (by ones, tens and hundreds) with straws, Popsicle sticks, or number blocks. The date may be used to experiment with number (for example, what are some different ways that we can name 15).

Community Circle Time

Community circle includes the times when we gather in a circle to share personal news, participate in some organized form of "show and tell," read Mr. Bear's journal, and have class meeting. Although sharing personal news and reading Mr. Bear's journal often precedes shared literacy at the beginning of the day, a full-day schedule allows for different times for special sharing and class meeting.

Shared Literacy Time

I believe that the most important whole-class group time is the morning shared literacy time. It is important to establish a daily routine for this meeting so the children can anticipate and count on certain procedures and rituals.

Choice Time and Workshop Time

Choice time can extend for a much longer time period in a full-day kindergarten. Teachers can schedule guided reading groups so that each child participates at least once a week. There is time for a workshop format, when the entire class focuses on a common activity or discipline at the same time. Many kindergarten teachers have told me that they love the engagement and commitment that generates when everyone is writing at the same time. Having a math workshop, when there is time to get out the many math manipulatives, encourages a variety of creative math opportunities. Class social studies and science projects can be explored in depth during a workshop time. On the day I visited Linda Sterns' kindergarten at the Kings Highway School in Westport, Connecticut, all the children had painted with watercolors and were writing about the experience. In a half-day kindergarten, many of these projects and activities are part of choice time or are not included in the curriculum at all.

Lunch, Rest, and Story Time

The day needs a variety of active and quiet times for children. I found that in first grade a quiet, independent reading time after the active time of lunch and recess was extremely successful, and kindergarten teachers have told me they have a similar routine in their classrooms. When the children come in they get their books and find a comfortable place in the room to read. In some classrooms the children have their own book boxes with favorite books that they are reading. The teacher moves about the room and reads with individual children.

Regardless of the length of the day, teachers have to make choices about how to use children's time. Appendix D describes some of the strategies and activities that individual teachers have found successful in both half- and full-day classrooms.

For Further Reading

Bridges, Lois. 1995a. *Assessment: Continuous Learning*. York, ME: Stenhouse.

———. 1995b. *Creating Your Classroom Community*. York, ME: Stenhouse.

Fisher, Bobbi. 1994. *Classroom Close-Up: Bobbi Fisher: Organization and Management*. Bothell, WA: The Wright Group. Videotape.

———. 1995. *Thinking and Learning Together: Curriculum and Community in a Primary Classroom*. Portsmouth, NH: Heinemann.

Miletta, Margaret. 1996. A *Multiage Classroom: Choice & Possibility*. Portsmouth, NH: Heinemann.

Peterson, Ralph. 1992. *Life in a Crowded Place*. Portsmouth, NH: Heinemann.

18

Language Arts

This chapter expands and elaborates on the theory and practice of reading and writing discussed the first edition of *Joyful Learning*. The first section revisits shared reading. The next section offers further suggestions for helping and assessing individual readers and writers during choice time.

Currently educators are using the term language arts when referring to reading, writing, speaking, and listening. From their experience working with children and from their own learning, they understand that these four components are interdependent and do not operate in isolation. They also are aware that at any given time one may predominate and the focus constantly shifts from one to another.

- We're singing "Old MacDonald" as we come to the rug area. The primary focus is oral, although some children look at the words and read as I point.
- We are working on a group guided writing about our field trip to the library. Although writing predominates, we are rereading what we have written and listening to see if it sounds right and makes sense, and speaking about what we want to say and the writing conventions we want to use.
- As I read *Lilly's Purple Plastic Purse* (Henkes 1996) to the class, the children listen and "read" the pictures. Occasionally I stop and we speak about the story and the children listen to each other.
- During writing time, Tanya, who brings a pink plastic purse to school each day, writes about her purse.
- Stephen selects to read this book to a group of friends during choice time. He tells the story and points to the speech bubbles as they appear in the text.
- Hillary and Stefan are talking (and listening to each other) about what to buy in our classroom greenhouse. Stefan, the salesperson, is writing up a sales slip.

When we keep meaning at the center of learning throughout the day, the interplay between reading, writing, speaking, and listening is natural and seamless. During shared literacy, reading predominates, and writing, speaking, and listening continually emerge and sometimes take precedence. The focus at choice time varies, depending on the choices the children make: reading dominates in the reading area and writing at the writing table; speaking and listening predominate at the sand table, block areas, and environmental play areas, although children often read and write as part of their play. During sharing time, reading, writing, speaking, and listening are all in play as presentation and dialogue move back and forth between the performer and audience.

My goal is for the children to become successful independent readers and writers for a variety of meaningful purposes. One of my jobs is to help them integrate the language cueing systems and apply the necessary skills and strategies to reach this goal. During shared literacy I am continually demonstrating the natural application of the cueing systems, pragmatic, semantic, syntactic, and grapho-phonemic, as we read and discuss text:

1. Pragmatic: context of the reader (What do you know about the topic?)
2. Semantic: meaning of the text (Does it make sense?)
3. Syntactic: interrelationships between words, sentences, and paragraphs in a text (Does it sound right?)
4. Grapho-phonemic: relationship between the sounds and written forms of language (Does the word look right? Does the word match what we are saying?)

Kindergarten children come to school with a wide range of understandings about stories and how they work, and about the conventions of print. A few are already independent readers and integrate the cueing systems, but many are still working this out and need focus work on grapho-phonics. Therefore, throughout shared literacy time we are continually focusing on graphemes (the twenty-six letters of the alphabet), phonemes (the forty-four sounds that make up English words), and phonemic awareness (ability to hear the sounds that make up words), and how to use them strategically within a whole text. During choice time the children practice what they are learning as they read, write, and play.

Shared Literacy

I now use the term shared literacy instead of shared reading for the whole-class group time during which we use songs, poems, and big books for literacy learning because we are engaging in a variety of literacy events, for example speaking, listening, writing, mathematics, and music, not just reading. We learn and express ourselves not just through the language arts, but through music art, movement, and mathematics and discover the richness and depth of learning. I want to provide opportunities for children to express themselves in multiple intelligences: linguistic, musical, logical-mathematical, spatial, bodily kinesthetic, interpersonal, and intrapersonal (Gardner 1983). I want them to see the connections between written and artistic expression (Ernst 1994).

I weave multiple ways of knowing naturally into the fabric of shared literacy and the children respond as learners as one knowledge system generates another. For example, we start singing a song and the children create a dance to go with it. Increasingly, teachers are becoming cognizant of multiple ways of knowing and of their possibilities for in depth learning, not just during shared literacy, but throughout the day as children generate curriculum.

Teachers are also aware that offering children a variety of ways to express themselves is especially helpful for ESL students as they make connections between their home language and English. They bring in props and artifacts, which the children can touch and talk about, that relate to the books they are reading.

During shared literacy teacher and children engage together in a process similar to the way parent and child enjoy a story at bedtime. The conditions include joyfulness, an engaging text that the child wants to hear again and again, repeated readings, observations of concepts about print, discussions of reading strategies such as pointing and rereading, and conversations about the story and pictures. Although writing is not as integral a part of the bedtime story, children observe adults at home writing for a variety of purposes: making lists, filling out forms writing letters and reports, and occasionally composing prose and poetry During shared literacy, teachers demonstrate these different forms of writing.

Recently teachers have acknowledged the value of reading a wide selection of literature, in both trade book and big book form, from the following categories: poetry and song, storybook, information book, information storybook, biography. This section gives examples of ways that I have used big books, charts and trade books during shared literacy to help children develop as life long learners while they learn reading and writing skills and strategies.

Songs and Poems

When I call the children to the rug area for shared literacy I am inviting them to engage in a variety of literacy experiences in a risk-free environment. There are many reasons that I have chosen singing as the signal in my class. It suggests that a joyful community is forming and it keeps me from using my "teacher voice," which is more demanding and controlling. It gives children the opportunity to finish what they are doing before joining but allows those of us already gathered to get going without spending our time waiting for "latecomers."

Singing at this time enables us to become familiar with many texts that we will use throughout the year. I write most of the songs in enlarged print on charts, but some are in big book form or from a trade book. I like to sing three or four songs, as well as read a few poems, and by the time we've finished, everyone has gathered. Sometimes we have stopped along the way to talk about something on the chart and other times we have sung them through for enjoyment and community, much like at camp, church, or a concert. Regardless, I trust that each child is working at her/his developmental level, selecting, self-monitoring, and self-correcting what he/she needs to make meaning. As the children become accustomed to this gathering procedure, they often select the songs and poems for the day and are in charge of starting the singing.

"Singing in the Rain"

I'm singing in the rain,
Just singing in the rain.
What a glorious feeling,
I'm hap-hap-happy again.
    Thumbs up! (thumbs up)
Sh, sh, sh, sh, sh, sh,
Sh, sh, sh, sh, sh, sh,
Sh, sh, sh, sh, sh, sh, sh,
Sh, sh, sh, sh, sh, sh.
    Elbows out! (elbows out)
    Knees bent! (knees bent)
    Tongue out! (tongue out)

Teachers have shared with me many different ways they enjoy "Singing in the Rain" with students. In my class, we all stand and move about while singing and carrying out the different actions, each time adding a new movement. By the end, laughter fills the room as we attempt to do everything at once. One rainy day I kept my raincoat on and we sang the song as the children entered the classroom.

Aside from giving the children an opportunity to stretch and take a break from sitting on the floor, this song lends itself to many innovations, or text substitutions. In the following stanza, written by a kindergarten class in New England, all the cueing systems were in play (see Figure 18-1). We wrote it as a group interactive writing experience, with me writing some of it and individual children taking the marker and writing what they knew. We discussed what we knew about snow and shared our experiences (pragmatic). We kept checking to see if what we were writing made sense (semantic) and sounded right (syntactic), both within the individual lines and as part of the entire stanza. We discussed letters and sounds as we wrote the words on the chart (grapho-phonemic).

Working over time with a repetitive song such as this one provides children with many opportunities to apply skills and strategies, particularly phonemic awareness, in a variety of meaningful ways

- Work with *onsets*, the initial consonant or consonant cluster at the beginning of a word (in stomping)
- Work with *rimes*, the vowel and consonant cluster at the end of a word (/ump/ in place of *jump*)
- Extend vocabulary (What other words could we use that mean about the same as glorious in this text?)
- Focus on high-frequency words (repetition of a word in the chorus)

Adding various actions encourage children to use multiple intelligences (particularly linguistic, musical, spatial, bodily kinesthetic) and to express themselves through different sign systems, specifically music and drama.

Morning, Noon, and Night

Morning, Noon, and Night: Poems to Fill Your Day, selected by Sharon Taberski. Taberski is a second-grade teacher at the Manhattan New School in New York City. The text is illustrated with colorful, lively drawings by Nancy Doniger and comes in big book form with accompanying little books and a tape. The first time I introduced this book to a class, I gave pairs of children a copy of the little book and asked them to look through and choose a poem that they would like us to read as a group. About fifteen minutes later, after much conversation and discussion, we began. I read from the big book and the children continued to refer to their little books. They indicated their choices in a variety of ways: page number, description of the picture, location in the book, and title name. They also explained to the class the reasons for their choice which usually had to do with a detail in the picture.

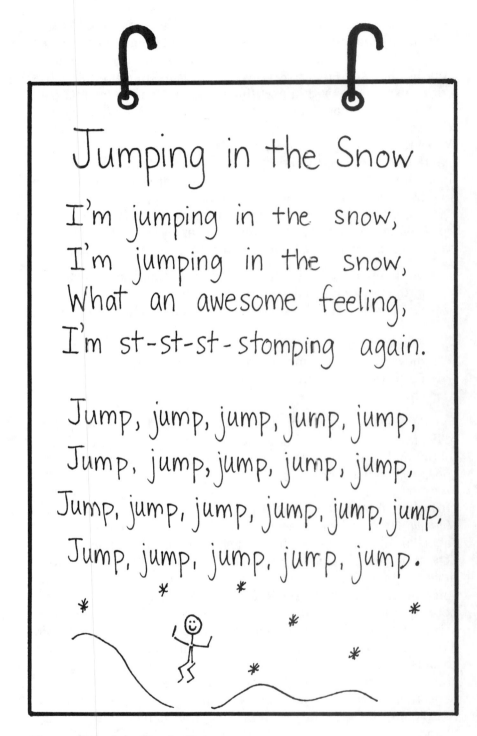

Figure 18-1 Jumping in the snow

For the next few weeks the books were available in the reading area for independent reading. After the children had ample time to explore the book, I added the tape to the listening center. We continued to read some of the poems during shared literacy every day, stopping to comment on the text and focus on the semantics, syntax, and graphophonics. Over time we discussed the title and how we felt the selected poems related to morning, noon, and night. That developed into a close look at the table of contents, which is broken up into categories. Eventually the children noticed that some of the authors have poems in other poetry books.

Becoming very familiar with an anthology such as this one provides children with many opportunities to apply skills and strategies in a variety of meaningful ways.

- Experience different ways to go about reading poetry books
- Use a table of contents and find page numbers in a book
- Work with rimes and common spelling endings
- Use the poems as models for writing class and individual poems
- Use the anthology as a model for a class or individual poem

Storybooks

Storybooks, with both fantasy and realistic fiction, comprise the largest group of books we read to kindergartners. When we read storybooks to young children we talk about characters, setting, place, mood, and plot. Children begin to understand that stories have a beginning, middle, and end, and conflict and resolution. During shared literacy we explore story in detail through the repeated readings of big books. In addition, throughout the day we read many storybooks that receive less focused study and discussion.

This Is the Bear

This Is the Bear (Hayes) is the story of a bear who is put in the trash by a little boy's dog and the ensuing adventure of the boy and dog to get him back from the dump. The illustrations closely match the text and quotation bubbles tell what the characters are saying or thinking. There are about seven words to a page and the text is written in large boldfaced letters, which makes it easy for beginning readers to follow or point to the words as they read.

This book did not need a long introduction because the children brought much background knowledge to the reading. Therefore, I introduced it through a brief discussion of the three characters on the cover, the bear, a boy, and a dog, all of whom appear to be friends. The children concluded that the picture did not help us specifically predict what the story might be about. Very quickly one child commented, "Let's turn the page," and I knew it was time to start reading.

This rhyming text lends itself to predicting what the last word in each rhyming set will be. I put sticky notes on each final rhyme and as we read we predicted what the word would be and discussed our choice in the context. For example, with the text,

> This is the man who picked up the sack.
> This is the driver who would not come *back*.

I might start with the following questions, "Does *back* make sense in the sentence? Does it sound right? If the word is *back*, what letter will it begin with?" Then someone would peel off the post-it and we'd look at the whole word to verify that it looked like the word we had chosen.

Becoming familiar with a storybook such as this one with a limited number of words in text and supportive illustrations provides children with many opportunities to apply skills and strategies in a variety of meaningful ways:

- Point to the text and read the predictable, rhythmic text
- Notice similar spelling patterns in rhyming words
- Discuss how the illustrations support and enrich the text (In this book the story is also told from the point of view of the dog through the illustrations.)
- Discuss the storybook structure of "home/adventure/home," in which the character starts at home, has an adventure, and returns home at the end

The Three Billy Goats Gruff

Children enjoy the readers theater version of *The Three Billy Goats Gruff*, retold by Betty Jane Wagner. The characters, with an accompanying rebus, are listed at the front of the big book. The appropriate rebus precedes each line of the text: one for each of the four main characters, a book for the storyteller, and two masks for helpers, who say "trip-trip" throughout the story. A frame around the illustrations gives the effect of a stage.

The group of kindergartners to whom I introduced this book were already familiar with the story. We briefly discussed the different rebuses and then read the story together, changing our voices to correspond to the storyteller, the helpers, and each character. At subsequent readings individual children took different parts. This book became a favorite during choice time. Various groups of children would gather together their own casts and arrange chairs for the audience. The teacher was able to step back.

The vocabulary in this text is extremely rich and descriptive, and provides many opportunities for the children to expand their spoken and written vocabulary. For example, the repeated phrase, "the green hillside lush with delicious grass," initiated a discussion on authors' word choices. First we discussed what the phrase meant in the story and shared personal experiences that it brought to mind. Then we made a list of other words the author might have used instead of *lush* (*filled, soft, fresh*) and *delicious* (*sweet, yummy, tasty*). As with many vocabulary discussions, I ask, "If you were the author, what word would you use?"

Becoming very familiar with a popular traditional tale provides children with many opportunities to apply skills and strategies in a variety of meaningful ways:

- Make comparisons between different versions of the story
- Dramatize the story and integrate multiple intelligences, specifically linguistic, bodily kinesthetic, and interpersonal
- Learn about dialogue

Information Books

Information books give factual information and are written as nonfiction. Children come to kindergarten with a wealth of information and an intense interest in the world about them, especially in the area of science. They are easily engaged in information books, and many children learn to read from them.

How Spiders Live

This book is one of three in a series about spiders written by Fred and Jeanne Biddulph and is published in big and little book form. Each has a table of contents and index and contains photographs and illustrated diagrams. The text is simple but gives a great deal of information.

One way I introduce this book is to explain to the children that when I get a new information book, I usually leaf through to get an idea what the book is about and what is in the book. Then I ask them to notice something that interests them as I quickly turn the pages of the book. Afterwards, they tell the class what they noticed and we go to the page and read and discuss.

I have also introduced this book by reading the contents and having a child pick one of the topics for us to read. We then turn to the page and read and discuss. At subsequent readings we follow the same procedure using the index.

Becoming familiar with an information book such as this one provides children with many opportunities to apply skills and strategies in a variety of meaningful ways:

- Find specific information
- Understand the specific benefits of photographs, illustrations and diagrams
- Learn to read diagrams
- Use as a model for their own inquiry projects
- Apply knowledge of the alphabet in using the index

Information Storybooks

Recently more and more informational storybooks are being written for young children. They provide science and social studies information as part of a story. Many of these books serve as models for inquiry projects both in kindergarten and subsequent grades.

Bear Facts

Bear Facts is an informational storybook with song and lyrics by Norma Gentner, a kindergarten teacher who loves music and science. With the help of her students she has written seven other science-related big books with accompanying little books and tapes. The illustrations, by different artists, accurately portray the scientific concepts introduced in the books. The repetitive tunes are catchy and easy to learn. The illustrations in *Bear Facts* show us the first year of life of two black bear cubs from birth to maturity as the seasons change. The text describes where these black bears live, their babies, what they eat, what they look like, and what they do throughout the year.

I have introduced *Bear Facts* in different ways to different groups of children. I select a starting strategy, and then continue observing the children as we go along to get a sense of when to begin reading the story.

My favorite introduction to *Bear Facts* is through a discussion of the title. Before showing the children the book or telling them the title, we discuss what a fact is:

- Something you know
- Something you can tell
- Information
- A machine that sends messages (This child was thinking of a fax machine.)

Next I write the title on my teaching easel and as the children share facts they know about bears, I write them underneath. I ask both open-ended questions, which elicit the children's prior knowledge, and specific questions, which focus the discussion of the text we are going to read. I usually start with the open-ended one, "What facts do you know about bears?"

More specific questions ask for particular facts that will show up in the text, such as, "Where do bears sleep?" or "What do we call their babies?" I often do this when the children can't come up with many facts about bears, or when they focus on bears attacking human beings. In that case we acknowledge that when bears are frightened they might attack us. Then I refocus the discussion through specific questions.

It is always my call how much I want to "tell" the children ahead of time about what is in the text or whether I want to leave more of the discovery up to them through subsequent readings. There's no right or wrong way but I always caution myself that by being too specific I can ruin that personal discovery, the "aha," that I believe gives ownership to the learner and provides a deeper sense of learning.

Finally, after I show the cover of the book and we comment on the picture, we read (sing) the book straight through. I like to read a big book through twice on the first sitting, but before the second reading, I ask the children to tell the class something that they noticed and that they are going to look for again. "I noticed that the cubs get bigger on each page. . . . I notice that there are the seasons. . . . I noticed a question mark." We read again, stopping for a while at each page to take in all that is there. Individual children might share with the group, or share quietly with the person next to them, or sit quietly, reading the pictures, doing their "silent" reading. This noticing exercise always reaffirms for me that we are all teachers. The children notice things that I haven't noticed, and might never notice on my own.

Next (often the next day) we try to remember the different facts that were in the book and I write them on a web. We reread the story and add and delete facts on the web so that it accurately reflects the text (see Figure 18-2). Then we compare and check off the facts in the book with the original facts sheet we made before the first reading.

At other times I introduce this book through a focus on letters and sounds. I start at my teaching easel with pen in hand and tell the children that I am slowly going to write the beginning letter of the new big book we are going to read. As I move my pen I ask them to say all the possible letters I could be writing. Usually I hear letters with straight lines such as T, M, and P. As I start the rounded part of the B,

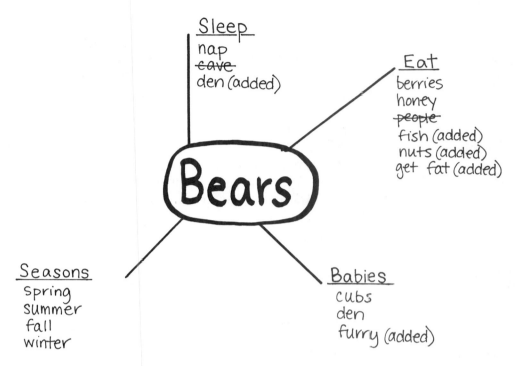

Figure 18-2 **Bear Facts** *web*

the possibilities narrow and I hear P, B, R, and D. I stop at different points and ask, "If I stopped here what would it be?" (P) "If I kept going what could it be?" (B or R) This is a clear example of demonstration and participation in dynamic action. I am demonstrating through writing and speaking as each child participates at his or her developmental level in what sounds like unison response (Holdaway 1979).

I am continually assessing during this procedure. If I hear children say C or O, I know that they need more demonstrations of different letters. If I hear numerals, I know that some children don't understand the difference between a letter and a numeral. I don't stop and correct anybody but make clarifying comments to the group in general, such as "I start writing an uppercase B with a straight line, and then I add two half circles. . . . A seven is a number; words start with letters." I trust that over time, with repeated demonstrations during shared literacy and writing opportunities during choice time, the children will sort out the various distinctions. Through a variety of experiences, they will make different hypotheses about the way text works, sample possibilities, confirm their predictions, or disconfirm and self-correct (Goodman, Watson, and Burke, 1987) and refine their understanding.

After we have established that the title of the book begins with

B, I tell the children that the book is about an animal that begins
with B. I list their suggestions on chart paper, starting each word
with an uppercase letter to correspond to the first letter in the title.
Sometimes we stop with about five possibilities, and other times I
write down many more (see Figure 18-3). When our list is complete,
I make a variety of predicting statements to narrow down to the
word "Bear" and children come up and put a line through the animals as we eliminate each one. The statements I select depend on
the skills I want to reinforce (see Appendix B-10).

Biographies

There are not many biographies written for kindergartners, but increasingly, biographical stories are being published for young children. When we read various kinds of biographies we can discuss the
different points of view that the authors took. I have found that biographies often need a careful explanation and discussion before I
read the story, as well as during the reading.

The Baby Sister

Tomie DePaola has written many stories drawn from his experiences as a young child. He wrote *The Baby Sister*, in the third person

Animals (B)	Other Animals	Other B words
Bee	Turkey	Book
Bear	Snake	Bottle
Bug	Cow	Bus
Beetle		
Baboon		
Butterfly		
Bunny		

Figure 18-3 Predicting words for Bear Facts

from his memory of the anticipation and arrival of his sister Maureen into his family.

The Story of Ruby Bridges
Ruby Bridges was the first black child to attend William Frantz Elementary school in New Orleans as part of a court order to integrate the school in 1960. Robert Coles spent years interviewing children and families involved in the integration process, and wrote this book from his research.

Mr. Lincoln's Whiskers
Karen B. Winnick, the author of *Mr. Lincoln's Whiskers*, is a student of Abraham Lincoln. Although the incidents in this story never happened to Lincoln, Winnick included what she knew about Lincoln and his times into this piece of historical fiction.

Supporting Literacy During Choice Time

Choice time in the natural learning classroom model is the time when the children practice what has been demonstrated during shared literacy and teachers work with children individually and in small groups. Chapters 7–12 describe the wide array of choice-time activities that support learning in kindergarten. Chapters 8 and 9 focus specifically on reading and writing and Chapter 14 describes my assessment procedure. The material in these three chapters, as well as the following suggestions and strategies, apply to both half- and full-day kindergarten.

Reading
Don Holdaway discovered that early readers spent time at home practicing "reading" the bedtime stories that were read to them. We need to build this practice time into our daily schedule. Reading was an I CARE in my half-day kindergarten. Children were expected to spend time with books each day. In a full-day kindergarten I would schedule a time when everyone would be reading, probably after recess or lunch. Children would be able to relax as they enjoyed books, and I would have time to listen to them read and assess their progress.

Book Selection
If we want children to develop as successful readers who love to read, we must allow them to choose the books they read and then honor those choices. It is our responsibility to talk to them about their specific interests and to provide books and magazines to support those interests.

It is also our responsibility to introduce children to new topics and offer them opportunities to pursue new interests. One of the ways we do this is through the wide selection of books we have in our classrooms and read during shared literacy.

Guided Reading

I have found that when children are involved in both shared literacy and independent reading and writing every day, most of them grow in their literacy learning. Teacher assessment, both formal and informal, along with portfolio assessment of children's work over time, provides confirmation that they are developing into successful readers and helps us plan what we need to teach in order to support continued growth. This includes working with children within a guided reading format, either individually or in a small group with selected texts that support their particular needs. It builds upon the foundation of intensive and extensive daily shared reading, during which children are learning "how to use independent reading strategies successfully" (Fountas and Pinnell, p. 2).

"The purpose of guided reading is to enable children to use and develop strategies 'on the run' " (Fountas and Pinnell, p. 2). Therefore, whether reading with a small group or individual children, I select a text with which they will feel successful and yet challenged.

A guided reading group

A guided reading group is composed of three, four, or five children with similar reading processes who can read texts of similar levels. Grouping remains flexible because children's reading needs vary and the teacher's teaching goals change as she assesses and plans specific instruction. The number depends on the level of activity of the children, and the amount of individual attention they need. I have found that with ESL students I like to work with no more than four children at a time so I can immediately attend to their language needs. Often a small group takes less time. Also, very active children benefit most from small groups that meet for a short time several times a week. As the school year goes on the time can be lengthened.

The following describes a guided reading lesson on *My Home* (Cowley) that I conducted with a group of kindergartners. (See Appendix B-11 for sample guided reading procedures.)

The book *My Home* (Cowley) tells about different animals and their homes and ends with a space girl taking off in her spaceship home. The seven word text is repetitive except for a different animal on each page: " 'I like my home,' said the ———."

1. Introducing the book and activating prior knowledge—
   Before showing the children the book, I asked them to describe their own homes, and name a favorite animal and
   describe that animal's home.

2. Predicting through discussion of the cover of the book—
   Next I held up the book and we talked about the homes
   of the turtle and bird on the cover. (I had not given the
   children their own book yet.) Throughout our discussions
   I referred to animals liking their homes, relating the word
   like, an important word in the text, to the meaning of the
   book.

3. Talking through the book—Our discussion continued as
   we focused on each page. I asked the children to pretend
   they were the animal and say, "I like my home." For example, when they took the role of the bunny they scrunched
   up their noses and sniffed as they spoke. We also discussed the word *space girl*. Some wanted to call it *space
   woman*, which would have made sense (semantic cue) and
   sounded right (syntactic cue), but wasn't the word that Joy
   Cowley chose. I wrote the words *woman* and *girl* on the
   chalkboard and we discussed the grapho-phonemic elements in each.

4. Reading individually—Finally I gave the children individual copies of the book and asked them to point to the
   words as they read and to keep the book flat on the floor
   so I could watch them. This is when I can assess what
   the children are doing and help them individually. Three
   children were reading word for word and I left them to
   continue on their own. One child responded to my support when I took his hand in mine and we pointed and
   read together. I continued to watch him to decide
   whether he would benefit from a book with fewer words
   on a page.

5. Sharing with the group or in pairs—As the children finished
   I asked them to read the book again to themselves and then
   pick a favorite page to read to the person next to them.

Guided reading with individual children

When I do guided reading with individual readers, I use many of the
same procedures I employ for a guided reading group. But I am
able to be more flexible and follow the children's leads more
closely because I can observe carefully what they do and support
them very specifically in developing their skills and strategies.

Every minute I spend with an individual child is directed toward what that child is doing as a self-monitoring learner. In essence, each child has a bedtime story with me.

Writing

I am very committed to a daily writing time when children write (and draw) about topics of interest. This daily writing builds upon the experiences of shared literacy. Once children get into the routine of daily writing, they develop ownership over their work. They gain control over their writing when they can choose their own topic, paper, and format, whether to work alone or with a friend, and how to file and share their work. During writing conferences we talk about their writing and sometimes we work on a collaborative writing piece. When children are involved in creating their own writing portfolios and when they sit in the author's chair, they think of themselves as writers.

In my half-day sessions, daily writing was an I CARE and took place during choice time. In other kindergartens, the entire class moves into writing workshop after shared literacy. This has been especially successful in full-day kindergartens.

Children also write for meaningful purposes during their work in different areas of the classroom. For example, when they create through a variety of media at the art area, build in the block area, and express their interests dramatically at the puppet theater or in the play environment.

Modeling writing

I start at the very beginning of the year modeling different ways of writing by stating that "we all write differently when we first start learning to write. Some of us start like this _____." I model different stages, from scribble to conventional writing, and then explain that my writing looks like the writing in a book because I have been practicing for a long time. The children become very comfortable and proud of their writing because they know that their stage of writing is acceptable. I never have children tell me that they can't write; they know they are learning to be better writers by practicing and it is rewarding to see them make progress.

Innovations and extensions

Children often draw and write about books as a follow-up to individual or small-group guided readings or shared literacy experiences with the entire class. Sometimes teachers assign innovations or extensions as an I CARE during choice time, or as projects for writing workshop. Often children choose on their own to do an innovation on a text (see Appendix D).

Assessing Letters and Sounds

It is important that children develop letter knowledge and phonemic awareness as they grow as readers and writers. Some kindergarten teachers believe that doing some form of letter of the week is an appropriate solution to teaching these skills, although they usually integrate it with many of the holistic strategies described in this book. As I explained in my response in Chapter 16 to the question, "Do you do letter of the week?" and in a subsequent article (Fisher 1996), I believe that *any* form of a letter of the week program is ineffective because it does not support children in integrating successfully the language cueing systems, and it controls the content of the curriculum.

Teachers who still do letter of the week tell me that it assures them that they are covering the letters and sounds and that they want to be accountable. Without a doubt it is important that they assess this aspect of children's literacy learning and keep track of what the children know, but covering the letters does not assure that children learn them. When teachers assess children's application of the grapho-phonemic cueing system as part of the reading/writing process, they learn how children are using these skills to read and write and they obtain information that will inform instruction.

Teachers have shared with me different ways that they keep records of the skills and strategies they demonstrate during shared reading, and that individual children use as they read and write. Some make a list of the alphabet and keeping an on-going tally of the letters and sounds they focus on during shared reading. They record at the end of the day or include the children and ask them to help fill in the chart (see Figure 18-4). Many teachers make a chart for each of the children and periodically record the letters that they use in their writing and the phonics they apply when they read. Some keep more detailed records for shared reading and individual children, including discussion and use of onsets, such as initial consonant or consonant clusters, and rimes, such as /at/, /ake/, /ing/ (see Figure 18-5).

During the kindergarten year children make great progress in all the areas of language arts, reading, writing, speaking, and listening. Often the results of this progress are not apparent in kindergarten but appear in first grade as children develop independence in reading and demonstrate conventional writing for an audience. A kindergarten program that integrates language arts and includes other sign systems and multiple ways of learning

Shared Reading
Tally of letters and sounds

	Sept.	Oct.	Nov.
a		I	
b	IIII	II	III
c	II	III	II
at		II	I
ing	I		II
cl			I

Figure 18-4 Tally of Letters and Sounds

builds a foundation for literacy as children develop a love for learning.

For Further Reading

Graves, Donald. 1994. *A Fresh Look at Writing*. Portsmouth NH: Heinemann.

Fisher, Bobbi. 1996. *Inside the Classroom. Teaching Kindergarten and First Grade*. Portsmouth, NH: Heinemann.

————. 1997. *Classroom Close-Up: Bobbi Fisher: Developing Young Readers*. Bothell, WA: The Wright Group. Videotape.

————. 1997. *Classroom Close-Up: Bobbi Fisher: Guiding Young Authors*. Bothell, WA: The Wright Group. Videotape.

Fountas, Irene, and Gay Su Pinnell. 1996. *Guided Reading: Good First Teaching for All Children*. Portsmouth, NH: Heinemann.

Individual Application of letters in writing

	a	b	c	d	
Amanda		l	ll	l	
Boyd		l			
Carlos	l	ll	lllll		
Francie	ll	lllll	l	lll	

Figure 18-5 Individual application of letters in writing

Mills, Heidi, Tim O'Keefe, and Diane Stephens. 1992. *Looking Closely: Exploring the Role of Phonics in One Whole Language Classroom*. Urbana, IL: National Council of Teachers of English.

Moustafa, Margaret. 1997. *Beyond Traditional Phonics: Research Discoveries and Reading Instruction*. Portsmouth, NH: Heinemann.

Tompkins, Gail E., and Lea M. McGee. 1993. *Teaching Reading with Literature: Case Studies to Action Plans*. New York: Macmillan.

19

Generative Curriculum

This chapter further examines the importance of dramatic play environments described in Chapter 12 and discusses ways of melding the teacher's and children's interests, as well as the prescribed school curriculum, into a dynamic "generative curriculum."

In 1986 Ken Goodman wrote that "Language learning is easy when it's whole, real, and relevant; when it makes sense and is functional; when it's encountered in the context of its use; when the learner chooses to use it" (1998, p. 26). His words supported me as I developed my beliefs about how children learn and continue to ring true for teachers ten years later as they work toward creating a curriculum that is meaningful and integrated. Later studies on classrooms and schools that work (Gardner 1991, Rose 1995, Brown 1991) point to successful efforts by teachers to relate the curriculum to the interests and lives of the children. Implicitly and explicitly stated is the active role of the children in initiating and crafting the curriculum.

Classroom teachers and researchers, working side by side, are continually developing new ways of looking at curriculum. For example, inquiry, multiple intelligences, different sign systems, intertextuality, theme integration, and simulations are becoming part of the everyday vocabulary and practice of many knowledgeable teachers. Since kindergarten is the first public school experience for many children, kindergarten teachers have the opportunity to provide children with their first formal encounter with what Pat Cordeiro and I call a generative curriculum.

Pat and I first heard the term generative curriculum from Don Holdaway in 1988 when he suggested generative or developmental curriculum as the next way of looking at what goes on in classrooms. Subsequently Pat and I wrote about generative curriculum (Fisher and Cordeiro 1994; Cordeiro 1995; Fisher 1995) and we are continuing to develop our own understandings and theories.

For me, generative curriculum is a conceptual model with a strong theoretical base, which allows for differences in specific curriculum content (social studies and science) and individual management and organizational styles. At the heart of a generative curriculum are the conditions of natural learning (Cambourne 1988) and their application to the classroom as delineated in the natural learning classroom model (Holdaway 1979, 1986). Demonstration, participation, practice/role-play, and performance are in dynamic action and it is often difficult to observe where one begins and another ends. Children, as well as teachers, become demonstrators and everyone is a learner. The principles of trust, risk taking, choice making, and inquiry stay constant but in a generative curriculum one idea or interest generates another and curriculum takes off in many directions.

Curriculum takes on the unique context of the particular classroom. For example, each situation adapts to the general developmental understandings of the age range of the children, the cultural and political situation of the particular school and school system, the interests, style, and personality of the teacher and students, and the requirements of the school-wide curriculum.

It is the teacher's job to watch carefully and support interests through demonstrations and conversation, by allowing time for genuine inquiry, and by providing a conducive learning environment and appropriate materials. Teachers and children create a variety of management and organizational procedures to give form and structure to the day. They organize the curriculum around specific procedures, such as the inquiry cycle (Short, Harste, and Burke 1996), the project approach (Katz and Chard 1989), Scottish Storyline (Creswell 1997), theme immersion (Manning, Manning, and Long 1994) and dramatic play environments, described in Chapter 12 and elaborated upon in this chapter.

In Kindergarten

Specifically, generative curriculum in kindergarten includes what we know about kindergartners: that they learn best when offered exploratory experiences and hands-on activities; that they learn through play; that they are developing a literacy set; that shared reading helps them learn how print works; and that invented spelling helps them as they focus on the grapho-phonemic cueing system. Teachers and children would then generate what is actually happening in the classroom: incidental learning, mini-studies and class-wide studies.

Some experiences are short and include all the incidental learning that goes on throughout the day: we read *The Rooster's Gift* (Conrad), but never consciously extend it beyond that first enjoyable reading; Mariah brings in a dead beetle she found, a few children look at it, and she writes about it; we take some time to watch the first snowfall and then go back to our work. Other happenings are longer and become mini-topics: the entire class, a small group of children, or an individual might delve into the topic of dinosaurs and make a mural; we read several books by Eric Carle; a group creates a model of a space city; one child continues to construct a tunnel with pattern blocks. Some of the topics stay open for a long time as the entire class generates a study that might last for a month or extend for the entire year: a few children start playing hospital and an on-going dramatic play environment is set up; we begin a list classifying animals and add to it every time we read about a new animal; we study the family as part of the required school curriculum.

As the year goes on, topics are reopened and new intertextual connections are made. We place fertile eggs in our incubator and Tyrone remembers *The Rooster's Gift*. We read it again and place it near the incubator with other books about chickens. As we discuss what chickens eat, Mariah recalls the beetle she brought in and wonders if chickens eat beetles. I introduce the book *Chickens* (Snowball) and some children use it as a model to make their own pop-up book. The block area is transformed into a farm and favorite farm books are brought into the area and used as "plans" for building.

Curriculum Models

There are several curriculum models that support a generative curriculum and that kindergarten teachers have adapted to fit their particular situation. The curriculum model I used was the dramatic play environment, and as I've continued to consider curriculum, I've found that this model, as well as other models, fulfills the criteria of a generative curriculum. Some of the essential elements in the models described below are also important in dramatic play environments. In this section I describe some of these models and give examples of ways that they relate to the recycle center we created in my kindergarten.

Authoring Cycle
Short, Harste, and Burke (1996) use the authoring cycle as a curricular framework, with inquiry the focus of curriculum no matter what the topic or subject. In setting up the recycle center, we "build from the known" by sharing our personal stories about recycling. As we examined the insignia at the bottom of different pieces of plastic, "questions for inquiry" arose as we wondered why some pieces didn't have a number.

Project Approach

In a project approach children create projects in which they can interact and play as they learn, "activities that engage their minds fully in the quest for knowledge, understanding, and skill" (Katz and Chard 1989, p. xi). For the recycle center, I made copies of the triangle insignia found on the bottom of recyclable materials and the children added the appropriate numbers. They decided to use the hollow big blocks for the recycle barrels and taped a sign on each one (see Figure 19-1).

Scottish Storyline

With Scottish Storyline, the teacher and children work together as collaborative storymakers. The teacher chooses a topic and the children build a setting for the story in the classroom. Characters are made for the story. Sometimes each child has a character and sometimes the class creates a few large characters. Then things begin to happen to the characters in the setting. Sign systems, language, visual arts, music, drama and movement, science and

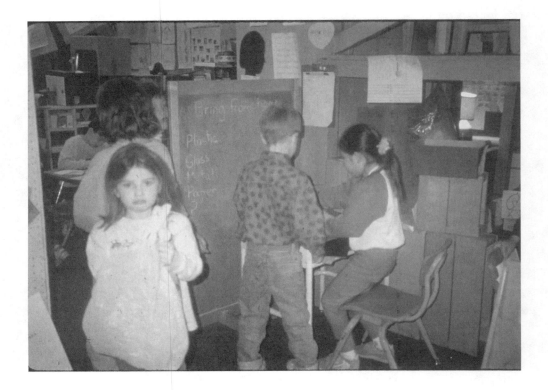

Figure 19-1 Recycle center

mathematics all are used to develop the story, pose problems, and develop the plot. A culminating event allows the children to share their learning with family and friends. When the children played in the recycle center in my kindergarten, they created stories as they took on the roles of manager and citizen.

Theme Immersion

Theme immersion involves an in-depth study of a topic, issue, or question in which children and teachers plan together throughout and "make connections between their activities in the classroom and the real world of today and tomorrow" (Manning, Manning, and Long 1994, p. 2). When we took recyclable materials from our classroom and homes to the town recycling center, we participated in important ecology issues of today and tomorrow.

Dramatic Play Environments

In a generative curriculum, teachers impart the general management routines and attitudes for learning that form the foundation and support of what they believe. From this framework together with the children, they generate curriculum to meet the individual and immediate needs of the situation. These routines and attitudes include organizing the physical space and materials; applying conditions of the natural learning model; building community through problem solving. Regardless of the model that kindergarten teachers use as a framework for curriculum in their classrooms, I believe that dramatic play must be a central part of it.

Physical Space and Materials

In arranging the room, the teacher must create physical spaces where children can play. I like to have two separate areas, so that different kinds of dramatic play can go on at the same time. Sometimes there is a specific play environment in one of the areas, while the other is left free for children to create new ones each day. Often the children change this free area and eventually make it part of the current dramatic play environment.

Teachers must also provide materials conducive to dramatic play. Many kindergartens are supplied with blocks and housekeeping props, and reading and writing materials are available in schools. When we start a new dramatic play environment I usually provide some initial materials. We talk about the different props we will need and the children gather things that are available in the classroom. As the environment develops, new materials are added and often the children bring in things from home. It is important to remember that the environment grows and changes over time as the children play. Creating the environment is an integral part of the process.

In my classroom, we started with a farm underneath the loft. My assistant brought in a small wheelbarrow, a milk pail, some farm tools, seeds, and a seed bag, and demonstrated their uses. The children extended the space next to the loft and created a vegetable garden, using plastic food models and the tools. They started converting the upper part of the loft into the farmhouse. When we set up a veterinarian's office, the children brought stuffed animals and doctor kits from home. We all brought plant cuttings from home to contribute to our greenhouse environment.

In all of these cases, one idea generated another and our collective thoughts created rich dramatic play environments. If I had been the only one contributing materials, we would have lost many opportunities for learning. If we as teachers are the only ones creating curriculum and contributing materials, we are confined to our unique but limited ideas. Children become engaged when they are actively involved in developing play environment. In fact, when teachers do all the planning, children often become disengaged.

The Natural Learning Classroom Model in Action

In a generative curriculum the natural learning classroom model is in dynamic action, and nowhere is this more apparent than in a dramatic play environment. Throughout the day there are repeated opportunities for demonstrations and participation, practice/role-play, and performance/sharing. During shared literacy I read books and poems on the current topic and the children participate in discussions. During choice time they incorporate new pertinent information into their play. They share what they have learned both informally, as they play, and formally during class discussions or when visitors are invited to the classroom.

When we created a veterinarian's office in my class we obtained demonstrations from two main sources, books and a visit to a local vet. Before our visit we read an information book about veterinarians, discussed the photographs, and generated a list of questions to ask the vet. Throughout the time the environment was in action, we would refer to the book and recall our visit. The class decided to set up the office and waiting room underneath the loft and place the examining room above. During choice time six children were selected to start setting up the area and then report back to the class and ask for further suggestions. (See Figure 19-2).

After the field trip, we determined three different roles that children could take: secretaries, vet, and pet owners. The children decided that they would not take the role of an animal, but would

Figure 19-2 Veterinarian's office

bring in stuffed animals from home to use as patients. Since everyone wanted to be secretaries, and vets, I kept a list of those who had had a turn. At the beginning of choice time we selected two vets and four secretaries for the day. For the first half hour a vet and two secretaries played, while the other three did their I CARES. They reversed the procedure for the second half hour. (There was room for everyone to be pet owners as often as they liked.)

As the children played, they added new materials and procedures. For example, they placed chairs and books in the waiting room. During shared literacy one day we decided that our veterinarian office would specialize in domestic animals only. This led to classifying our classroom library according to domestic, farm, woodland, plains, and jungle animals, and placing only stories about domestic animals in the waiting room. The secretaries gave the owners a slip of paper to take up to the vet when they were called. The vet wrote out prescriptions for the pets and used instruments from play doctor kits brought from home. We tore up fabric and used wood from the recycle materials in the art area for bandages and splints.

The children shared what they were learning as they incorporated it into their play. They also wrote thank you letters to the vet, drawing a picture and dictating to me something that they learned on their visit. Before we sent the letters, they read their sentences to their classmates as part of a language experience exercise. We also made a big book entitled *Veterinarian Party*, an innovation on *The Monsters' Party* (Cowley). In answer to the repeated question, "What does this veterinarian do?" our text read: "She sets bones, that's what this veterinarian does."

Building Community Through Problem-Solving

As children develop dramatic play environments, they learn about the world around them. They expand their knowledge of social studies and science as they apply the conventions and processes of different sign systems and modes of expression. They learn how to solve problems and come to consensus through the natural and authentic experiences that arise during play.

I have found that the use of dramatic play environments has minimized discipline problems and disruptive behavior in my kindergarten primarily because when children are engaged in work and play that is meaningful to them, they act responsibly and with integrity. They want to solve problems and arguments so they can get on with their play. As they work through the immediate problem, they acquire life-skill strategies to use throughout their lifetime.

During the veterinarian environment one day there was a great deal of noise and confusion in the waiting room. I called everyone to the rug and as we went around the circle, children told their version of what was going on. Emily summed up the problem by commenting, "Well, people are fooling around because we are having to wait too long in the waiting room!" (This authentic problem is one we all meet from time to time in our adult lives.) We then discussed appropriate waiting-room behavior that we notice when we go to the doctor, and came up with alternative things to do there, such as draw, read, and talk quietly. The class decided to try these alternatives rather than limit the number of pet owners allowed at one time.

Another whole class discussion focused on a problem in the examining room. Children reported that sometimes the owners were taking the vet's instruments and acting as if they were the vet. First, anyone who wanted to comment on the problem was given the chance. Next we discussed how they and their parents act when they go to the pediatrician. This seemed to solve the problem, although from time to time we did need to recall and review our discussion.

As we started our farm environment many of us were distracted by the sound of many cats meowing. It was disturbing the teaching and learning going on in the rest of the classroom and was encour-

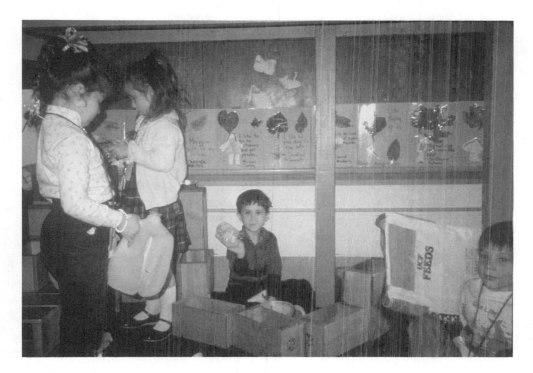

Figure 19-3 The farm

aging cat fights rather than farm play. Our group discussion led to listing different farm animals (and farmers) and deciding how many of each animal we should have on our farm. I made signs for each and we hung them with clothespins on a rope on the loft. Children selected an animal and wore the sign clipped to a piece of yarn around their neck (see Figure 19-3). This control of the number and kinds of animals helped guide productive, focused farm play. Over time the environment became a dairy farm and the children incorporated into their play some of the information in *The Milk Makers*, by Gail Gibbons, which I read to the class. It also included a vegetable garden, which generated our next environment, a greenhouse.

Suggestions for Dramatic Play

The following suggestions, which come from kindergarten teachers throughout the country, might generate ideas for your classroom. Once you decide on an environment topic, ask the children for suggestions and create it together.

- Pizza parlor. Have waiters set the tables and take the orders from the customers. The chefs make the pizza. They can use cardboard rounds, which are painted red, and add cheese, pepperoni, onions, mushrooms, etc., made out of construction paper.

- Habitats. Create different habitats in various play areas, with animals, plants, and terrain appropriate to the ecosystem.
- Weather station. Make a very simple weather station, with clipboards, weather graphs, thermometers, graph paper, crayons, pencils, a phone, and a desk.
- Airport. Set up an airport and get materials and props from one of the airlines.
- Tent camping. Put up a tent with camping materials— cups, forks, candles, flashlights, lanterns, sleeping bags, fishing pole, nets, and a camera.
- Thrift shop. Stock the store with "yard sale" items brought from home that the children can "buy" and keep. First sort and price the items in $1.00 increments. For a week everyone gets $2.00 a day to spend at the store during choice time. They can buy something outright or put it on "layaway." The teacher acts as head cashier and helps the other cashiers make change and write receipts. At the end of the week have a "clear-a-rama" sale.
- Post office area. Create a post office area in the classroom with a rural mailbox and mailboxes for each child. In the beginning of the year the area is filled with paper, envelopes, stamps, a classroom directory with the children's names and pictures, and as the year goes on add new supplies such as a box of trimmed greeting cards, scraps of paper, card stock, and happy birthday and get well cards. In the morning and during free-choice time the children can copy prepared messages or write their own, and mail them to classmates or take them home to family and friends.

Summary

This chapter has focused on dramatic play environments as a meaningful curriculum model for kindergarten. Play shouldn't be confined to the dramatic play area of the classroom, just as reading and writing shouldn't be limited to those areas. Many teachers put book boxes and writing baskets filled with different sizes and colors of both lined and unlined paper, pens, markers, and pencils in all the areas of the classroom, including art, music, sand table, blocks, and workbench. Reading and writing in one area generates reading and writing in another as children take on different roles. Regardless of the curriculum model the teacher chooses, children will generate play.

For Further Reading

Cordeiro, Pat. 1995. *Endless Possibilities: Generating Curriculum in Social Studies and Literacy*. Portsmouth, NH: Heinemann.

Creswell, Jeff. 1997. *Creating Worlds, Constructing Meaning: The Scottish Storyline Method*. Portsmouth, NH: Heinemann.

Gardner, Howard. 1983. *Frames of Mind: The Theory of Multiple Intelligences*. New York: Basic Books.

Glover, Mary K. 1997. *Making School By Hand*. Urbana, IL: National Council of Teachers of English.

Manning, Gary, Maryann Manning, and Roberta Long. 1994. *Theme Immersion: Inquiry-Based Curriculum in Elementary and Middle Schools*. Portsmouth, NH: Heinemann.

Short, Kathy, Jerome C. Harste, with Carolyn Burke. 1996. *Creating Classrooms for Authors and Inquirers*. 2d edition. Portsmouth NH: Heinemann.

Epilogue to the
Second Edition

Teachers today are facing intensifying professional and social demands. Among other things, they must respond to children who come to school hungry, homeless, and feeling unsafe, manage large class sizes with no adult assistance, adhere to growing school-wide curriculum requirements with few resources and limited time, and prepare their students for increasing state and national assessment tests and standards. In spite of these demands, teachers continue to do everything they can to support the emotional, social, intellectual and physical well-being of their students. They treat them as individuals who come into their classrooms day after day, eager to learn, to be cared for, and to be loved.

As we move into the twenty-first century, how do teachers continue to maintain effective and rigorous learning in their classrooms in the midst of increasing stress and pressure? Inside the classroom they take the time to sing songs, laugh, and listen to children. Outside the classroom they give themselves permission to climb a mountain, read a novel, go to a concert, develop a new hobby, and enjoy some solitude. They nurture themselves as well as the children so there will be joyful learning for all.

As Joy Cowley says in a letter to teachers in *Whole Learning: Whole Child.* "So thank you, dear teacher, for all the knowledge and love you are investing in future generations. Like Atlas, you carry the world on your shoulders, and at times you will be aware of the weight. But don't allow an occasional negative response to damage your faith in yourself. You are a remarkable person doing the greatest job on this earth" (1994).

Epilogue to the First Edition

My first exposure to reading as a process was during the course I took at Lesley College in 1984 with Don Holdaway and Mary Snow. I had been teaching for fifteen years and had never really defined what reading meant to me. I believed that it was good to read to kids and that letters and sounds were very important. After all, that's what kindergarten teachers were supposed to teach, so that the children would be "ready" for "real" reading in the basals and be able to "do" phonics workbooks in first grade.

The course, entitled "The Evaluation of Emergent and Initial Readers," started me thinking about reading as a process of constructing meaning from print. I read *Foundations of Literacy* (Holdaway 1979), *Essays into Literacy* (Smith 1983), *The Early Detection of Reading Difficulties* (Clay 1985), and *Reading, Writing, and Caring* (Cochrane, Cochrane, Scalena, and Buchanan 1984), and started applying this new knowledge as I began to watch the children in my classroom.

I made copies of "Observations for a Reading Development Continuum" (in Cochrane, Cochrane, Scalena, and Buchanan 1984) and "Stages of Development in a First-year Programme" (in Holdaway 1979, p. 107) and placed them on my desk. I asked individual children to use my pointer and read me a big book they knew and liked. After they read, I would go over to my desk and try to match the characteristics described by Cochrane and Holdaway to the reading behaviors I had just observed. I'd record the title of the book, the reading stage that I felt most accurately described the child's reading, and any informal observations I had made. I would also watch children during shared reading and during choice time when they were reading independently, and record what they did.

As I read, watched, and learned, I noticed that I was making up my own terms for different reading behaviors. They described more closely what I understood the children were doing, so I began writing them on the assessment forms I had created and referring to them during parent conferences and conversations with colleagues.

One day I realized that I couldn't have reading process going on in my classroom without writing process. So I read *Writing: Teachers and Children at Work* (Graves 1983) and *Lessons from a Child* (Calkins 1983). I started the children writing every day, and I included demonstrations of writing during shared reading.

It is a process for me, just as learning is a process for the children I teach. I know that these descriptors, as well as many of the classroom procedures I have described, will continue to change as I read, attend workshops, talk with other teachers, and work with the children in my class.

My hope is that teachers will be helped by this book to accept the challenge to examine their belief systems, to carry out research in their classrooms, and to develop their own classroom routines, activities, and strategies; reading, writing, and math descriptors; and checklists. Most of all I hope that the teachers reading this book will also go beyond their classrooms and share their teaching beliefs and practices with others. That's what it's all about.

Appendices

Appendix A
Reproducible Forms

NAME _____ DATE _____

WHAT I HAVE SHARED

MY PICTURE

A.1 Sharing Form

© 1998 by Bobbi Fisher from *Joyful Learning*, rev. ed. Portsmouth, NH: Heinemann

A.2 Masks

A.3 Developmental Reading Stages Form

THE IMPORTANT THING

ABOUT _____

IS THAT

_____

_____

_____

_____

_____.

BUT

THE IMPORTANT THING

ABOUT _____

IS THAT

_____.

A.4 Innovation of The Important Book

JOB INTERVIEW

1. Your name: _____

2. Your job: _____

3. Why is your job important?
    a) _____
    b) _____
    c) _____
    d) _____

4. What are some of the important things that you do in your job?
    a) _____
    b) _____
    c) _____
    d) _____

5. Why is the office at your job important? (For example, for
    answering the telephone, ordering materials, printing materials.)
    a) _____
    b) _____
    c) _____
    d) _____

6. What do you like about your job? _____
    _____

7. Would you be willing to visit the class and share what you do at
    your job? _____

8. Is there anything you can send in from your job to share with the
    class? _____

A.5 Job Interview Form

© 1998 by Bobbi Fisher from *Joyful Learning*, rev. ed. Portsmouth, NH: Heinemann

CELEBRATING ME

HERE I AM

Name:	Address:
Birthday:	My Family:
My Pets:	
My mom is from:	My dad is from:

THESE ARE A FEW OF MY FAVORITE THINGS

Book: Food:

TV Show: Game:

Color: Animal:

My collections:

My interests:

What I like to do inside:

What I like to do outside:

How I am like other people:

How I am different from other people:

What I want to do when I grow up:

The most special thing about me:

A.6 Celebrating Me

	Interest in Books	Retells a story	Watches text during Shared Reading	Recognizes name	Recognizes other's names	Recognizes upper case letters	Recognizes lower case letters	Sound/symbol Correspondence	School/class library	Reading stage

A.7 Class Assessment Profile: Reading

© 1998 by Bobbi Fisher from *Joyful Learning*, rev. ed. Portsmouth, NH: Heinemann

	Interest in writing	Elaboration of drawing	Drawing tells a story	Spelling stage	Reads back own writing	Writes a sentence	Writes first name	Writes last name	Pencil grip and direction	Uses some lower case letters

A.8 Class Assessment Profile: Writing

© 1998 by Bobbi Fisher from *Joyful Learning*, rev. ed. Portsmouth, NH: Heinemann

	Interest in math	Develops own ideas	Counts to ___	Recognizes numbers	Writes numbers	One-to-one correspondence	Conserves number	Uses math language	Creates patterns	Classifies

A.9 Class Assessment Profile: Math

NAME_____   TEACHER_____

Key: 1= Most of the time   2= Some of the time   3= Not noticed yet
    *= Has full command   += In control   o= Needs time

READING ASSESSMENT Date				
• Interest in books				
• Retells a story				
• Watches text during shared reading				
• Recognizes name in various contexts				
• Recognizes other children's names				
• Recognizes upper case letters				
• Recognizes lower case letters				
• Sound/symbol correspondence				
• School/class library				
• Reading Stage				

WRITING ASSESSMENT

• Interest in writing				
• Elaboration of drawing				
• Drawing tells a story				
• Spelling stage				
• Reads back own writing				
• Writes a sentence				
• Writes first name				
• Writes last name				
• Pencil grip and direction				
• Uses some lower case letters				

MATH ASSESSMENT

• Interest in math				
• Develops own ideas				
• Counts to___				
• Recognizes numbers				
• Writes numbers				
• One-to-one correspondence				
• Conserves number				
• Uses math language				
• Creates patterns				
• Classifies				

A.10 Individual Assessment Profile

A.11 Class Checklist

© 1998 by Bobbi Fisher from *Joyful Learning*, rev. ed. Portsmouth, NH: Heinemann

A.12 Anecdotal Class Grid

Name of Child _____ Date _____

Name of Interviewer _____

A. General warm-up questions

1. What are some of the things that you like to do?

2. What are some of the things that you can do well?

3. What kinds of stories do you like best?

4. What is your favorite book? Books? Why?

5. What special book or kind of story would you like me to read in school and/or get for our classroom library?

READING

B. Being read to at home

1. Are you read stories at home?

2. How many a day?

3. Who reads to you?

4. When are you usually read to?

5. Where are you read to?

6. Who picks the stories, you or the reader or both?

7. What do you do while you are being read to?

C. General reading knowledge

1. What is reading?

2. Who do you see who reads? What are they reading?

3. Why do people read?

4. What are they doing while they read?

5. What do good readers do?

6. Can people learn to read by themselves?

D. The child's reading

Can you read? Tell me about it. (If the child answers "yes," ask questions 1–8. If the child answers "no," ask questions 9–12.)

A.13 Beginning of the Year Reading and Writing Interview

1. What can you read?

2. When did you learn to read?

3. How did you learn to read?

4. Did someone help you learn to read or did you learn by yourself?

5. When you are reading and come to something you don't know, what do you do?

6. What goes on in your head when you read?

7. Can you read a book you have never heard before?

8. Was it easy or hard to learn to read?

9. What do you do when you look at books?

10. Can you tell in your own words the story of a book you know?

11. How do you think you will learn to read?

12. Will it be easy or hard to learn to read?

WRITING

E. General writing knowledge

1. What is writing?

2. Who do you see who writes?

3. What are they writing?

4. Why do people write?

5. What are they doing when they write?

6. What do good writers do?

F. The child's writing

Most children believe they can write. If necessary, I explain that writing can be scribbling, writing random letters, writing the letters that they hear in a word, inventive spelling, and more conventional forms.

1. What can you write?

2. When did you learn to write?

3. How did you learn to write?

4. When you are writing and come to something you don't know, what do you do?

5. What goes on in your head when you write?

1. Tell me about your reading.

2. How did you learn to read?

3. What did we do in school to help you read?

4. Which helped you the most, the songs and charts, the big books, or both?

5. Which was the most important big book (or chart) for you? Why?

6. What other big books were helpful to you?

7. Which big books can you read?

8. What other books can you read?

9. Did having to read a book during work time every day help? How?

10. Did you learn more about reading from shared reading, from independent reading time, or both?

11. Did you learn to read more from reading by yourself or with a friend?

12. Can you read a book you have never read before?

13. Could you read before you came to kindergarten?

14. Do your parents know that you can read? How do they know?

15. Can you write?

16. Which can you do better, read or write?

17. Did writing every day help you to read? How?

18. Do you think everyone in this class can read? Write? How do you know?

A.14 *End of the Year Reading and Writing Interview*

Name				Tel. No.
	Strengths	Areas for Growth	Parent Goals for School Year	
Intellectual				
Social				

Conference Times

Most Convenient Times	Least Convenient Times

A.15 Parents' Goals Form

© 1998 by Bobbi Fisher from *Joyful Learning*, rev. ed. Portsmouth, NH: Heinemann

Kindergarten News Week of	
Monday	**Tuesday**
Wednesday	**Thursday**
Friday	**Notices**

A.16 Weekly Newsletter

PARENT CONFERENCE PLANNING FORM

Child's Name:_____ Parent's Name_____
Date:_____
Time:_____

Introductory Comments

• Social Competency
• Intellectual Competency

Primary areas for discussion

• Social
• Intellectual

Specific plans to support growth and development

• Social
• Intellectual

Follow-up contact with parents

A.17 Parent Conference Planning Form

WEEKLY PLANNING

Week of

Special notes and plans
Dramatic Play Environment

Monday
Special notes and plans
Shared Reading
Choice

Tuesday
Special notes and plans
Shared Reading
Choice

Wednesday
Special notes and plans
Shared Reading
Choice

Thursday
Special notes and plans
Shared Reading
Choice

Friday
Special notes and plans
Shared Reading
Choice

A.18 Weekly Planning Sheet

DAILY PLANNING SHEET

Date

Notes, Plans, Specialists, Visitors

Community Circle Time
Opening Story

Shared Reading		
Text	Strategy/Skill	Artifact

Choice Time
Teacher choice   I CARES
Reading
Writing
Math
Other
Student Choice
Dramatic Play Environment

Sharing Time

End of Day
Outside Play
Story

A.19 Daily Planning Sheet

✓	Date	Title	Name

A.20 Library Book Sign-out Sheet

Appendix B
Letters and Charts

September

Dear Children and Parents,

Mrs. Fisher found me at a little store in Vermont during her vacation this summer, when she was spending a week at a lake with her husband and two children.

Now that school has begun, she has suggested that I spend a night with the children in her kindergarten class. I have come with a toothbrush so I can brush my teeth, and a journal so you can write about what we did together at your house.

Since a different child will be expecting to take me home each night, please be sure that I come to school each day. Also, I don't want to miss what is going on in school.

Your friend,

Mr. Bear

B.1 Letter Accompanying Mr. Bear

Who would like to mask . . . ?

- a letter they know
- a word they know
- the letter with which their first/last name begins
- a letter in their name
- their favorite letter
- the letter with which their friend's name begins
- the letter _____
- the letter with the sound _____
- the letter before _____
- the letter after _____
- the letter between _____ and _____
- a lowercase _____
- an uppercase _____
- a small word
- a medium-sized word
- a large word
- a word with one [two, three, and so on] letters
- a word that begins with _____
- a word that ends with _____
- a word with the blend _____
- the word _____
- a word that means about the same as _____
- a word that is the opposite of _____
- a compound word
- a color word
- an action word
- the name of a person, place, or thing
- a word with the ending *ing* [*ly, ed*, and so on]
- a period [question mark, quotation marks, and so on]
- the contraction for "I am"
- the first word on the page we are going to read
- the last word on the page we are going to read

B.2 Masking Questions

Homes

- Apartment
- Farm
- House
- Trailer

Offices and Factories

- Architect's office and construction site
- Bank
- Chicken farm/hatchery
- Doctor's office
- Invention factory
- School office
- Space center
- Veterinarian's office
- Science laboratory

Public Service

- Fire station
- Highway department
- Hospital
- Library
- Police station
- Post office
- Town dump
- Town Hall

Recreation Areas

- Aquarium
- Bowling alley
- Children's museum
- National Audubon Farm
- Zoo

Stores and Shops

- Department store
- Farm stand
- Greenhouse and nursery
- Grocery store
- Ice cream parlor
- Restaurant
- Shoe store
- Book store

Demonstration

- Field trips
- Speakers
  expert in the field
  another student in the school
  middle or high school student
  another teacher in the school
  parent
- Artifacts
- Filmstrip, movie, video, computer program
- Books, magazine and newspaper articles
- Songs, poems, and chants

Participation

- Children interacting with the demonstration
- Class discussions
- Children participating by
  telling what they know
  sharing what they notice
  asking questions
  bringing in artifacts and books

Role-play/Practice

- Setting up and playing in environments
- Artwork
  constructions
  drawings and paintings
- Writing reports, stories
- Science investigations
- Applying math
- Musical activities

Performance

- Inviting people to visit the environment
- Displaying artwork in the rooms, halls, school library, town library
- Publishing books, pamphlets, newspapers
- Displaying scientific investigations
- Putting on a play for another class, parents, the school, senior
  citizens

B.4 Dramatic Play Environment Planning Guide

Haynes School Kindergarten
Sudbury, Massachusetts

August

Dear [name of child],

School will be starting in a few weeks, and I hope you are as excited about our year together as I am.

On Thursday, September 6th, you will be coming to school on the kindergarten bus with your mom and/or dad or a friend. Mrs. Kurth, the kindergarten assistant, and I will meet the bus and show you to our room.

When we get to the classroom, first, please look for the I CARE hook board in the reading area of the room. Hang a white I CARE on the hook under your name to show everyone that you are here. Also, sign in on the piece of paper on the green table. I am sure you can remember to do this every day when you come to school.

Next, look around the room and find a card with your name on it. Bring it to me so I can meet you and learn your name. If you have a nickname, please let me know.

Have your mom or dad weigh and measure you (shoes off, please) and record the results on the chart near the scale. At the end of the year, we will see how much you have grown.

Then, explore our classroom, choose something to do (you can paint, build with blocks, play in the loft, and so on) and meet some of the new friends you will be with throughout the year.

Before you take the bus home, you will meet Mr. Delani, the school principal, and have some juice and cookies while I talk with your parents.

See you soon!

Love,

Haynes School Kindergarten
Sudbury, Massachusetts

August

Dear Parents,

Welcome to the Haynes School Kindergarten. Mrs. Kurth, the kindergarten assistant, and I are anticipating a stimulating and happy year with your children.

Please plan to take the kindergarten bus with your child on Thursday, September 6th. This will assist the bus driver in learning the route and help your child feel safe and secure about getting to and from school.

When you get to the classroom, please help your child be successful in the tasks I have suggested in the enclosed letter. Also, a packet of forms with your name on it will be waiting for you. These may be filled out immediately or sent back to us with your child the following day.

You are invited to borrow a book or article on parenting and other issues relating to young children. This material will be displayed in the classroom and available throughout the school year.

During this orientation day, while the children are getting to know Mr. Delani, the principal, we will have the opportunity to meet together. At that time I will briefly describe the kindergarten program and answer questions. Particular items that I will cover include the following areas:

1. SNACK. Your child may bring a simple snack each day. (A snack should take no more than five minutes to eat.)

2. CLOTHING. Whenever possible, we will be going outside to play, so please have your child dress accordingly. In order to foster independence, select coats and boots that your child can handle with the least amount of assistance from adults. (Please label clothing with name tapes.)

3. TRANSPORTATION. If you are going to pick your child up or if she/he is to get off the bus at a different stop, you must send a note each time stating the change.

4. BIRTHDAYS. We love them and are happy to celebrate if you wish to send a special snack for everyone. (You do not need to let us know in advance.)

5. TEACHER CONTACT. If you need to get in touch with me, call the school office or send a note. I will get back to you promptly.

I look forward to meeting you on the 6th, and working with you throughout the year.

Sincerely,

B.6 *Welcoming Letter to Parents*

In class

- Plan a project (art, science, math, language) and work with small groups of children.
- Help with a teacher-planned project.
- Cook. We have some utensils, large cookie sheets, school ovens, and a hot plate. We would appreciate it if you would bring the ingredients and the recipe written on a large piece of paper.
- Read with children.
- Act as a scribe for class books.
- Sew. Help children make pillows or sleeping bags for their stuffed animals.
- Take pictures of class events and activities.
- Share a hobby or tell about your job.
- Other _____

At home

- Bake for class celebrations.
- Use your computer to type ready-to-publish books the children have written.
- Use your computer to type "About the Author" bibliographies that the children have dictated in class. I will print multiple copies for each child.
- Copy "About the Author" bibliographies on chart paper.
- Mend torn dress-up clothes.
- Get recycled materials from the Children's Museum.
- Get recycled paper from Flexcon in Spencer, Massachusetts.
- Other _____

Name: _____

Throughout the year we can use the following items:

- Recycled materials for the art area
- Wood for the workbench
- Yogurt containers for paint
- Writing supplies (envelopes, paper, wallpaper, leftover note cards)
- Paper (a variety of sizes, colors, and textures, including computer paper)
- Fabric, yarn, felt, large needles for sewing
- Dress-up clothes
- Appliance boxes
- Cardboard boxes
- Games and puzzles
- Other (use your imagination)
- Suggestions for local field trips (perhaps where you have a personal connection or interest)

B.8 Contributions from Home

September

Dear Parents,

Parents often ask me to suggest books that address various aspects of child growth and development. In order to respond to this need, I have set up a classroom lending library.

   The "Bibliography of Books for Parents" describes the books I have available to lend. Please look it over and send me a note requesting the book(s) you would like to borrow. Also, as the year goes on, please let me know if there are other books you would like to read.

   Please try to return the books within two weeks, so they can circulate among the more than forty families represented in the two kindergarten classes.

Sincerely,

B.9 *Letter to Parents on Lending Library*
© 1998 by Bobbi Fisher from *Joyful Learning*, rev. ed. Portsmouth, NH: Heinemann

Focus on grapho-phonics

- The word has two vowels.
- The word has an *e*.
- The word does not have the vowel *u*.
- The word has four letters.
- The word has one part [claps, syllables].
- The word does not have two [three] parts.
- The word does not end with a vowel.
- The word does not have a set of double letters.
- The word does not have an /i/ sound at the end
- The word ends with a /r/ sound.
- The word ends with an *r*.

Focus on semantics

- The animal is a mammal.
- The animal is not an insect.
- The animal has fur.
- The animal has paws.
- The animal does not hop.
- The animal cannot fly.
- The animal is bigger than a bunny.
- The animal is smaller than a horse.

B.10 Sample Predicting Statements
© 1998 by Bobbi Fisher from *Joyful Learning*, rev. ed. Portsmouth, NH: Heinemann

1. **Introducing the book and activating prior knowledge**
   - Discuss the subject of the book.
   - Tell about personal experiences.
   - Show the children artifacts mentioned in the book
   - Relate the book to poems and other fiction and nonfiction.
   - Involve the children through puppets, music, and drama.

2. **Predicting through discussion of the cover of the book**
   - Use the suggestions above but relate them specifically to the book's title and the illustrations on the cover.
   - Write the title on the board and discuss print concepts (number of words, number of letters, common spelling patterns, upper- and lowercase letters).

3. **Talking through the book**
   - Use the suggestions above but relate them specifically to the text and the illustrations on the page.
   - Encourage the children to use the language in the book.
   - Write words on the chalkboard that might be difficult for the children when they read independently.
   - Discuss selected print conventions (letters, upper- and lowercase letters, words, common spelling patterns, high-frequency words, spaces between words, punctuation).

4. **Reading individually**
   - If appropriate, ask the children to point as they read so you can assess their progress.
   - Demonstrate reading strategies.
   - Work with individuals as needed by holding their fingers, helping them point, reading with them, helping them apply cueing systems (looking at pictures, beginning sounds, etc.).
   - Assess for immediate teaching and to plan future instruction.

5. **Sharing with the group or in pairs**
   - Read the story together.
   - Read the story in pairs.
   - Talk about the story.
   - Have each child read a favorite page.
   - Talk about what children noticed as they read.
   - Discuss reading strategies the children used.
   - Relate story to other books and to personal experiences.

B.11 Sample Guided Reading Procedures
© 1998 by Bobbi Fisher from *Joyful Learning*, rev. ed. Portsmouth, NH: Heinemann

Appendix C

Supplies and Materials for the Classroom

This section lists most of the supplies and materials that are referred to in this book. A list of professional resources for ordering materials follows. Please keep in mind that I don't put all the materials out at once, but add supplies and artifacts as the interests and needs arise from the children. I also encourage the children to contribute to the classroom environment. For example, they are encouraged to lend games, books, and props for the dramatic play environments and to bring in recycled materials for the art area.

Reading Area

The reading area is a very important place in my room. Aside from shared and independent reading, it is the place where we gather together as a classroom community to share what is important in our lives, to plan for choice time, to talk about what we have done during the day, and to get ready for clean-up. Therefore, I have listed the supplies that go along with all the activities that take place in the area (reading, calendar, I CARE board clean-up chart, and sharing table) in this section. Many of the big books and supportive readers are available in Spanish.

Furniture and Storage
   Author's chair
   Book shelves
   Box to hold big books
   Containers for storing books (according to author, genre, subject) in place of shelves. I use plastic dishpans, files, crates, and cardboard boxes.
   Display shelf for books
   Pillows

Pocket chart
Rocking chair
Sharing table
Teaching easel

Supplies

Books
Chalkboard, chalk, eraser
Chart paper, with and without lines. One of my favorites is
    24" × 36" tagboard.
Dry-erase board, markers, eraser
Framing materials (highlighter tape, sticky notes, masks
    [see Appendix A-5])
Musical instruments (bells, drums, rhythm sticks, tam-
    bourines)
Overhead projector and screen
Pointers (I have them available for the children to use dur-
    ing choice time.)
Puppets
Tape recorder, book and song tapes
Writing utensils: pen, pencils, markers, crayons

Listening Area

Headphones
Song tapes and copies of the songs
Story tapes and copies of the accompanying book. I store
    each tape and book in a sealable plastic bag.
Table and chairs for three to six children
Tape recorder

Management Materials

Alphabet chart
Birthday chart
Calendar
Charts indicating number of school days
I CARE board area. Mine is a 40' × 60' pegboard that serves
    as the back of a shelf in the art area. On it I hang
        I CARE board with name labels and a hook for each
            child
        I CARE circles: about 30 each of white, green, yellow, red,
            blue, and orange, hanging from six pegboard hooks
        Index cards with each child's name in alphabetical order
            indicating the leader of the day

Large I CARE in each color to indicate which I CARES
are to be done on a given day
Clean-up chart
Weather chart

Books

My Ten Favorite Big Books from the First Edition

Brown Bear, Brown Bear What Do You See? Bill Martin, Jr., and
John Archambault. (Holt)
Dan the Flying Man. Joy Cowley. (Wright Group)
The Enormous Watermelon. Brenda Parkes and Judith Smith.
(Rigby)
I Am Freedom's Child. Bill Martin Jr. (DLM)
Greedy Cat. Joy Cowley. (Richard C. Owen)
Hairy Bear. Joy Cowley. (Wright Group)
I Like the Rain. Claude Belanger. (Rigby)
The Little Red Hen. (Scholastic)
Mrs. Wishy-washy. Joy Cowley. (Wright Group)
Who's in the Shed? Brenda Parkes (Rigby)

Other Favorites of Mine and the Children

The Circus Is in Town. Claude Belanger. (Rigby)
Farm Concert. Joy Cowley. (Wright Group)
Fire! Fire! Said Mrs. McGuire. Bill Martin, Jr. (Harcourt Brace)
I Was Walking Down the Road. Sarah E. Barchas. (Scholastic)
The Little Yellow Chicken. Joy Cowley. (Wright Group)
Monday, Monday, I Like Monday. Bill Martin, Jr. (Holt)
Number One. Joy Cowley. (Richard C. Owen)
One Cold Wet Night. Joy Cowley. (Wright Group)
Teddy Bear. Nellie Edge. (Nellie Edge)
What Shall I Do? (DLM)

My Ten Favorite Big Books Published in the 1990s

Ants Ants, Ants. Norma Gentner. (Wright Group)
Bear Facts. Norma Gentner. (Wright Group)
Chickens. Diane Snowball. (Mondo)
Creature Features. David Drew. (Rigby)
Goodnight, Goodnight. Brenda Parkes. (Rigby)
Gravity. Norma Gentner. (Wright Group)
Morning, Noon, and Night: Poems to Fill Your Day. Selected by
Sharon Taberski. (Mondo)
The Three Billy Goats Gruff. Retold by Betty Jane Wagner
(SRA)

This Is the Bear. Sarah Hayes. (Candlewick Press)
Zoo Looking. Mem Fox. (Mondo)

Trade Books—A Variety of the Following:
Biography
Information books
Informational storybooks
Poetry
Storybooks

Texts from the Following Genres:
ABC books
Almanacs
Atlases
Counting books
Dictionaries
Different languages
Fables
Fairy tales
Magazines
Newspapers
Plays
Poetry books
Science books
Social studies books
Song books

Readers with Supportive Texts for Emergent and Initial Readers
Book Bank (Wright Group)
Book Shop (Mondo)
Books for Young Learners (in English and Spanish) (Richard C. Owen)
Literacy 2000 (in English and Spanish) (Rigby)
Literacy Tree (in English and Spanish) (Rigby)
Little Celebrations (Celebration Press)
Ready to Read (Richard C. Owen)
Story Box (in English and Spanish) (Wright Group)
Sunshine Series (in English and Spanish) (Wright Group)
Twig Books (in English and Spanish) (Wright Group)
Visions: African-American Experiences (Wright Group)
Voyagers (SRA)

Favorite Song Tapes

The Color Song and *Together Again.* Paul Ippolito (Box 128, Chester, VT, 05143).

Family Tree. Tom Chapin.

Friendship Train. Jim Valley.

Kids Songs. Nancy and John Cassidy.

Rise and Shine. Raffi.

Teaching Peace. Red and Kathy Grammer.

This Pretty Planet. Peter and Mary Alice Amidon. (8 Willow Street, Brattleboro, VT 05303)

You'll Sing a Song and I'll Sing a Song. Ella Jenkins.

Writing Area

Although most of the writing materials are stored in this area, it is important to put paper and writing utensils in all areas of the room.

Furniture and Storage

Box for recycled paper

Bulletin board where children can display their work

Desk, which we call "The Quiet Table," where a child can work alone

File box and folders where children file their work

Message board

Post boxes

Shelves for paper and writing materials

Table and chairs

Upper- and lowercase alphabet on a bulletin board at eye level for the children to see and touch

Paper

Colored and white

Different sizes

Envelopes, canceled stamps, advertisement stamps, and stickers

Greeting cards and postcards

Lined and unlined

Memo pads

Notebooks

Paper stapled together into books

Recycled computer paper

Sticky notes

Writing Utensils

Ball point pens
Colored pencils
Crayons (primary and standard size)
Lead pencils (primary and standard size)
Markers (I put these out for special occasions because I
   don't have a big supply and they get used up quickly. I
   also want the children to use crayons because I like the
   effect and control they provide.)

Other Supplies

Alphabet, upper- and lowercase (alphabet strips, card with
   pictures of initial sound)
Class list (I hang one on the bulletin board and laminate
   several others so the children can use them when they
   are writing.)
Date stamp and stamp pad
Letter, number, and design stamps
Rulers
Scissors
Stapler/staples

Math Area

Furniture, Storage, and Supplies

Floor space
Numerals 1 through 10 on a bulletin board at eye level for
   the children to see and touch
Paper and pencils
Shelves to store math manipulatives and games
Table and chairs

Favorite Math Manipulatives

Attribute blocks
Chip trading
Color cubes
Counters (animals, chips, teddy bears)
Cuisenaire Rods
Dice
Geoboards
Pattern blocks
Recycled materials for sorting and patterning
Tangrams
Unifix Cubes

Other Math Manipulatives
Beads/strings
Board games (Connect Four, tic tac toe, checkers, memory)
Dominoes
Number puzzles
Parquetry blocks
Pegboards/pegs
Puzzles

Unit Blocks
Animals (circus, jungle, farm, woodland)
Blocks for six children
Books (about buildings, construction, transportation; if the children start building farms, we add farm books)
Paper, pencils, crayons for making signs and writing plans
People (multicultural families, community workers, other occupations)
Road signs
Storage shelf
Vehicles (airplanes, boats, cars, spacecraft, trucks)

Science Area

Water Table
The water table can be filled with Styrofoam, sand, artificial rice (I try to use food only for eating, not for playing), tennis balls, you name it. See *Sand and Water* (Beaty and De Rusha) for an extensive list.

Boats
Books about water, water life, shells, and boats
Graduated cylinders, measuring cups, buckets, pitchers
Paper, pencils, and crayons for writing signs and recording experiments
Plastic transparent water tub that fits on a table
Sand and water wheel
"Sink and float" materials found around the room
Siphons, tubing, water pumps
Soap for bubbles
Water table on legs with drain

Sand Table
Books about water animals, the beach, and the ocean
Graduated cylinders, measuring cups, buckets, and pitchers

Paper, pencils, and crayons for writing signs and recording
   experiments
Scoops, shovels, molds
Sifters and funnels
Small plastic sea animals

Other Science Supplies

Aquarium
Books and magazines
Bug boxes
Containers
Cooking utensils
Food coloring
Glass fish tank for a terrarium, or a temporary home for
   crickets, filled with soil, sticks, leaves
Magnets
Magnifying glasses
Microscopes
Plants
Prisms
Rocks
Rulers, yardsticks, and measuring tapes
Scales and balances
Seeds, pots, and soil
Thermometers
Things from nature that the children and I bring in (nests,
   shells, leaves, snake skins)

Art Area

Furniture and Storage

Bulletin board
Display table
Drying rack for paintings
Shelf to hold art supplies and recycled materials
Table and chairs
Two easels, preferably side by side with trays to hold paint
   containers

Paint

Finger paint
Tempera paint and brushes
Watercolors and brushes

Paper
Cellophane
Construction paper
Crepe paper
Finger paint paper
Foil
Mylar
Tagboard
Tissue paper
White and manila paper

Other Supplies
Colored pencils
Crayons
Cray-Pas
Markers
Paste and glue
Plasticine
Playdough
Rulers
Scissors
Stamps and stamp pads
Stapler
Stencils

Recycled Materials
Buttons
Fabric
Metal
Things found in nature
Paper
Plastic
Styrofoam
Wood
Yarn

Workbench
I put a carpet on top to muffle the hammering sound.

Construction Materials
Glue
Nails, screws, washers, nuts, bolts
Pieces of metal, pipes, wire, broken machines, and gadgets
Sand paper
Tools (hammer, saw, drill, screwdriver, wrench)

Vice
Wood

Dramatic Play Environments

Most of the equipment for dramatic play environments is already available in the classroom, can be found at home, or can be made from recycled materials at school. For example, when we set up the veterinarian's office, children brought in stuffed animals, old sheets for bandages, and collars from home. They made an X-ray machine and a thermometer in the art area. I also keep in mind possible themes as I order kindergarten supplies, attend yard sales, and find things around the house.

Big Blocks and Trucks
Highway signs
Hollow blocks
Large trucks that the children can sit on and ride

Housekeeping (Materials to Reflect Many Cultures)
Dolls
Dress-up clothes
Furniture
Kitchen utensils
Reading and writing materials (newspapers, coupons, writing paper, notepads for lists)
Telephone and telephone book

Snack Table and Chairs

Outside Play

Large Equipment
Cart that holds two children
Jungle gym
Riding trucks
Sandbox
Seesaw
Swings
Wagon that holds three children

Small Equipment
Balls
Jump ropes
Sand toys

Appendix D
Learning from
Each Other

At workshops I have given throughout the country, teachers have shared with me activities and strategies that have been successful in their classrooms. Many teachers wrote down classroom ideas that have worked for them. This appendix describes some of their ideas that are particularly appropriate to kindergarten. Throughout the appendix, I have tried to retain each teacher's voice and spirit.

Although I refer to parents here, for some children the significant caregivers may be other relatives, such as grandparents, aunts and uncles, foster parents, and in some cases close family friends.

Materials and Supplies

Velcro boundaries
Put colored loop Velcro, instead of masking tape, on the rug to mark areas and boundaries or to create Venn diagrams on the floor.

Umbrella display
Display students' writing and pictures from umbrellas. This is a great way to utilize high ceilings.

Pipe displays
Use PVC pipe to hang materials such as charts, art easels, and murals, or to use for big book stands. (See Figure D-1.)

Shoe bag storage
Use the pockets of a shoe bag to store a variety of things: puppets, pointers, mystery objects, or number games.

Big Book Holder

6 U joints used

2 connecting joints used

D-1 Pipe Displays

Storing and Hanging Charts

Hanging charts with Velcro
Attach a Velcro strip all across the top of your chalkboard and put
the opposite Velcro pieces on the back corners of charts.

Writing with dry-erase markers
Laminate the charts that you want to write on over and over again.
Use a dry-erase marker and erase with nail polish remover or a spe-
cial solution made for dry erasing.

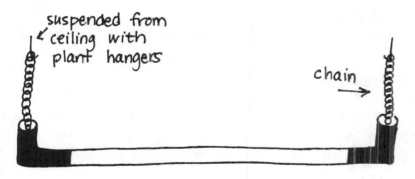

suspended from
ceiling with
plant hangers

chain

Hang charts over pipe from hangers.

Drill holes and use thick clothesline rope. Loop it around the metal bars by the ceiling tiles.

Overheads

Make overheads of favorite songs and poems. The children can use pens to highlight different parts of the text. The overheads can be used again and again.

Pointers

A variety of pointers

Use feather pointers, back scratchers, wands, little sticks that come in new shoes, or wooden spoons. The children like to pick their own pointer to keep track of print when they "read the room."

Decorative erasers
Create unusual erasers by attaching decorative erasers to the ends of many dowels.

Special pointers for special texts
Make special pointers for certain poems and songs. Some examples are a paper sun stapled onto a tongue depressor for "Mr. Sun," or a paper rainbow for "The World Is a Rainbow." My class loves them and it motivates them to point and read.

Flashlight
Use a flashlight to spotlight letters and words.

Writing Materials

Storing magic markers
Make "marker sticks" to store markers. Drill holes in a piece of wood to match the size of Crayola Classic Markers. Glue the lids into the holes, and when they dry put the markers in. This keeps the markers fresh. In one year seven sets of markers served twenty-four children. (See Figure D-2.)

Color coded date stamps
Change the date stamp pad color each month. September could be green, October orange, November brown, December red. This will help you find things easily.

Building Community

Caring About Each Other

Kindness journals
Maintain a kindness journal in which children write and draw about acts of kindness they have observed or done both in the classroom and at home. Sometimes the teacher can contribute to it.

The Ouch Book
Have children write or draw about their scrapes, bumps, and bruises in *The Ouch Book*. This gives them a chance to express their feelings and cuts down on whining and little complaints. Some will write nearly every day.

The Wiggly Tooth Book
Develop writing skills using those very important loose teeth that children always want everybody to know about. *The Wiggly Tooth Book*

marker
caps set
in glue

marker

cap

Wood

D-2 Storing Magic Markers

provides a place for children to write and draw in and then share
with teacher and classmates.

Reading sofa
Furnish the reading center with a small child-sized sofa. Each day
two children can choose a book and the teacher can read to them,
sitting between them on the sofa. As the year goes on, the children
can read short predictable books to the teacher.

Sign-in and Attendance

First and last name sign-in
Make up a master sheet with the names of the children at each
table group, and create a new master each time the seating
arrangement changes. Every day, have children sign in at their tables. Using a new copy of the same master each day gives the children a model to follow.

Vary the contents of the master throughout the school year.
During the first part of the year, the master might list first names

only. By the middle of the year, the master might list first and last names. At the end of year, the master could be blank and the children be expected to write their names on their own. This is wonderful for showing the children's development during the school year. (See Figure D-3.)

Computer names

Make a computer class list in very large print so that it is several pages long. The list should be in alphabetical order, with a line after each name where the children can sign in. At the beginning of the school year this helps those who are not yet able to recognize their names. Later, different fonts can be used so the children see their names written in different kinds of type. They can either copy the font or write their names in their usual handwriting.

Dry-erase marker

Have a large board with two sections labeled Home and Here. Write each child's name on a plastic-coated name card, large enough for students to write their own names underneath with a dry-erase marker. The children then hang their cards on hooks under Here. At the end of the day they erase their names and place the card back under Home.

Sorting sign-in

Hang two pocket charts by the door. One side is labeled Home and the other School. First, the children find their names on the home side and move it to the school side. On the school side you can sort the names in various ways. In the beginning of the year you might sort by sharing groups. Later, you can sort by using the alphabet. For example, the children can put their names in a *yes* or *no* column by answering a question such as "Do you have an *a* in your name?" After you have gone through the alphabet, you could sort by all kinds of other things. Often, children will come up with categories on their own: hair or eye color, shoe types, shoelaces or Velcro, suspenders or belts, long or short sleeves, and the like. (See Figure D-4.)

Mr. Bear

Writing briefcase

Send Mr. Bear home with a writing briefcase filled with crayons, pencils, markers, and paper for the children to use while he is visiting.

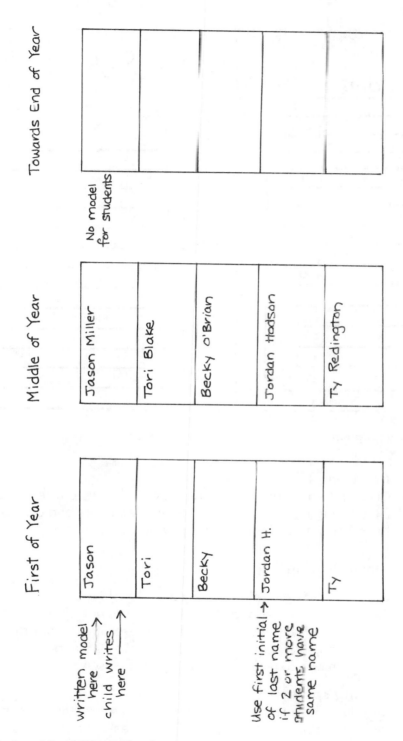

Towards End of Year

No model
for students

Middle of Year

Jason Miller

Tori Blake

Becky O'Brian

Jordan Hodson

Ty Redington

First of Year

Jason

Tori

Becky

Jordan H.

Ty

written model
here →
child writes
here →

Use first initial →
of last name
if 2 or more
students have
same name

D-3 First and Last Name Sign-in

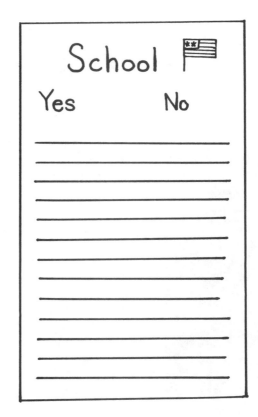

D-4 Sorting Sign-in

Book bag
Give Mr. Bear a book bag of favorite class books to take home. The child taking the bag home can select a few books and can also ask the other children for reading suggestions.

Class Meetings

Class meeting
Call a class meeting once a week to discuss how things are going. Talk about what is going well and solve conflicts from the classroom or playground. Often you can role-play situations to help the kids learn how to take responsibility for themselves.

Feeling sponges
Introduce three large sponges: red for anger, blue for sadness, yellow for happiness. Explain them at three separate circle times. Each child might hold a sponge and tell about a feeling. The sponges can be used at different times when there is a need to verbalize feelings or solve problems between children.

Sharing with a friend

Say, "It looks like we have a lot to say about this Take a minute or two to share your ideas with friends around you." It seems there is never enough time to listen to everything that children have to share, and this approach helps when there is a lot of talking about a subject during group time. The children feel validated and they all get a chance to express themselves.

Doughnut circle sharing

Have students sit in two circles, one within the other. The students in the center circle sit facing out, so that each one faces a student from the outer circle. They may spend a few minutes sharing and talking with each other. Then those in the middle rotate to the right one spot so everyone has a new person to talk with. This is a great way for everyone to have a chance to share important events in their lives.

Problem Solving

Talker/listener chairs

Mark one chair *Talker* and another one *Listener*. When kids have a problem, they can discuss it in these chairs. Each child gets a turn in both chairs. Children often do a great job of working things out and the teacher seldom has to intervene.

Negotiation table

Designate a negotiation table where children can sit to talk over conflicts and arrive at solutions.

The Record Keeper Book

When children want to tell about conflicts concerning themselves or other children, ask them to fill out a page in *The Record Keeper* Book. They name the incident, write the date, time, and location, and describe what happened. Later the teacher can talk with everyone involved.

The End of the Day

Clean-up song

Play a song (about three minutes long) on the tape player at clean-up time. The kids will memorize the song after about a week, and it gives them a time frame within which to clean. I love not having to nag or quiet them down to direct them to clean up.

Daily, weekly, and yearly review

At the end of each day write about what you did and learned that day. The next morning at group time reread what you wrote. By the end of the week you will have a class story, and at the end of the year a class book. Some years you might make weekly copies for the children to take home. Other years you might prefer to wait until the end of the year and make a book of all the weekly stories.

Review and a look ahead

Each day do a review of the classroom's news and events. You might also include something that will happen the next day. Children are always eager to know what they can look forward to the following day.

Individual review

At the end of every day ask the children to draw or write about something special they did at school. At the end of the week invite the children to take their work home. In this way their families learn about what is going on at school and receive a weekly writing sample.

Language Arts

Innovations and Extensions

I Like the Rain (Belanger 1988)

> I like the rain,
> I like the rain,
> R-A-I-N
> I like the rain.

Encourage children to create many innovations for this song: I like to jump, skip, read, swim, ride, bike, walk, talk, do math, go east, go west, come, boss, find, cook, sing, kick, meet, peek, care, hide, race, bowl, kiss, love, and play. Put the words on cards. In that way it is easy to rearrange the words, add more, put them in alphabetical order, sort them phonetically, put them into different categories, and so on. One day we wanted to end with the longest word we could think of. Margaret thought of "pretend," but later in the day she came up with "subtract." The next day we classified by number of syllables, which initiated an interesting discussion of why all the words except subtract had only one syllable. Another day we classified the words in nouns, verbs, and adjectives, and that led us to wonder why all the words we had come up with could be classified as verbs.

"Old MacDonald"

Make a friendship book based on "Old MacDonald." The asterisk indicates where to fill in a unique trait of the friend.

My friend Mary had a *smile. F-R-I-E-N-D
And with her smile she made new friends. F-R-I-E-N-D
With a new friend here and a new friend there
Here a friend, there a friend
Everywhere she makes friends F-R-I-E-N-D

Use "Old MacDonald" also to teach the vowels:

Old MacDonald had some vowels. A-E-I-O-U.
And on his farm he had a cat
With an *a, a* here, and an *a, a* there
Here an *a*, there an *a*, everywhere an *a, a*
Old MacDonald had some vowels. A-E-I-O-U

Mary Wore Her Red Dress (Peek)
On the first day of school, give the children an 11″ × 18″ sheet of paper with the outline of a human figure. They can draw their features and what they are wearing and the teacher can add the text, writing the color word in that same color. For example, "Linnea wore her blue [write *blue* in blue color] jeans, blue jeans, blue jeans, Linnea wore her blue jeans on the first day of school."

Time for Bed (Fox)
Ask the kids to paint something to say good night to. Attach a sentence strip and display the drawings on the wall before putting them together in a book. For example, "It's time for bed, little ————, by Renee."

Bear Facts (Gentner)
On large paper write the text from *Bear Facts* and leave blanks wherever there is specific information about bears. Using facts about different animals, such as horses or rabbits, the children explain how to fill in the blanks. A lot of research goes into these projects. (Variation: Make copies with the blanks and have the children fill in their own stories.)

You might create a bulletin board outside your room entitled "Oh did you know, did you know, did you know?" Children may post any news and include an illustration. For example, news could be that Dustin is six, Reeva lost her first tooth, Nevil and Mariel are friends, Mrs. Martin is proud of the books her class made, two and two equals four, or London is the capital of England. The news items can be left up for a while and then placed in a class book to sing the news as a group. These items can also be part of a class newsletter each Friday in a "Oh, Did You Know" column.

At the end of the year you can write First Grade Facts and sing, "Oh yes we know, yes we know, yes we know that . . . we can read books, Africa is a continent," and so on.

Group Writing

News journal

Write a news journal with your students. Include things that happen in the classroom, news about losing teeth, and information about pets. At the end of the month you will have a beautiful big book to add to your library.

Interactive writing activity

About twice a week, do an interactive writing activity based on a book you have just read. Discuss the important ideas and the vocabulary the author has used and come up with a sentence about the book. The teacher can write some of it and the class leader can write some of it. This enables the teacher to demonstrate the way in which a word is written, word spacing, phonics, punctuation, and sentence structure. A group of children can add illustrations and these can be put into a class book.

Whole class stories

To make whole class stories, write the words in enlarged print and have some of the children illustrate them. Sometimes you can make a little book. Either make copies for the children to illustrate or have the children copy the words themselves. Read these over and over so the children learn the stories.

Reading/Writing Connection

Reading the room

Hang up all of the song, poem, and daily news charts and have the children go to these when they "read the room." They can work in pairs, one using a pointer and pointing to different texts and the other wearing special "glasses" and reading.

Writing the room

Invite children to take a clipboard and go around the room writing down different things, sometimes at random and sometimes by category (such as all the words beginning with a certain letter).

Class writing logs

Leave writing logs (I use three-ring binders with clear plastic covers, which the children illustrate) with different titles around the room. The children enjoy writing in these journals throughout the day and sharing with their friends what they have written. Some of the writing logs our class has are *Pet Peeves* (observations of pet activities, both in class and at home), *Terrific Trips* (details of places and people), *Movie Madness* (descriptions and reviews of movies), *Tell a Joke*, and *Tooth Tales*.

Audiotaping poems

Type up the poems read in class and then have the children illustrate them. They can read the poems aloud into a tape recorder, and at the end of the year the children will have a recording of their reading progress and an accompanying poetry anthology.

Letters, Words, and Sounds

Alphabet swat game

First, write the alphabet in large letters on two big (3' × 3') pieces of butcher paper, putting about half the alphabet on each page. Then, remove the centers of two fly swatters and decorate the swatters with glitter and sparkly streamers. To play the game, one child calls out a letter and holds up a card showing that letter. Two children, each holding a fly swatter, kneel in front of the butcher paper and swat the letter when they find it.

Teaching the alphabet

To teach the alphabet, take green, yellow, and red electrical tape and place it under the alphabet. I use green for letters A through I, yellow for letters J through Q, and red for letters R through Z. A child picks a letter and asks, "Is it at the beginning, middle, or end of the alphabet?"

Letters and names

Introduce most letters of the alphabet by reading and spelling everyone's name. Laminate a card with each child's name and randomly choose five or six a day to spell and read. After a while the children associate the letters with familiar names. All lessons can be taught in English and in Spanish.

Name book

Early in the year, make an alphabet book featuring the letters in all the students' names. Start at the beginning of the alphabet and add two or three letters a day. On a teaching easel put a large piece of paper with an upper- and lowercase letter at the top. Give the children their name cards. If you are working on the letter *a*, ask, "I'm looking for an *a*. Does anyone have an *a* in their name?" Write each name on the paper and have each child come up and highlight the letter *a* in his or her name.

Sign language and finger spelling

Use American Sign Language with songs and texts. Signing helps children learn phonemic awareness. In addition, the teacher can finger spell with the children. The class can learn songs, words, the alphabet, and numbers. My kids love it; they teach their own families and also teach other classes in our school.

One teacher's approach

A kindergarten teacher in Alabama shares some of the meaningful classroom activities that help her students learn about letters.

> I don't do "letter of the week." I have found that a combination of other things seems more appropriate.
>
> Early in the year, as the children are learning to write their names, we talk about the beginning letters, looking to see how many names begin with the same letters and then graphing our findings. Gradually, as clay, paint, collage materials, and templates are introduced in the art center, we use them to explore different ways to make the letters that start children's names. In other areas of the room, plastic, wooden, or magnetic letters are available for sorting. More activities continue to be added all year.
>
> We explore alphabet books and then some children decide to make one of their own. Everyone is welcome to contribute pages for their "initial" letter. Soon we add the other letters as well. The kids make a variety of alphabet books throughout the year, including whole alphabet books, letters-only books, books using a different medium or technique on each page (print making, rubber stamps, chalk, rubbings, collage, finger paint), theme alphabet word or picture books, alphabet riddle books, or adaptations of other alphabet books.
>
> We make charts for the word wall with words that begin with the same letter. We also make phone books including all of our names, addresses, and phone numbers (including mine), and talk about the need for alphabetizing.
>
> We learn to make our own dictionaries. I give the children books of blank pages with a letter written on each page. Every time they get a new word, they write it in their dictionary on the proper page. Gradually, they notice that they have more words on some of the pages. We share and discuss our findings.

I introduce "key words" and the children keep their favorite words on index cards on a key ring. Later in the year, after each child has collected a number of words, they take the words off the rings and sort them. Many sort by initial letter, some alphabetize by the first letter, and others categorize in others ways, such as by topic or letter length. The children often work in pairs and discuss the activity as they go along.

Reading

Audiotape assessment

Give all the children their own audiotape. Periodically they can record the date and title of a favorite book and then read either the entire book or short selection. Accept whatever reading is appropriate for them. In the beginning of the year it will often be a retelling but as the year goes on you will get a more specific indication of their reading development.

Backpack reader program

Sponsor a "backpack reader" program, in which the children select books to take home each day from a special group of predictable language books in the classroom. Hang a chart on the door with a book pocket for each child. Each day children can choose books from the backpack reader shelf, sign the library cards in the back of the books and place the cards in their door pockets, and put the books in their backpacks to take home to read with their families. The next day, as they come into class, they pick up the cards from their pockets and put them back in the books, return the books to the shelf, and pick out new ones. Having the chart on the door prompts children to return their books and sign out new ones. Although the children only have to sign their names, the cards become running records of what books they are reading. (See Figure D-5.)

Book boxes

Create book boxes to keep books for silent reading. Cover laundry detergent boxes with contact paper and put the children's names on index cards, which they can decorate and paste on their boxes. Each week, with the teacher's help, students can choose up to fifteen books to put in their boxes: several that they can read, some challenging ones, a few magazines, and a school-mandated basal, for example. Children will love having the boxes to touch and use throughout the day. During silent reading they

D-5 Backpack Reader

can bring them to the circle; the teacher sets the timer, and the class reads.

Author book tubs

In the authors' corner, have plastic tubs for different authors' books. Decorate each tub with the name and photograph of an author, pictures of the author's books, and some of the characters (pictures can be obtained from book order flyers). The children will enjoy being able to find their favorite authors, and this project gives them the responsibility to put the books back in the right tubs. The tubs usually stay in a specific corner, but sometimes a pair of children use a tub somewhere else in the room.

Generative Curriculum

Generating Topics

Individual interests

At the beginning of the school year ask each child to bring in a list of two things that he or she would like to learn about during the year. Make a chart of all the children's interests and refer to it during the year.

Future careers

Ask the children to imagine what they are going to be when they grow up. For one or two days or a week focus on one profession. As a class, research the career and find out the actual steps that are commonly taken to achieve it. This helps students see what to expect when they choose career paths and gives them the confidence to pursue their goals. For example, you could learn what is involved in becoming a school principal or what one has to do to become a judge. Often, exploration of one profession will lead to interest in other careers; some of the children who cannot decide early in the year may be able to think of careers as the year goes on.

Group interests

Make an announcement to the class about a student's area of interest and invite anyone interested to join in on the study. This accommodates a variety of lessons and taps into the interests of the students. Usually seven to ten children join a classmate's study. For example, one day in my mixed-age bilingual classroom (K–2), a child approached me with a new book on Australian animals and wanted to know about the Tasmanian Devil. I said to the class, "Joey has asked about the Tasmanian Devil of Australia. Anyone interested in learning about it can come join us in the carpet area." At the end of that group lesson, which integrated language arts, science, social studies, and math, everyone in the group had to teach the rest of the class about the animal.

While the group lesson is occurring, the rest of the children can keep working on their own projects. That is part of their power to choose and be independent. However, I find that the rest of the class gets very quiet because they all want to listen and learn and still keep working on their projects all at the same time.

As the year goes on the children make the announcements, gather books for the study group before we begin, and take over more and more of the leadership.

Curriculum Projects

Surveys

During fire safety week make up a form with a picture of a fire extinguisher, alarm box, fire siren box, and exit sign. Walk with the children through the school and make tally marks under the ones they find.

Hug a tree

The kindergarten classes in our school were studying trees. We decided to plant three trees in front of our school because there weren't any near enough for us to watch closely every day. The kids chose what kind of tree to buy and where to plant them. We discussed the tree changes we thought we would see through the seasons; we made up a song about trees and danced around the site where the trees would be planted; then we took a trip to the local greenhouse to buy the trees. We planted them, and sang and danced again. The trees were hugged by the children as they got on the bus each day.

The Saturday after Thanksgiving our school was vandalized and two of the trees were stolen right out of the ground. Our tree was bent and cut. We were all upset, so we wrote about our feelings. Then some of the kids went out and sketched pictures of what the tree looked like and made a painting from that picture. I posted their painting and quotes about their feelings in the hall. Six children wrote a note to parents to let them know what had happened to the trees. We posted that in the hall, too.

Their writing instigated a strong reaction in our school community. A parent, who read the note, called the local news station and someone came and did a story about our trees. The nursery where we bought the trees offered to donate new ones after seeing the story on the news. People we didn't even know came to us to help and to express their caring.

Signs of spring

In the spring, grow grass in large plastic containers, which you can decorate with paper. The grass takes about three weeks to grow five inches. Observe and measure the growth each week, drawing pictures and finishing the sentence, "I noticed this week _____." Some children may bring in nests they've found and place them in their containers. Others may make springtime decorations like bunnies and eggs. They love to "mow the lawn" and cut the grass in various ways. At the end of the project they can make the grass a permanent part of their lawns at home.

Sharing

Friday at the Movies

On a roll of plain paper, which I mark off in frames, have the kids write (or dictate) a movie and illustrate the scenes. In scroll fashion "project" the movie by illuminating the back of the paper with a light bulb. These movies are viewed during "Friday at the Movies" in my class.

Parade

To show off curriculum projects that take place in your classroom, have a parade for the whole school. For example, as the culminating activity for our theme cycle on homes, we showed different types of homes that our ancestors lived in and made models of our own homes. The class was filled with photographs, pictures, our own paintings and models, and different artifacts

Communicating with Parents

Starting the School Year

Poem on a postcard
Start the school year by writing a poem on a postcard and sending it home before school starts. The same poem is on a chart when the children come on the first day.

Setting up the room
In the letter you send home to incoming students, give some dates and times when you will be setting up the classroom and invite parents and children to help. This begins community and ownership of the classroom, as people get to know each other informally.

Learning Projects

Story tape
Record a story, along with sound effects (*Noisy Nora* is a good choice), on a tape. Put the book, tape, and a parent/student comment sheet in a sealable plastic bag and send it home with a different child each night.

Puppet bags
Send home a puppet and a book to go with it. Some of these can be specific story characters, such as Clifford or Curious George. Others can be general characters, such as a pig to accompany *The Three Little Pigs*.

The writer's briefcase
Invite children to take turns bringing home a writer's briefcase, which teachers can fill with paper (lined, blank construction, computer, newsprint, fluorescent), writing instruments (pencils, markers, crayons, watercolors, colored pencils, picture and letter stamps), index cards, two sizes of clipboards, a stapler, and ideas for publishing (flip books, bound books, pop-up books). Some teachers include information for parents, such as articles about writing and reading, suggestions of materials to have at home, and

book lists. Often the children share their projects when they bring back the briefcase. One teacher wrote, "Many of my children don't have access or the availability of writing materials, and the enjoyment that families have with the briefcase has encouraged them to get some writing materials for their children at home."

Activity bags
Make a set of six or seven activity bags that children take turns bringing home (each child takes home one bag per week). The bags might contain activities relating to something you are studying in class (for example, patterning with nuts, seeds, and dried moss; a puppet and story book; magnetic letters). One teacher sends home a science bag with a simple experiment and directions. After about six weeks, when everyone has taken all the bags, you can change what is inside. The children love to help create the activities.

Family book making
Send home a blank book and suggest that the student and a family member create a story with illustrations. On the cover they write the title, author, and illustrator. Place the books in the classroom library for independent and paired reading.

Vacation diary
Children have a great deal to share when they return from long school breaks. Ask students to keep a personal diary at home to record events during their breaks. They may draw pictures or write, and include items such as photographs, menus, and travel folders. After the break, the children can share their diaries with each other before they are placed in our classroom library until the next vacation.

Autograph book
To make a class autograph book, have the children take home a page to fill out with their family. The family members sign the book, and the children either draw a picture or paste in a photograph of them. Put the pages in plastic sleeves in a loose-leaf notebook, and when it is complete the children may take turns sharing it with their families.

Home/school sharing bag
Send a canvas sharing bag home with children. In it place class books, photos from a field trip, and anything else to share with parents. When a child brings the bag back to school, he or she can include something from home to share with the class. After each child has taken the bag home, you can put new things inside and

start again. This way each child gets a special sharing day once every twenty or so days.

Sharing bag

Have children take turns taking a sharing bag home. With the family's help, each child can decide what to put into the bag and then write down three clues about it. When the child returns to school, he or she can sit in the teacher's chair and read aloud the clues. Classmates can ask questions and try to guess the contents. (Children can also say clues "out of their head" if they do not get support from home.) Many teachers send a calendar home so parents know when their child's sharing date will be. Sometimes a teacher might opt to solicit certain kinds of items such as things from nature or from the child's cultural background. Other teachers vary topics throughout the year, asking for objects related to science, personal collections, or favorite books. Often, teachers leave the subject open ended and let the children decide.

Teacher Communications with Parents

Newsletter questions

Once a week send home a newsletter to tell the parents what the class has been doing and why. Include questions parents can ask their children, phrases to use, and language to help their children open up and talk about school. You can also report on loose and lost teeth, birthday events, and other happenings at school.

Monthly newsletter

Once a month send out a kindergarten newsletter. You might take the whole day to work on it, and expect all the children to cooperate and discuss what should be included. The children can draw pictures, interview other children, and so on. At night the newsletter can be put in the computer, where a template has been set up. The pictures can be photocopied and included in the newsletter. A copy can be sent home with each child, a copy to the principal, and one to the superintendent. I always include

- a "Ten Best List" chosen by the children (ten favorite cafeteria foods, ten books we like, ten things we like to do at school)
- a list of upcoming events, holidays, birthdays, and new babies in the family
- themes for the month with drawings by the children (for example, "Ocean Sea Picture by Miguel")

- children's reviews of a favorite book or a special thing they learned
- news of parent volunteers
- parent contributions (perhaps recipes)
- a personal anecdote

Overnight express

Every night have the children take home clear plastic envelopes with their names on them. The envelopes might contain notices, books, and notes, and the children should bring them back to school every day. Parents will rely on getting the envelope and the children will learn the beginning responsibilities of homework: taking something home and bringing it back to school.

Home/school notebooks

Use spiral notebooks as communication tools between parents and teachers. The children can turn them in every morning, and the teachers can check for messages and set aside time to write during their free period in the day. (Teachers might write in a few notebooks every day.) Teachers could also send hand-outs from the office and other notices in the notebooks, giving teachers and parents a dated record of communication.

Leave me a message

Have a paper and pencil available on a desk near the door to the classroom. When parents come into the room to tell you something during class time, ask them to write it down so you can remember it. This frees you from conversations with parents when you want to be talking with the children.

Student-led parent conferences

Four times a year teach the children to lead the parent conferences. They can take their parents to the different areas of the room (reading, writing, math, science, art, dramatic play), show their work, and tell their goals for the next months. In each area, post questions for the parents to ask that the children have been prepared to answer, such as, How did you get better at reading? What strategies do you use when you get stuck on a word? How has your writing changed? What are some of the ways the blocks help you add and subtract? What have you learned from observing the gerbils? What did you have to know to make your art construction? Parents will enjoy this special time with their children and get a very clear picture of what they are doing in school, and the children will get a great deal out of the experience.

Parents in the Classroom

Open house

Involve families and students during open house in a productive and enjoyable routine. Create a checklist of activities with the children, and give every child a copy. The students can then guide their family members to various activities and check off each activity when completed. This way, during the busy social time you can make sure that students share important aspects of the class community with their families. (See Figure D-6.)

Welcome

☐ Writing Folder

☐ Pet gerbil

☐ Pattern Blocks

☐ Big Books

☐ U.S.A. Puzzle

☐ Discovery Lab

☐ Clay Table

☐ Play environment /
    Greeting card factory

D-6 Open House

Helper suggestions

Post a brightly colored paper with a generic list of things that parent helpers can do, such as fill the stapler, make some blank writing books, or fill the glue bottles. Parents look to see what needs to be done when they come in to help.

Kid watching

Encourage parents to participate in classroom procedures. When they come to visit, provide them with a "kid watcher" form to fill out. This helps them focus on important things that the teacher wants them to notice (use of phonics, attention to concepts about print, interests of the children) and gives the teacher some feedback. This very successful strategy also gives parents a better understanding of all the teaching and learning that is going on.

Family traditions

Invite parents to join us at our morning meeting and share a family tradition with the class. The class can interview them and ask questions. (Variation: Guest storytellers, scientists, politicians)

Including the school community

Invite members of the school community to come in and read their favorite picture books. The children can generate a list of people and help schedule the visits. After the visit, a child can write (or dictate) a review of the book and draw a picture. Mount the review and photograph of the visit on construction paper and make a book of the visits.

Lunch with the teacher

Invite a child and his or her parents to have lunch in the room with you. They will love the calm of the class and it's a way to spend quality time with each child. You can even put a tablecloth and other decor of the child's choice on the table.

Bibliographies

My Favorite Children's Books

Ahlberg, Janet, and Allan Ahlberg. 1978a. *Each Peach Pear Plum*. New York: Scholastic.

———. 1978b. *The Jolly Postman*. New York: Scholastic.

Aker, Suzanne. 1990. *What Comes in 2s, 3s, and 4s*? New York: Simon and Schuster.

Alborough, Jez. 1992. *Where's My Teddy*? Cambridge, MA: Candlewick.

Angelou, Maya. 1993. *Life Doesn't Frighten Me*. New York: Stewart, Tabori and Chang.

Anno, Mitsumasa. 1977. *Anno's Counting Book*. New York: Thomas Y. Crowell.

Arnold, Tedd. 1987. *No More Jumping on the Bed*. New York: Dial.

Arnold, Tedd. 1992. *The Signmaker's Assistant*. New York: Dial.

Asch, Frank, and Vladimir Vagin. 1989. *Here Comes the Cat!* New York: Scholastic.

Avison, Brigid. 1993. *I Wonder Why I Blink and Other Questions About My Body*. New York: Kingfisher Books.

Aylesworth, Jim. 1992. *Old Black Fly*. New York: Henry Holt.

Baer, Gene. 1989. *Thump, Thump, Rat-a-Tat-Tat*. New York: Harper and Row.

Bagert, Brod. 1997. *Gooch Machine: Poems for Children to Perform*. Honesdale, PA: Boyds Mill Press.

Baskwill, Jane. 1989. *Pass the Poems Please*. Halifax, NS: Wild Things Press.

Bayer, Jane. 1984. *A My Name is Alice*. New York: Dial.

Baylor, Byrd. 1986. *I'm in Charge of Celebrations*. New York: Scribner.

Bedard, Michael. 1992. *Emily*. New York: Doubleday.

Blumenthal, Deborah. 1996. *Chocolate-Covered-Cookie Tantrum*. New York: Clarion.

Branley, Franklyn. 1986a. *Air Is All Around You*. New York: Harper and Row.

———. 1986b. *Snow Is Falling*. New York: Harper and Row.

———. 1986c. *What Makes Day and Night*? New York: Harper and Row.

Brett, Jan. 1989. *The Mitten*. New York: G. P. Putnam.

———. 1992. *The Trouble with Trolls*. New York: G. P. Putnam.

Brown, Margaret Wise. 1947. *Goodnight Moon*. New York: HarperCollins.

———. 1949. *The Important Book*. New York: HarperCollins.

Brown, Ruth. 1981. *A Dark Tale*. New York: Dial.

Browne, Anthony. 1989. *The Tunnel*. New York: Knopf.

Bucknall, Caroline. 1988. *One Bear in the Picture*. New York: Dial.

Bunting, Eve. 1989. *The Wednesday Surprise*. New York: Clarion.

———. 1991. *Fly Away Home*. New York: Clarion.

Burningham, John. 1985a. *Colors*. New York: Crown.

———. 1985b. *John Burningham's 1 2 3*. New York: Crown.

———. 1996. *Shopping Basket*. Cambridge, MA: Candlewick.

Burton, Virginia Lee. 1942. *The Little House*. Boston, MA: Houghton Mifflin.

————. 1976. *Mike Mulligan and His Steam Shovel*. Boston, MA: Houghton Mifflin.

Cannon, Janell. 1993. *Stellaluna*. New York: Harcourt Brace.

Carle, Eric. 1981. *The Very Hungry Caterpillar*. New York: Philomel.

————. 1990. *The Very Quiet Cricket*. New York: Philomel.

————. 1993. *Today Is Monday*. Philomel. New York.

————. 1996. *Little Cloud*. New York: Philomel.

Carlson, Nancy. 1994. *How to Lose All Your Friends*. New York: Viking.

————. 1996. *Sit Still!* New York: Viking.

Chase, Edith Newlin. 1996. *Secret Dawn*. Buffalo, NY: Firefly Books.

Christelow, Eileen. 1996. *Five Little Monkeys with Nothing to Do*. New York: Clarion.

Christensen, Bonnie. 1994. *An Edible Alphabet*. New York: Dial.

Cohen, Miriam. 1967. *Will I Have a Friend?* New York: Macmillan.

Conrad, Pam. 1989. *The Tub People*. New York: Scholastic.

————. 1996. *The Rooster's Gift*. New York: HarperCollins.

Day, Alexandra. 1989. *Carl Goes Shopping*. New York: Farrar, Straus and Giroux.

DePaola, Tomie. 1989. *The Art Lesson*. New York: G. P. Putnam.

————. 1996a. *Baby Sister*. New York: G. P. Putnam.

————. 1996b. *Strega Nona*. New York: G. P. Putnam.

de Regniers, Beatrice. 1988. *Sing a Song of Popcorn*. New York: Scholastic.

Diller, Harriet. 1996. *Faraway Drawer*. Honesdale, PA: Boyds Mill Press.

Dorros, Arthur. 1991. *Follow the Water from Brook to Ocean*. New York: Harper and Row.

————. 1992. *This Is My House*. New York: Scholastic.

Dunrea, Olivier. 1989. *Deep Down Underground*. New York: Macmillan.

Duvoisin, Roger. 1962. *Our Veronica Goes to Petunia's Farm*. New York: Knopf.

Eastman, P. D. 1960. *Are You My Mother?* New York: Random House.

————. 1961. *Go Dog Go!* New York: Random House.

Ehlert, Lois. 1987. *Growing Vegetable Soup*. New York: Harcourt Brace Jovanovich.

————. 1991. *Red Leaf, Yellow Leaf*. New York: Harcourt Brace Jovanovich.

Ehrlich, Amy. 1993. *Parents in the Pigpen, Pigs in the Tub*. New York: Dial.

Elting, Mary, and Michael Folsom. 1980. *Q is for Duck*. New York: Clarion.

Emberley, Ed. 1967. *Drummer Hoff*. New York: Prentice Hall.

Eovalsi, Maryann. 1987. *The Wheels on the Bus*. Boston, MA: Little, Brown.

Flack, Marjorie, and Kurt Wiese. 1933. *The Story About Ping*. New York: Viking.

Fox, Mem. 1989. *Koala Lou*. New York: Harcourt Brace.

————. 1993. *Time for Bed*. New York: Harcourt Brace.

————. 1995. *Tough Boris*. New York: Harcourt Brace.

————. 1996. *Zoo-Looking*. Greenvale, NY: Mondo.

Frasier, Debra. 1991. *On the Day You Were Born*. New York: Harcourt Brace.

Freeman, Don. 1964. *Dandelion*. New York: Viking.

Geisel, Theodore. 1957. *The Cat in the Hat*. New York: Random House.

Gibbons, Gail. 1985. *The Milk Makers*. New York: Macmillan.

Giganti, Paul, Jr. 1992. *Each Orange Had 8 Slices*. New York: Greenwillow.

Greenfield, Eloise. 1972. *Honey, I Love*. New York: Thomas Y. Crowell.

————. 1991. *First Pink Light*. New York: Black Butterfly Children's Books.

Hague, Michael. 1992. *Twinkle, Twinkle, Little Star*. New York: Morrow.

Hale, Sarah Josepha. 1990. *Mary Had a Little Lamb*. New York: Scholastic.

Harley, Bill. 1996. *Sitting Down to Eat*. Little Rock, AR: August House.

Harris, Robie H. 1996. *Happy Birth Day!* Cambridge, MA: Candlewick.

Hartman, Gail. 1991. *As the Crow Flies: A First Book of Maps*. New York: Bradbury.

Hayes, Sarah. 1986. *This Is the Bear*. Cambridge, MA: Candlewick.

Heller, Ruth. 1981. *Chickens Aren't the Only Ones.* New York: Grosset and Dunlap.
———. 1991. *Chrysanthemum.* New York: Greenwillow.
Henkes, Kevin. 1996. *Lilly's Purple Plastic Purse.* New York: Greenwillow.
Hest, Amy. 1995. *In the Rain with Baby Duck.* Cambridge, MA: Candlewick.
———. 1996. *Baby Duck and the Bad Eyeglasses.* Cambridge, MA: Candlewick.
Hill, Eric. 1981a. *Spot Visits His Grandparents.* New York: G. P. Putnam.
———. 1981b. *Spot's First Walk.* New York: G. P. Putnam.
Hoban, Tana. 1989. *Of Colors and Things.* New York: Greenwillow.
———. 1990. *Exactly the Opposite.* New York: Greenwillow.
Hoberman, Mary Ann. 1978. *A House Is a House for Me.* New York: Scholastic.
Hopkins, Lee Bennett. 1988. *Side by Side: Poems to Read Together.* New York: Simon and Schuster.
Houston, Gloria. 1992. *My Great Aunt Arizona.* New York: Harper and Row.
Howe, James. 1984. *The Day the Teacher Went Bananas.* New York: E. P. Dutton.
———. 1986. *There's a Monster Under My Bed.* New York: Atheneum.
Hutchins, Pat. 1968. *Rosie's Walk.* New York: Macmillan.
———. 1972. *Goodnight Owl.* New York: Macmillan.
———. 1986. *The Doorbell Rang.* New York: Greenwillow.
Isherwood, Shirley. 1996. *Something for James.* New York: Dial.
Jeunesse, Gallimard. 1994. *Pyramids.* New York: Scholastic.
Johnson, Angela. 1989. *Tell Me a Story, Mama.* New York: Orchard.
Johnson, Dolores. 1994. *Papa's Stories.* New York: Macmillan.
Johnston, Tony. 1996. *Once in the Country: Poems of a Farm.* New York: G. P. Putnam.
Jonas, Ann. 1989. *Color Dance.* New York: Greenwillow.
Kandoian, Ellen. 1989. *Is Anybody Up?* New York: G. P. Putnam.
Kellogg, Steven. 1988. *Johnny Appleseed.* New York: Morrow.
Killilea, Marie. 1992. *Newf.* New York: Philomel.
Kinsey-Warnock, Natalie. 1992. *Wilderness Cat.* New York: Dutton.
Komaiko, Leah. 1990. *My Perfect Neighborhood.* New York: Harper and Row.
Kovalski, Maryann. 1987. *The Wheels on the Bus.* Boston, MA: Little, Brown.
Krasilovsky, Phyllis. 1993. *The Woman Who Saved Things.* New York: Tamourine Books.
Kraus, Robert. 1967. *Come Out and Play Little Mouse.* New York: Greenwillow.
———. 1970. *Whose Mouse Are You?* New York: Macmillan
———. 1986. *Where Are You Going Little Mouse?* New York: Greenwillow.
Krauss, Ruth. 1945. *The Carrot Seed.* New York: Harper and Row.
Leaf, Munro. 1988. *Wee Gillis.* New York: Viking.
Lear, Edward. 1991. *The Owl and the Pussycat.* New York: G. P. Putnam.
Legge, David. 1994. *Bamboozled.* New York: Scholastic.
LeSieg, Theo. 1961. *Ten Apples Up on Top.* Boston, MA: Random House.
Lewin, Betsy. 1996. *Chubbo's Pool.* New York: Clarion.
London, Jonathan. 1996a. *I See the Moon and the Moon Sees Me.* New York: Viking.
———. 1996b. *Let the Lynx Come In.* Cambridge, MA: Candlewick.
MacDonald, Amy. 1990. *Little Beaver and the Echo.* New York: G. P. Putnam.
Manushkin, Fran. 1990. *Latkes and Applesauce.* New York: Scholastic.
Martin, Jane Read, and Patricia Marx. 1996. *Now I Will Never Leave the Dinner Table.* New York: HarperCollins.
Martin, Bill, Jr. 1993. *Old Devil Wind.* New York: Harcourt Brace.
———. 1994. *Wizard.* New York: Harcourt Brace.
Martin, Bill, Jr., and John Archambault. 1986. *Barn Dance!* New York: Henry Holt.
———. 1988. *Listen to the Rain.* New York: Henry Holt.
Martin, Mary Jane. 1996. *From Anne to Zach.* Honesdale, PA: Boyds Mill Press.

Mayer, Mercer. 1987. *There's an Alligator Under My Bed*. New York: Silver, Burdett and Ginn.

McBratney, Sam. 1994. *Guess How Much I Love You?* Cambridge, MA: Candlewick.

———. 1996. *Dark at the Top of the Stairs*. Cambridge, MA: Candlewick

McDermott, Gerald. 1974. *Arrow to the Sun*. New York: Viking.

McDonald, Megan. 1995. *Insects Are My Life*. New York: Orchard.

Merriam. Eve. 1993. *Twelve Ways to Get to Eleven*. New York: Simon and Schuster.

Micklethwait, Lucy. 1993. *Child's Book of Art: Great Pictures, First Words*. New York: Dorling Kindersley.

Murrow, Liza Ketchum. 1989. *Good-Bye, Sammy*. New York: Holiday House.

Nikola-Lisa, W. 1994. *Bein' with You This Way*. New York: Lee and Low.

Opie, Iona, ed. 1996. *My Very First Mother Goose*. Cambridge, MA: Candlewick.

Pallotta, Jerry. 1986. *The Icky Bug Alphabet Book*. Watertown, MA: Charlesbridge.

Peek, Merle. 1985. *Mary Wore Her Red Dress*. New York: Clarion.

———. 1987. *The Balancing Act*. New York: Clarion.

Penn, Audrey. 1993. *Kissing Hand*. Washington, DC: Child Welfare League of America.

Perkin, Rex. 1948. *The Red Carpet*. New York: Macmillan.

Peterson, Cris. 1996. *Harvest Year*. Honesdale, PA: Boyds Mill Press.

Potter, Beatrix. 1901. *Peter Rabbit*. New York: Viking Penguin.

Prelutsky, Jack. 1983. *The Random House Book of Poetry for Children*. New York: Random House.

Quackenbush, Robert. 1973. *Go Tell Aunt Rhody*. New York: Lippincott.

Rogers, Fred. 1996. *Let's Talk About It: Divorce*. New York: G. P. Putnam.

Rosen, Michael. 1989. *We're Going on a Bear Hunt*. New York: Margaret K. McElderry Books.

Rounds, Glen. 1990. *I Know an Old Lady Who Swallowed a Fly*. New York: Holiday House.

Royston, Angela. 1992. *Eye Openers: Sea Animals*. New York: Macmillan.

Rylant, Cynthia. 1985. *The Relatives Came*. New York: Bradbury Press.

———. 1996. *Old Woman Who Named Things*. New York: Harcourt Brace Jovanovich.

Sampson, Michael, and Mary Beth Sampson. 1997. *Star of the Circus*. New York: Henry Holt.

Schwartz, David M. 1985. *How Much Is a Million?* New York: Scholastic.

Sendak, Maurice. 1962. *Chicken Soup with Rice*. New York: Scholastic.

Shea, Pegi Deitz. 1996. *New Moon*. Honesdale, PA: Boyds Mill Press.

Shelby, Anne. 1991. *Potluck*. New York: Orchard.

Sis, Peter. 1989. *Going Up*. New York: Greenwillow.

Slate, Joseph. 1996. *Miss Bindergarten Gets Ready for Kindergarten*. New York: E. P. Dutton.

Small, David. 1994. *George Washington's Cows*. New York: Farrar, Straus and Giroux.

Smith, Sarah. 1995. *The Library*. New York: Farrar, Straus and Giroux

Snowball, Diane. 1995. *Chickens*. Greenvale, NY: Mondo.

Steig, William. 1969. *Sylvester and the Magic Pebble*. New York: Trumpet Club.

Stevenson, Robert Louis. 1990. *My Shadow*. New York: G. P. Putnam.

Stoeke, Janet Morgan. 1994. *Hat for Minerva Louise*. New York: E. P. Dutton.

———. 1996. *Minerva Louise at School*. New York: E. P. Dutton.

Taberski, Sharon, ed. 1996. *Morning, Noon, and Night: Poems to Fill Your Day*. Greenvale, NY: Mondo.

VanAllsburg, Chris. 1988. *Two Bad Ants*. New York: Houghton Mifflin

Voake, Charlotte. 1996. *Ginger*. Cambridge, MA: Candlewick.

Waddell, Martin. 1991. *Farmer Duck*. Cambridge, MA: Candlewick.

———. 1992. *Owl Babies*. Cambridge, MA: Candlewick.

———. 1994. *When the Teddy Bears Came*. Cambridge, MA: Candlewick.

———. 1996. *You and Me, Little Bear*. Cambridge, MA: Candlewick.

Wagner, Betty Jane. 1997. *The Three Billy Goats Gruff*. Columbus, OH: SRA.

Walsh, Ellen Stoll. 1989. *Mouse Paint*. New York: Harcourt.

Ward, Cindy. 1988. *Cookie's Week*. New York: G. P. Putnam.

Wells, Rosemary, 1973. *Noisy Nora*. New York: Scholastic.

Wescott, Nadine. 1988. *The Lady with the Alligator Purse*. Boston, MA: Little, Brown.

———. 1990. *There's a Hole in the Bucket*. New York: Harper.

Wickstrom, Sylvie. 1988. *The Wheels on the Bus*. New York: Crown.

Wolcott, Patty. 1991. *Where Did That Naughty Little Hamster Go?* New York: Random House.

Wood, Don, and Audrey Wood. 1984. *The Napping House*. New York: Harcourt Brace Jovanovich.

Yashima, Taro. 1983. *Crow Boy*. New York: Puffin.

Yolen, Jane. 1987. *Owl Moon*. New York: Philomel.

Young, Ed. 1992. *Seven Blind Mice*. New York: Philomel.

Zemach, Margot. 1976. *Hush Little Baby*. New York: E. P. Dutton.

Professional Resources

Books and Resources for Teachers and Children

Candlewick Press
2067 Massachusetts Avenue
Cambridge, MA 02140
(617) 661-3330

Carol Hurst's Children's Literature
    Site
http://www.carolhurst.com

Celebration Press
1900 East Lake Avenue
Glenview, IL 60025
1-800-792-0550

Heinemann
361 Hanover Street
Portsmouth, NH 03801-3912
1-800-793-2154

Henry Holt and Company, Inc.
115 West 18th Street
New York, NY 10011
(212) 886-9200

Mondo Publishing
One Plaza Road
Greenvale, NY 11548
1-800-230-3650

National Council of Teachers of
    English (NCTE)
1111 Kenyon Road
Urbana, IL 61801
1-800-369-6283

Nellie Edge
Resources for Creative Teaching
P. O. Box 12399
Salem, OR 97309
(503) 399-0040

Newbridge Educational Programs
P. O. Box 984
Hicksville NY 11802-0984
1-800-867-0307

Outside the Box, Inc.
P. O. Box 16751
Seattle WA 98116
(206) 932-1598

Richard C. Owen Publishers, Inc.
135 Katonah Avenue
Katonah, NY 10536
1-800-336-5588

Rigby Education USA
P. O. Box 797
Crystal Lake, IL 60039-0797
1-800-822-8661

Scholastic, Inc.
P. O. Box 7502
Jefferson City, MO 65102
1-800-325-6149

SRA/McGraw-Hill
220 East Danieldale Road
DeSoto, TX 75115
1-800-843-8855

Stenhouse
P. O. Box 360
York, ME 03909-0360
1-800-988-9812

Wright Group
19201 120th Avenue N.E.
Bothell, WA 98011-9512
1-800-523-2371

Professional Organizations, Journals, and Magazines

Book Links
434 W. Downer
Aurora, IL 60506
(708) 892-4695

Horn Book Magazine
14 Beacon Street
Boston, MA 02108
(617) 227-1555

International Reading Association
    (IRA)
The Reading Teacher
800 Barksdale Road
P. O. Box 8139
Newark, DE 19714

National Association of the
    Education of Young Children
    (NAEYC)
Young Children
1834 Connecticut Avenue, N. W.
Washington, DC 20009
1-800-424-2460

National Council of Teachers of
    English (NCTE)
*Language Arts, Primary Voices, School
    Talk*
1111 Kenyon Road
Urbana, IL 61801
1-800-369-6283

National Council of Teachers of
    Mathematics (NCTM)
The Arithmetic Teacher
1906 Association Drive
Reston, VA 22091-1593
(703) 620-9840

National Science Teachers
    Association (NSTA)
1840 Wilson Boulevard
Arlington, VA 22201-3000
1-800-722-6782

The New Advocate
The New Advocate
480 Washington Street
Norwood, MA 02062
(617) 762-5577

Storyline Design
The Storyline Connection
333 State Street #246
Lake Oswego, OR 97034

Teaching K–8
40 Richards Avenue
Norwalk, CT 06854
1-800-777-8600

Professional Books for Parents

Learning Theory

Goleman, D. 1995. *Emotional Intelligence: Why It Can Matter More Than IQ.* New York: Bantam.

Healy, J. 1990. *Endangered Minds: Why Children Don't Think and What We Can Do About It.* New York: Simon and Schuster.

Oglan, G. 1997. *Parents and the Whole Language Classroom.* Urbana, IL: National Council of Teachers of English.

Smith, F. 1995. *Between Hope and Havoc: Essays into Human Learning and Education.* Portsmouth, NH: Heinemann.

Reading and Writing

Barron, Marlene. 1990. *I Learn to Read and Write the Way I Learn to Talk.* Katonah, NY: Richard C. Owen.

Clay, Marie. 1988. *Writing Begins at Home: Preparing Children for Writing Before They Go to School.* Portsmouth, NH: Heinemann.

Cowley, Joy. 1994. *Whole Learning: Whole Child.* Bothell, WA: The Wright Group.

Edwards, S. A., and R. W. Maloy. 1992. *Kids Have All the Write Stuff: Inspiring Your Children to Put Pencil to Paper.* New York: Penguin.

Gentry, Richard. 1996. *My Kid Can't Spell: Understanding and Assisting Your Child's Literacy Development.* Portsmouth, NH: Heinemann.

Graves, Donald, and V. Stuart. 1985. *Write from the Start.* New York: New American Library.

Hill, M. 1989. *Where Reading and Writing Begin.* Portsmouth, NH: Heinemann.

Martens, Prisca. 1996. *I Already Know How to Read: A Child's View of Literacy.* Portsmouth, NH: Heinemann.

Parenting

Carlsson-Paige, Nancy, and Diane E. Levin. 1990. *Who's Calling the Shots? How to Respond Effectively to Children's Fascination with War Play and War Toys.* Philadelphia, PA: New Society Publishers.

Kohn, Alfie. 1993. *Punished by Rewards: The Trouble with Cold Stars, Incentive Plans, As, Praise, and Other Bribes.* New York: Houghton Mifflin.
Trelease, Jim. 1995. *The New Read-Aloud Handbook.* 4th edition. New York: Penguin.
Walmsley, Sean, and Bonnie B. Walmsley. 1996. *Kindergarten: Ready or Not? A Parent's Guide* Portsmouth, NH: Heinemann.

Social Issues

Berliner, David C., and B. J. Biddle. 1995. *The Manufactured Crisis: Myths, Fraud, and the Attack on American's Public Schools.* Reading, MA: Addison-Wesley.
Coles, Robert. 1997. *The Moral Intelligence of Children.* New York: Random House.
Routman, Regie. 1996. *Literacy at the Crossroads: Crucial Talk About Reading, Writing, and Other Teaching Dilemmas.* Portsmouth, NH: Heinemann.

Children's Books Mentioned in the Text

Chapter 1

Archambault, John. 1989. *Counting Sheep*. Allen, TX: DLM.
Cowley, Joy. 1980. *Hairy Bear*. Story Box in the Classroom, Stage 1. San Diego, CA: The Wright Group.
———. 1986a. *The Birthday Cake*. Story Box in the Classroom, Stage 1. San Diego, CA: The Wright Group.
———. 1986b. *Mrs. Wishy-washy*. Story Box in the Classroom, Stage 1. San Diego, CA: The Wright Group.
Cowley, Joy, and June Melser. 1980. *In a Dark, Dark Wood*. Story Box in the Classroom, Stage 1. San Diego, CA: The Wright Group.
Cutting, Jillian. 1988. *Faces*. The Sunshine Series. San Diego, CA: The Wright Group.
Fox, Mem. 1984. *Wilfred Gordon McDonald Partridge*. Brooklyn, NY: Kane/Miller.
Hill, Eric. 1981. *Spot's First Walk*. New York: G. P. Putnam.
Martin, Bill Jr., and John Archambault. 1970. *I Am Freedom's Child*. Allen, TX: DLM.

Chapter 2

Cowley, Joy. 1987. *The Teeny Tiny Woman*. Crystal Lake, IL: Rigby.
———. 1988. *Greedy Cat*. New York: Richard C. Owen.
Old MacDonald. 1989. Needham Heights, MA: Silver, Burdett and Ginn.
Parkes, Brenda, and Judith Smith. 1986. *The Enormous Watermelon*. Crystal Lake, IL: Rigby.

Chapter 3

The Little Red Hen. 1985. New York: Scholastic.
Martin, Bill Jr. 1995. *Fire! Fire! Said Mrs. McGuire*. New York: Harcourt Brace.

Chapter 4

Aliki. 1968. *Hush Little Baby*. New York: Simon and Schuster.
The Gingerbread Man. 1984. Crystal Lake, IL: Rigby.

Hutchins, Pat. 1972. *Good-night, Owl!* New York: Macmillan.

Martin, Bill Jr., and John Archambault. 1989. *Chicka Chicka Boom Boom*. New York: Simon and Schuster.

Morris, William Barrett. 1982. *The Longest Journey in the World*. New York: Holt, Rinehart and Winston.

Weiss, Nicki. 1989. *Where Does the Brown Bear Go?* New York: Greenwillow.

When Goldilocks Went to the House of the Three Bears. Book Shelf One. New York: Scholastic.

Chapter 5

Barchas, Sarah E. 1975. *I Was Walking Down the Road*. New York: Scholastic.

Belanger, Claude. 1988. *The Circus Is in Town*. Crystal Lake, IL: Rigby.

Cowley, Joy. 1983a. *Jigaree*. Story Box in the Classroom, Stage 1. San Diego, CA: The Wright Group.

———. 1983b. *The Monsters' Party*. Story Box in the Classroom, Stage 1. San Diego, CA: The Wright Group.

Parkes, Brenda. 1986. *Who's in the Shed?* Crystal Lake, IL: Rigby.

Vaughn, Marcia. 1986. *Tails*. Bookshelf Stage One. New York: Scholastic.

Chapter 6

Cowley, Joy. 1980. *Hairy Bear*. Story Box in the Classroom, Stage 1. San Diego, CA: The Wright Group.

———. 1983. *Dan the Flying Man*. Story Box in the Classroom, Stage 1. San Diego, CA: The Wright Group.

———. 1988. *Greedy Cat*. New York: Richard C. Owen.

Cutting, Brian, and Jillian Cutting. 1988. *What Am I?* Crystal Lake, IL: Rigby.

"Five Little Monkeys." 1984. In *The More We Get Together* edited by Jack Booth. New York: Holt, Rinehart and Winston.

Hutchins, Pat. 1968. *Rosie's Walk*. New York: Macmillan.

Martin, Bill Jr. 1983. *Monday, Monday, I Like Monday*. New York: Holt.

Parkes, Brenda, and Judith Smith. 1986. *The Enormous Watermelon*. Crystal Lake, IL: Rigby.

Smith, Judith, and Brenda Parkes. 1986. *The Three Billy Goats Gruff*. Crystal Lake, IL: Rigby.

Chapter 7

Chase, Edith Newlin. 1984. *The New Baby Calf*. New York: Scholastic.

Chapter 8

Brown, Margaret Wise. 1947. *Goodnight, Moon*. New York: HarperCollins.

———. 1949. *The Important Book*. New York: HarperCollins.

Cowley, Joy. 1983a. *Dan, the Flying Man*. Story Box in the Classroom, Stage 1. San Diego, CA: The Wright Group.

———. 1983b. *Jigaree*. Story Box in the Classroom, Stage 1. San Diego, CA: The Wright Group.

Cowley, Joy, and June Melser. 1980. *In a Dark, Dark Wood*. Story Box in the Class-room, Stage 1. San Diego, CA: The Wright Group.

Goss, Janet L., and Jerome C. Harste. 1981. *It Didn't Frighten Me*. Bookshelf Stage 2. New York: Scholastic.

Locker, Thomas. 1984. *Where the River Begins*. New York: Dial.

Martin, Bill Jr. 1982. *Brown Bear Brown Bear, What Do You See?* New York: Holt.

Chapter 9

Peet, Bill. 1972. *The Ant and the Elephant*. Boston, MA: Houghton Mifflin.

Chapter 10

Branley, Franklyn, and Eleanor Vaughan. 1956. *Mickey's Magnet*. New York: Thomas Y. Crowell.

Chapter 11

Carle, Eric. 1981. *The Very Hungry Caterpillar*. New York: Putnam.

DePaola, Tomie. 1974. *Charlie Needs a Cloak*. Englewood, NJ: Prentice Hall.

Freeman, Don. 1986. *Corduroy*. New York: Viking.

Jonas, Ann. 1989. *Color Dance*. New York: Greenwillow.

Kalan, Robert. 1981. *Jump, Frog, Jump*. New York: Scholastic.

Lioni, Leo. 1967. *Frederick*. New York: Random House

Chapter 12

Bartlett, Margaret F. 1961. *The Beginning of a Brook*. New York: Thomas Y. Crowell.

Lindbergh, Ann Morrow. 1944. *Gift from the Sea*. New York: Pantheon.

Locker, Thomas. 1984. *Where the River Begins*. New York: Dial.

———. 1986. *Sailing with the Wind*. New York: Dial

Chapter 17

Cowley, Joy. 1996. *A Long, Long Tail*. Bothell, WA: The Wright Group.

Chapter 18

Biddulph, Fred, and Jeanne Biddulph. 1990. *How Spiders Live*. Bothell, WA: The Wright Group.

Coles, Robert. 1995. *The Story of Ruby Bridges*. New York: Scholastic.

Cowley, Joy. 1996. *My Home*. Bothell, WA: The Wright Group.

DePaola, Tomie. 1996. *The Baby Sister*. New York: Putnam.

Gentner, Norma. 1993. *Bear Facts*. Bothell, WA: The Wright Group.

Hayes, Sarah. 1986. *This Is the Bear*. Cambridge, MA: Candlewick.

Henkes, Kevin. 1996. *Lilly's Purple Plastic Purse*. New York: Greenwillow.

Taberski, Sharon, ed. 1996. *Morning, Noon, and Night: Poems to Fill Your Day*. Green-vale, NY: Mondo.

Wagner, Betty Jane. 1997. *The Three Billy Goats Gruff*. Columbus, OH: SRA.
Winnick, Karen B. 1996. Mr. *Lincoln's Whiskers*. Honesdale, PA: Boyds Mills Press.

Chapter 19

Conrad, Pam. 1996. *The Rooster's Gift*. New York: HarperCollins.
Cowley, Joy. 1983. *The Monsters' Party*. Bothell, WA: The Wright Group.
Gibbons, Gail. 1985. *The Milk Makers*. New York: Macmilan.
Snowball, Diane. 1995. *Chickens*. Greenvale, NY: Mondo

Appendix D

Belanger, Claude. 1988. I *Like the Rain*. Crysal Lake, IL: Rigby.
Fox, Mem. 1993. *Time for Bed*. New York: Harcourt Brace.
Gentner, Norma. 1993. *Bear Facts*. Bothell, WA: The Wright Group.
Peek, Merle. 1985. *Mary Wore Her Red Dress*. New York: Clarion
Wells, Rosemary. 1973. *Noisy Nora*. New York: Scholastic.

Professional Bibliography

Areglado, N., and M. Dill. 1997. *Let's Write*. New York: Scholastic.

Avery, C. 1993. *And with a Light Touch: Learning About Reading, Writing, and Teaching with First Graders*. Portsmouth, NH: Heinemann.

Baker, A., and J. Baker. 1990. *Mathematics in Process*. Portsmouth, NH: Heinemann.

Baratta-Lorton, M. 1976. *Mathematics Their Way*. Reading, MA: Addison-Wesley.

Barron, M. 1990. *I Learn to Read and Write the Way I Learn to Talk*. Katonah, NY: Richard C. Owen.

Beaty, S., and K. De Rusha. 1987. *Sand and Water*. Lexington, MA: Early Education Curriculum.

Bergen, D., ed. 1987. *Play as a Medium for Learning and Development*. Portsmouth, NH: Heinemann.

Berliner, D. C., and B. J. Biddle. 1995. *The Manufactured Crisis: Myths, Fraud, and the Attack on America's Public Schools*. Reading, MA: Addison-Wesley.

Bissex, G. L. 1980. *Gnys at Wrk: A Child Learns to Write and Read*. Cambridge, MA: Harvard University Press.

Bredekamp, S., and C. Copple, eds. 1996. *Developmentally Appropriate Practice in Early Childhood Programs*. Revised edition. Washington, DC: National Association for the Education of Young Children.

Bridges, L. 1995a. *Assessment: Continuous Learning*. York, ME: Stenhouse.

———. 1995b. *Creating Your Classroom Community*. York, ME: Stenhouse.

Brown, R. G. 1991. *Schools of Thought: How the Politics of Literacy Shape Thinking in the Classroom*. San Francisco, CA: Jossey-Bass.

Buchanan, E. 1989. *Spelling for Whole Language Classrooms*. Katonah, NY: Richard C. Owen.

Butler, A., and J. Turbill. 1984. *Towards a Reading-Writing Classroom*. Portsmouth, NH: Heinemann.

Calkins, L. M. 1983. *Lessons from a Child*. Portsmouth, NH: Heinemann.

———. 1994. *The Art of Teaching Writing*. New edition. Portsmouth, NH: Heinemann.

Cambourne, B. 1988. *The Whole Story: Natural Learning and the Acquisition of Literacy in the Classroom*. New York: Ashton Scholastic.

Cambourne, B., and J. Turbill. 1987. *Coping with Chaos*. Portsmouth, NH: Heinemann.

Carlsson-Paige, N., and D. E. Levin. 1987. *The War Play Dilemma: Balancing Needs and Values in the Early Childhood Classroom*. New York: Teachers College Press.

———. 1990. *Who's Calling the Shots? How to Respond Effectively to Children's Fascination with War Play and War Toys*. Philadelphia, PA: New Society Publishers.

Cazden, C. 1988. *Classroom Discourse: The Language of Teaching and Learning.* Portsmouth, NH: Heinemann.

Clay, M. 1975. *What Did I Write?* Portsmouth, NH: Heinemann.

———. 1979. *Reading: The Patterning of Complex Behaviour.* Portsmouth, NH: Heinemann.

———. 1985. *The Early Detection of Reading Difficulties.* Portsmouth, NH: Heinemann.

———. 1988. *Writing Begins at Home: Preparing Children for Writing Before They Go to School.* Portsmouth, NH: Heinemann.

———. April 1986. "Constructive Processes: Talking Reading, Writing, Art and Craft." *The Reading Teacher* 39: 764–770.

———. 1991. *Becoming Literate: The Construction of Inner Control.* Portsmouth, NH: Heinemann.

———. 1993. *An Observation Survey of Early Literacy Achievement.* Portsmouth, NH: Heinemann.

Cochrane, O., D. Cochrane, S. Scalena, and E. Buchanan. 1984. *Reading, Writing, and Caring.* Katonah, NY: Richard C. Owen.

Coles, R. 1997. *The Moral Intelligence of Children.* New York: Random House.

Cordeiro, P. 1995. *Endless Possibilities: Generating Curriculum in Social Studies and Literacy.* Portsmouth, NH: Heinemann.

Cowley, J. 1994. *Whole Learning: Whole Child.* Bothell, WA: The Wright Group.

Crafton, L. 1996. *Standards in Practice: Grades K–2.* Urbana, IL: National Council of Teachers of English.

Creswell, J. 1997. *Creating Worlds, Constructing Meaning: The Scottish Storyline Method.* Portsmouth, NH: Heinemann.

Davidson E., ed.1986. *Interaction: Teacher's Resource Book.* Crystal Lake, IL: Rigby.

Department of Education-Wellington (New Zealand). 1985. *Reading in Junior Classes.* Katonah, NY: Richard C. Owen.

DeRusha, K. 1990. *Dramatic Play.* Lexington, MA: Early Education Curriculum.

Devonshire, H. 1988. *Printing.* Fresh Start Series. New York: Franklin Watts.

———. 1990a. *Drawing.* Fresh Start Series. New York: Franklin Watts.

———. 1990b. *Moving Art.* Fresh Start Series. New York: Franklin Watts.

Doake, D. B. 1985. "Reading-Like Behavior: Its Role in Learning to Read." In *Observing the Language Learner,* edited by A. Jaggar and M. T. Smith-Burke. Newark, DE: International Reading Association.

Durkin, D. 1966. *Children Who Read Early.* New York: Teachers College Press.

Durst, S. 1988. "Oscar's Journal." In *Understanding Writing: Ways of Observing, Learning and Teaching,* edited by T. Newkirk and N. Atwell. Portsmouth, NH: Heinemann.

Duthie, C. 1996. *True Stories: Nonfiction Literacy in the Primary Classroom.* York, ME: Stenhouse.

Dyson, A. H. 1997. *What Difference Does Difference Make?* Urbana, IL: National Council of Teachers of English.

Education Department of Western Australia. 1994. *First Steps: A Program for Linking Assessment with Teaching and Learning.* Portsmouth, NH: Heinemann.

Edwards, S. A., and R. W. Maloy. 1992. *Kids Have All the Write Stuff: Inspiring Your Children to Put Pencil to Paper.* New York: Penguin.

Elkind, D. 1981. *The Hurried Child: Growing Up Too Fast Too Soon.* Reading, MA: Addison-Wesley.

Ernst, K. 1994. *Picturing Learning: Artists and Writers in the Classroom.* Portsmouth, NH: Heinemann.

Fisher, B. 1988. "Home/School Journals." In *The Whole Language Teachers Association Newsletter*. Sudbury, MA: Whole Language Teachers Association.

———. 1990. "Children as Authorities on Their Own Reading." In *Workshop* 2, edited by N. Atwell. Portsmouth, NH: Heinemann.

———. 1994. *Classroom Close-up: Bobbi Fisher: Organization and Management* Bothell, WA: The Wright Group. Videotape.

———. 1995. *Thinking and Learning Together: Curriculum and Community in a Primary Classroom*. Portsmouth, NH: Heinemann.

———. 1996. *Inside the Classroom: Teaching Kindergarten and First Grade*. Portsmouth, NH: Heinemann.

———. 1997. *Classroom Close-up: Bobbi Fisher: Developing Young Readers*. Bothell, WA: The Wright Group. Videotape.

———. 1997. *Classroom Close-up: Bobbi Fisher: Guiding Young Authors*. Bothell, WA: The Wright Group. Videotape.

Fisher, B., and P. Cordeiro, eds. 1994. "Generating Curriculum: Building a Shared Curriculum." *Primary Voices K–6* 2(3).

Fountas, I., and G. S. Pinnell. 1996. *Guided Reading: Good First Teaching for All Children*. Portsmouth, NH: Heinemann.

Freeman, D. E., and Y. S. Freeman. 1992. *Whole Language for Second Language Learners*. Portsmouth, NH: Heinemann.

Freeman, Y. S., and D. E. Freeman. 1997. *Teaching and Writing in Spanish in the Bilingual Classroom*. Portsmouth, NH: Heinemann.

Gamberg, R., et al. 1988. *Learning and Loving It: Theme Studies in the Classroom*. Portsmouth, NH: Heinemann.

Gardner, H. 1983. *Frames of Mind: The Theory of Multiple Intelligences*. New York: Basic Books.

———. 1991. *The Unschooled Mind: How Children Think and How Schools Should Teach*. New York: Basic Books.

Garland, C., ed. 1990. *Mathematics Their Way Summary Newsletters*. Saratoga, CA: Center for Innovation in Education.

Gentry, R. 1996. *My Kid Can't Spell: Understanding and Assisting Your Child's Literacy Development*. Portsmouth, NH: Heinemann.

Glover, M. K. 1997. *Making School by Hand*. Urbana, IL: National Council of Teachers of English.

Goleman, D. 1995. *Emotional Intelligence: Why It Can Matter More Than IQ*. New York: Bantam.

Goodman, K. 1986. *What's Whole in Whole Language?* Portsmouth, NH: Heinemann.

———. 1993. *Phonics Phacts*. Portsmouth, NH: Heinemann.

———. 1996. *On Reading*. Portsmouth, NH: Heinemann.

Goodman, K., E. B. Smith, R. Meredith, and Y. M. Goodman. 1987. *Language and Thinking in School: A Whole Language Curriculum*. Katonah, NY: Richard C. Owen

Goodman, Y. 1984. "The Development of Initial Literacy." In *Awakening to Literacy* edited by H. Goelman and A. Oberg. Portsmouth, NH: Heinemann.

———. 1985. "Kidwatching: Observing Children in the Classroom." In *Observing the Language Learner*, edited by A. Jaggar and M. T. Smith-Burke. Newark, DE: International Reading Association.

———. 1986. "Children Coming to Know Literacy." In *Emergent Literacy: Writing and Reading*, edited by W. Teale and E. Sulzby. Norwood, NJ: Ablex.

Goodman, K., Y. Goodman, and W. Hood. 1989. *The Whole Language Evaluation Book*. Portsmouth, NH: Heinemann.

Goodman, Y., D. Watson, & C. Burke. 1987. *Reading Miscue Inventory: Alternative Procedures*. Katonah, NY: Richard C. Owen.

Graves, D. 1983. *Writing: Teachers and Children at Work*. Portsmouth, NH: Heinemann.

———. 1994. *A Fresh Look at Writing*. Portsmouth, NH: Heinemann.

Graves, D., and V. Stuart. 1985. *Write from the Start*. New York: New American Library.

Halliday, M. 1975. *Learning How to Mean: Explorations in the Development of Language*. Baltimore, MD: Edward Arnold.

Hansen, J., and D. Graves. 1983. "The Author's Chair." *Language Arts* 60:176–183.

Harste, J. C., V. A. Woodward, and C. L. Burke. 1984 *Language Stories and Literacy Lessons*. Portsmouth, NH: Heinemann.

Harste, J. C., and K. G. Short. 1988. *Creating Classrooms for Authors*. Portsmouth, NH: Heinemann.

Healy, J. 1990. *Endangered Minds: Why Children Don't Think and What We Can Do About It*. New York: Simon and Schuster.

Hill, M. 1989. *Where Reading and Writing Begin*. Portsmouth, NH: Heinemann.

Hill, S., and T. Hill. 1990. *The Collaborative Classroom: A Guide to Co-operative Learning*. Portsmouth, NH: Heinemann.

Hirsch, E. S., ed. 1984. *The Block Book*. Washington, DC: National Association for the Education of Young Children.

Holdaway, D. 1979. *The Foundations of Literacy*. Portsmouth, NH: Heinemann.

———. 1980. *Independence in Reading*. Portsmouth, NH: Heinemann.

———. 1984. *Stability and Change in Literacy Learning*. Portsmouth, NH: Heinemann.

———. 1986. "The Structure of Natural Learning as a Basis for Literacy Instruction." In *The Pursuit of Literacy: Early Reading and Writing*, edited by M. Sampson. Dubuque, IA: Kendall/Hunt.

———. 1988. "Towards Joyful Language Teaching Through Homely Models." *Whole Language Teachers Association Newsletter*, Fall 1988. Sudbury, MA: Whole Language Teachers Association.

———. 1990. The Social Dynamics of Acquisition Learning. Unpublished paper.

Hornsby, D., D. Sukarna, with J. Parry. 1986. *Read On: A Conference Approach to Reading*. Portsmouth, NH: Heinemann.

Hubbard, R. 1989. *Authors of Pictures, Draughtsmen of Words*. Portsmouth, NH: Heinemann.

Jenkins, C. 1995. *Inside the Writing Portfolio*. Portsmouth, NH: Heinemann.

Johnson, J., et al. 1987. *Play and Early Childhood Development*. Glenview, IL: Scott, Foresman.

Johnson, T. D., and D. R. Louis. 1987. *Literacy Through Literature*. Portsmouth, NH: Heinemann.

Katz, L. G., and S. C. Chard. 1989. *Engaging Children's Minds: The Project Approach*. Norwood, NJ: Ablex.

Kobrin, B. 1995. *Eyeopeners* II. New York: Scholastic.

Kohn, A. 1993. *Punished by Rewards: The Trouble with Gold Stars, Incentive Plans, As, Praise, and Other Bribes*. New York: Houghton Mifflin.

Laminack, L., and K. Wood. 1996. *Spelling in Use: Looking Closely at Spelling in Whole Language Classrooms*. Urbana, IL: National Council of Teachers of English.

Lindbergh, A. M. 1955. *Gift from the Sea*. New York: Pantheon.

Lynch, P. 1986. *Using Big Books and Predictable Books*. New York: Scholastic.

Manning, G., M. Manning, and R. Long. 1994. *Theme Immersion: Inquiry-Based Curriculum in Elementary and Middle Schools*. Portsmouth, NH: Heinemann.

Martens, P. 1996. *I Already Know How to Read: A Child's View of Literacy*. Portsmouth, NH: Heinemann.

Martin, B., Jr., and P. Brogan. 1972. *Sounds of Laughter*. Teacher's edition. New York: Holt.

Massam, J., and A. Kulik. 1986. *And What Else?* Bothell, WA: The Wright Group.

McCormick, C. E., and J. M. Mason. 1990. *Little Books*. Glenview, IL: Scott Foresman.

Midkiff-Borunda, S. S. 1989. *Reading Together: An Ethnographic Investigation of a Primary School Literacy Center*. Unpublished Ph.D. dissertation, Harvard University.

Miletta, M. M. 1996. *A Multiage Classroom: Choice and Possibility*. Portsmouth, NH: Heinemann.

Mills, H., T. O'Keefe, and D. Stephens. 1992. *Looking Closely: Exploring the Role of Phonics in One Whole Language Classroom*. Urbana, IL: National Council of Teachers of English.

Mills, H., T. O'Keefe, and D. Whitin. 1996. *Mathematics in the Making: Authoring Ideas in Primary Classrooms*. Portsmouth, NH: Heinemann.

Moline, S. 1995. *I See What You Mean: Children at Work with Visual Information*. York, ME: Stenhouse.

Mooney, M. 1990. *Reading To, With, and By Children*. Katonah, NY: Richard C. Owen.

Moustafa, M. 1997. *Beyond Traditional Phonics: Research Discoveries and Reading Instruction*. Portsmouth, NH: Heinemann.

Newkirk, T., and N. Atwell, eds. 1988. *Understanding Writing: Ways of Observing, Learning, and Teaching*. Portsmouth, NH: Heinemann.

Oglan, G. 1997. *Parents and the Whole Language Classroom*. Urbana, IL: National Council of Teachers of English.

Olson, J. L. 1992. *Envisioning Writing: Toward an Integration of Drawing and Writing*. Portsmouth, NH: Heinemann.

Ostrow, J. 1995. *A Room with a Different View: First Through Third Graders Build Community and Create Curriculum*. York, ME: Stenhouse.

Paley, V. 1990. *The Boy Who Would be a Helicopter*. Cambridge, MA: Harvard University Press.

———. 1992. *You Can't Say You Can't Play*. Cambridge, MA: Harvard University Press.

Pappas, C. C., B. Z. Kiefer, and L. S. Levstik. 1990. *An Integrated Language Perspective in the Elementary School*. New York: Longman.

Peterson, R. 1992. *Life in a Crowded Place*. Portsmouth, NH: Heinemann.

Piaget, J. 1962. *Play, Dreams, and Immitation in Childhood*. New York: Norton.

Pluckrose, H. 1987. "Fresh Start." New York: Franklin Watts.

———. 1987. *Crayons*. New York: Franklin Watts.

———. 1987. *Paints*. New York: Franklin Watts.

Renner, J. W., and E. A. Marek. 1990. *The Learning Cycle and Elementary School Science Teaching*. Portsmouth, NH: Heinemann.

Rose, M. 1995. *Possible Lives: The Promise of Public Education in America*. New York: Houghton Mifflin.

Routman, R. 1988. *Transitions: From Literature to Literacy*. Portsmouth, NH: Heinemann.

———. 1991. *Invitations: Changing as Teachers and Learners K–12*. Portsmouth, NH: Heinemann.

———. 1996. *Literacy at the Crossroads: Crucial Talk About Reading, Writing, and Other Teaching Dilemmas*. Portsmouth, NH: Heinemann

Smith, Frank. 1983. *Essays into Literacy*. Portsmouth, NH: Heinemann.

———. 1986. *Insult to Intelligence*. Portsmouth, NH: Heinemann.

———. 1988. *Joining the Literacy Club: Further Essays into Education*. Portsmouth, NH: Heinemann.

———. 1995. *Between Hope and Havoc: Essays into Human Learning and Education.* Portsmouth, NH: Heinemann.

Short, K. G., Harste, J. C., with C. Burke. 1996. *Creating Classrooms for Authors and Inquirers.* 2nd edition. Portsmouth, NH: Heinemann.

Snowden, C. 1985. *Developing Language Through Drama.* Albany, NY: Delmar Publishers.

Sowers, S. 1988. "Six Questions Teachers Ask About Invented Spelling." In *Understanding Writing: Ways of Observing, Learning, and Teaching,* edited by T. Newkirk and N. Atwell. Portsmouth, NH: Heinemann.

Spodek, B., ed. 1986. *Today's Kindergarten.* New York: Teachers College Press.

Strickland, D., and L. Morrow, eds. 1989. *Emerging Literacy: Young Children Learn to Read and Write.* Newark, DE: International Reading Association.

Teale, W., and E. Sulzby. 1986. *Emergent Literacy: Writing and Reading.* Norwood, NJ: Ablex.

Tompkins, G. E., and L. M. McGee. 1993. *Teaching Reading with Literature: Case Studies to Action Plans.* New York: Macmillan.

Trelease, J. 1995. *The New Read-Aloud Handbook.* 4th edition. New York: Penguin.

Vygotsky, Lev. 1986. *Thought and Language.* Cambridge MA: MIT Press.

Walmsley, S. A., and B. B. Walmsley. 1996. *Kindergarten: Ready or Not? A Parent's Guide.* Portsmouth, NH: Heinemann.

Weaver, C. 1994. *Reading Process and Practice: From Socio-Psycholinguistics to Whole Language.* 2d edition. Portsmouth, NH: Heinemann.

Wells, G. 1986. *The Meaning Makers: Children Learning Language and Using Language to Learn.* Portsmouth, NH: Heinemann.

Whitin, D. J., H. Mills, and T. O'Keefe. 1990. *Living and Learning Mathematics: Stories and Strategies for Supporting Mathematical Literacy.* Portsmouth, NH: Heinemann.

Wilde, S. 1991. *You Kan Red This! Spelling and Punctuation for Whole Language Classrooms, K–6.* Portsmouth, NH: Heinemann.

Wilde, S. 1997. *What's a Schwa Sound Anyway? A Holistic Guide to Phonetics, Phonics, and Spelling.* Portsmouth, NH: Heinemann.

Index